telling writing

telling writing

fourth edition

KEN MACRORIE

Professor Emeritus of English
Western Michigan University

BOYNTON/COOK PUBLISHERS, INC.

UPPER MONTCLAIR, NEW JERSEY 07043

The author would like to thank the proprietors for permission to quote from copyrighted works, as follows:

SAMUEL BUTLER: from *The Complete Works of Samuel Butler* and *The Notebooks of Samuel Butler*, published by Jonathan Cape Ltd. Reprinted by permission of the Executors of the Samuel Butler Estate.

TRUMAN CAPOTE: from *Writers at Work, The Paris Review Interviews*, edited by Malcolm Cowley. Copyright © 1957, 1958, by The Paris Review, Inc. Reprinted by permission of The Viking Press, Inc.

STUART CHASE: from "Writing Nonfiction," written for *On Writing, By Writers*, William W. West, Editor; copyright 1966 by Ginn and Company. Reprinted by permission of the publisher.

JOHN CIARDI: from "Work Habits of Writers," written for *On Writing, By Writers*, William W. West, Editor; copyright 1966 by Ginn and Company. Reprinted by permission of the publisher.

Library of Congress Cataloging in Publication Data

Macrorie, Ken, 1918–
    Telling writing.

    Bibliography: p.
    Includes index.
    1. English language—Rhetoric.   2. English language—Study and teaching.   I. Title.
PE1408.M33255   1985   808'.042   84–29296
ISBN 0–86709–153–3

For information address Boynton/Cook Publishers, Inc.
52 Upper Montclair Plaza, P. O. Box 860, Upper Montclair, NJ 07043

Printed in the United States of America

    87 88 10 9 8 7 6 5 4

preface

New in this fourth edition of *Telling Writing* are discussions in the very last pages of how useful are the practices of reading aloud in a writing class and employing Peter Elbow's "Believing Game" in critiquing sessions. Also in this edition are changes of the sexist uses of the word *he* for the designation of the universal person or author. In earlier revisions I failed to root out some of them from a book originally written in 1968. Also for this fourth edition I introduced many contractions such as *can't* and *didn't* for *cannot* and *did not*. My earlier failure to use contractions appropriate to a book informal in style is embarrassing to an author selling advice to other writers. When we teach or write textbooks, we want to sound authoritative, so we unconsciously use excessively formal language.

My experience in revising this book underlines my conviction that writing and speaking are to a large extent unconscious activities. At the moment of producing our best utterances, we're usually thinking of meaning, not word choice. And yet we're helped by stopping occasionally to think in a detached way about how we speak and write, or do anything else well. To live both subjectively and objectively, consciously and unconsciously, is to utilize our potential as higher animals. And this is true in all our endeavors, whether we are thinking at the most abstract level or playing in a mudpile. When I interviewed teachers in many different fields from kindergarten through graduate school for my book *Twenty Teachers,* I discovered that they addressed their learners, in writing or speech, in language that might be called their Mother Tongue, an informal, conversational dialect full of contradictions, with an occasional word from their learned, elevated vocabulary that created what I call in this book "the alternating current."

I point to *Twenty Teachers* here because although the people in it teach such different subjects as elementary school physical education and advanced university mathematics, they are often using methods like those presented in this book on writing. Good teaching in any field isn't a matter of employing gimmicks and choosing from a damn-fool encyclopedia of tricks to play on students on Monday, but a matter of setting up a climate friendly to learning and then challenging learners to connect their experience and ideas with those of the accepted authorities or producers. Students can't become truly educated unless they grow out of and beyond themselves. The program of *Telling Writing* gives them the indispensable base, a knowledge of themselves on which to grow.

In past editions of this book I've spoken my debt to scattered individuals who have helped me form and work out the program presented here, but this time I'd like to thank people who have worked for three of the most productive and exciting networks in the field of language learning. For the opportunity to work occasionally with National Writing Project summer institute people and for the privilege of their acquaintance and friendship, I thank Jim Gray, Mary K. Healy, Miles Myers, and Keith Caldwell. For the opportunity of learning from the staff and students of the Bread Loaf School of English, I thank Paul Cubeta, Dixie Goswami, Jimmy Britton, Nancy Martin, Peter Elbow, Don Graves, Jim Moffett, Shirley Brice Heath, Carol Elliott, and the many teachers who learn and teach with them. For the pleasure of working with rare publishers who have cared more about improving learning than making money, I thank Robert W. Boynton and the late S. William Cook, Jr.

contents

telling writing

introduction: words coming to you

THE UNCONSCIOUS IN WRITING

IF, LIKE ABOUT ninety percent of Americans, you feel you can't write, you're wrong.

Unintentionally, the school system has designed "English" classes to prevent you from writing strongly and then made you feel mistaken, bad, guilty, illiterate, and disgraceful for not doing so.

Traditionally English teachers practice students in only a part of the act that makes up writing. They have set the conscious to work and ignored the unconscious. When in either talking or writing, people begin a sentence of more than a half-dozen words, they don't know what words will end it. Right now, start talking or writing about what you did yesterday, and as you begin a sentence, try to predict what words will finish it. You won't be able to do that and yet when you move your lips or pen, you'll find the sentence developing and, eventually, ending.

Writing classes in high schools and colleges are titled "composition" courses. *Com·pose,* from Latin, meaning "put together." In truth, what happens is more a coming-to than a putting-together. When we write we have an idea of where we'd like our meaning to go, but we don't know what words or sentences will take us and our readers there. If we're traveling well, we don't know all the things or people we're going to run into on the way, what we'll pick up, what we'll learn—and especially, what events, sights, or insights will sneak up on us.

1

This is beginning to sound like an airy little fairy story and I don't want it to. When I say that words come *to* you more than you consciously choose them, I'm only reporting what professional writers have said for centuries, and what in many parts of the country a number of teachers have discovered in writing seminars made up of all kinds of students, ranging from ninth graders to fifty-year-old teachers returning to college for more learning. (Another funny word—*students,* from the Latin verb meaning to be eager, zealous, or diligent. Often school renders us bored, lazy, and careless because it doesn't ask enough of us and forgets that we walked in the door with powers of our own.) In the seminars, teachers found students actually eager, zealous, and diligent when they were freed to let words come to them, to allow their unconscious to do its thing. And then also, when other students responded to their writing and suggested improvements, to make the conscious do its thing.

Asked to write freely and strive for truths, seminar students told stories of their own experience. Week after week, semester after semester, a number of teachers have been observing how people write and respond to truthful writing. Our efforts amount to a kind of scientific study, like field work by anthropologists who spend a year or two in the South Seas observing how a people foreign to them carry out, say, their religious or marriage customs. For long periods we've made these observations—some teachers for five, ten, or fifteen years. These findings are not to be pushed aside casually.

STRATEGIES

In our seminars, we found again and again that when a paper was read aloud and praised by the group for strong expression, the writer was not aware of having used a certain device, for example, a comparison like a metaphor or simile,

> **I have only a vague memory of him, and I loved him. I felt as hard as the marble headstone.**

or alliteration,

> **I watched this guy who looked like he'd maybe *b*elonged to a motorcycle gang *b*efore *b*lundering into this place.**

or rhythms that intensify meaning,

> **I found a magazine, tore out a page, rolled it up and casually strolled over to the stove. Even when you're alone,**

it's just not cool to act too anxious. I turned on the gas, and it started off with a "foomp." Then I touched my homemade cigarette to the flame and puffed. Once, twice, "Ow!" Damn, look at that thing burn!

or sound effects of the utmost subtlety,

Her muscles bunched and smoothed in a rippling flow over the length of her body.

In the last example, the o's in *smoothed, flow, over,* and *body* make these sounds: *ooh, oh, oh, ah.* The word *bunch* tightens the tongue against the lower palate with its *ch,* and *smoothed* puckers the lips and moves the tongue forward to the teeth, just as the words denote bunching and smoothing in their meanings. Then *rippling* bespeaks that action, and the last six words slide away with an easy rhythm of unstressed syllables in pairs—o·ver the length of her bod·y." K.D. DeCelles, the student writer, didn't plan out those sound effects. But they're right for the purpose, which was to make us feel what the writer felt standing in a bog watching a moose run from a bear.

Over the years in these seminars, we've become aware that often powerful sound effects come to untrained writers, as if there's something built into human beings like a circuitry of an electronic machine that commands their language. A British educator once said that alliteration is a product of extreme emotion. "If you don't believe that," he said, "go home tonight and at dinner pour a glass of milk over your brother's head and listen to your father. You'll hear alliteration." A seminar student, recording a conversation between herself and her mother, wrote: "Mom, I *d*on't *d*epend on *d*ope." In writing as well as speech, alliteration appears to rise out of feeling or physical action as well as express them. But sometimes it seems simply musical, as in this sentence by another student:

The air is heavy with *w*ild summer grapes and rotten apples as Grandma *w*addles to one of the three *w*aiting cars.

One day a year or so ago I realized that, as I silently read words printed on a page, I usually hear them in my head. Subsequently, when I talked to teachers and students around the country, I asked my audiences how many people shared that experience. Invariably seventy-five to eighty-five percent of the audience raised their hands. Then I noticed that the same thing usually happens when I'm typing or forming words in handwriting. I hear them in my head as they're going down on paper. Not always does this voice pronounce words I'm reading or writing, but *usually*—when I'm really into what I'm reading or writing. What that "really into" signifies is as mysterious, and as real, as the voice in my head sounding out groupings of words.

I'd like you to hold these notions in mind as I cite some more examples of the way nonprofessional writers sometimes handle words. When I visited a fourth-grade class several years ago and asked ten-year-olds to write freely and truthfully, LaVerne produced a paper in which this passage appeared:

> **When I watered the calves I spilted the water on my self becose the two calves made me spell it and then I wen't up to tell my mom. The calves barn steks. And when the like you whith thay tung it tikls. And when they kike you it smarts. And when you feel then it fell's like bon's.**

One can deride that passage, saying that this terrible speller got the word *spell* right but only when she meant *spill*. When I read the paper I was looking for something else—which I found, *parallel construction*. Note the parallelism in these sentences:

> **And when they lick you with their tongue, it tickles. And when they kick you, it smarts. And when you feel them, it feels like bones.**

A great deal of sensuous truth about calves is packed into those sentences, and with the clarity and punch that parallel construction gives a statement. You can guess that this girl with her spelling disability doesn't write except under command. But she knows how to sound out language as if she had been given that ability along with her bones and flesh. I don't know if that's true. She may have had such patterns of words print on her brain slowly as she picked them up from the air. They may have accumulated there over the ten years that belonged to her since she left her mother's womb. But whether she was born with them or acquired them, they are there, as I believe they are for all of us.

We human beings have so badly misunderstood, or failed to understand, the way language works in us (I use that phrasing rather than "the way we control words") that we haven't heard that our spoken and written words speak to each other within our sentences, which are alive and growing. Our minds catch and stutter on a word, and the results may be powerful or weak. For example, this passage from a seminar writing overworks the word *hard*.

> **Frances started to slow down with years, and I *hardly* saw her but twice that year. We *hardly* talked, we never did**

except for questions and small talk. For some reason it was
hard for Frances. . . .

I know that editors notice such weak repetition and some English
teachers mark it with red ink, but the same teachers don't recognize
that our unconscious has the power to repeat sounds and words powerfully as well as to get hung up on them. Here's a seminar writer repeating a word powerfully. I don't say that the repetition was unconscious, but that it came to her, and she was relaxed enough to
accept the gift as she related a bicycle accident:

> Over a bump, and I watched the last ray of sun *sparkle*
> on my bike generator as it fell off the front wheel frame
> into the spokes. It's *sparkling*; I'm flying. Slow motion. I
> remember . . . somersaulting through the air. . . .

Our words speak to our words in both sounds and meanings.
Mindy Stiles wrote in her journal of walking toward a dormitory door
to go out in the snow.

> A voice called out, "Hey little kitten, you've lost your
> mitten." I turned around and faced a smiling guy holding
> my mitten in his paw. "Thank you." As I reached to get it,
> I accidentally scratched him.

One can say that Mindy's choice of the word *paw* instead of *hand*
was highly conscious, but our seminar experience suggests it wasn't.
The word *kitten* helped her say *paw,* but that connection was probably not in her mind as she began to write the passage. I imagine that
she started writing knowing she was going to make the point that
scratching the guy was a kittenish act, but I'll wager that the word
paw came to her just as she put down "my mitten in his. . . ." My
own experience has been that such wordplays or metaphors come to
people who let them come and record them before their fearful conscious selves edit or censor them. For the first thirty years of my life I
suffered from metaphor paralysis. I thought that live and surprising
comparisons issued exclusively from professional writers. My mother
never played with words or used fresh metaphors. My father did, but
he died when I was twelve. So for many years my written words seemed
to have been typed by a computer. I must have exerted a great effort
to break the natural connections in my brain between things and words,
and words and words. In the seminars, metaphors appear frequently:

> My sister is in love with exclamation points. She starts off
> her letters with "Hi!!!" and ends them with "Love, Joan!"
> and finishes every other sentence with them, too. . . . She

talks the same way. Sometimes I expect an exclamation point to drool out of her mouth when she finishes speaking.

YOUR LIBRARIES OF LANGUAGE

Almost always in the seminars, writers who are praised for metaphors and similes say that the expressions that struck their listeners visited them as they were writing. They didn't hunt for, plan, or contrive them.

So there you can also be, like these untrained seminar writers, sitting innocently at a desk or table, being visited by literary and rhetorical strategies that people have been taught to believe belong only to professionals. The saying is, "Writers are born, not made." Some truth there, but I'd have to add, "And we're all writers, at times." Words don't select a few deserving or anointed persons to call on. They come to us all, and sometimes splashing brilliance. Naturally, we'll write better if we keep the door open and take care of our guests when they arrive.

But it's all so preposterous, you may be thinking. I couldn't have such abilities. I can't even spell. (Remember ten-year-old LaVerne.) Where would I get the patterns? The slots to put words in? I don't read books. But you've been exposed to many skillful word patterns. Perhaps you were brought up on the King James Bible, with its Elizabethan sonorities and parallelisms; or the *Peanuts* comic strip with its marvelous economy in words. You've read the terse directions for using a pinball machine or opening a can of beer. The flimsiest and shoddiest novel you've read may have known how to begin and end, how to make you want to turn the page. Much street talk and disc jockey patter is stylish. One doesn't have to be what cultivated people call "a reader" to be familiar with language. Hearing a first-rate but popular television show, you may be exposed to pointed dialogue, to a humor not of gag lines but of situation and character. At times our seminar students write with these language patterns, some of which must have printed on their brains, or wherever their libraries of language are shelved.

We've found that asking students to write freely, putting down as fast as they can what comes to their minds, without worrying about grammar, punctuation, or spelling, and to try for truths—big or small, just not anything phony—often excites their word-making circuits and delivers sentences with charge. This initial free writing frees them to write more strongly on assignment.

TRUTHTELLING

But it's truthtelling that does the most to release language powers. We ask for truths to the world out there, which can be verified; and truth to the world inside, the writer's feelings, which no one can verify. A double obligation, but one that miraculously frees our seminar writers. I don't altogether understand why or how. Perhaps when they're telling truths (as *they* see and feel them, not as super-humans with absolute truthtelling powers), they concentrate first on what they're saying and second on what others will think of it. They may be doing that because truthtelling puts them on solid ground.

This is not to say that our words don't often speak beyond their literal meanings, and sometimes opposite to our intentions. But I'm distinguishing between the effort to tell our truths and someone else's. When we write ours, we hear the people we've known, and remember the things we've seen. They belong to us. The voice we hear making the words on the page is one of ours: it sounds in us like conscience. And so in a way we are objective, supported by the memory traces of those objects and persons we're calling up. The experiences we remember, but no longer are we in them as we were when they occurred.

Other benefits come to writers striving to tell truths. We find they seldom use clichés or trite phrases. They seldom waste words. And by some power that I can't name they're given the specific, telling details that most English teachers plead for. Sample:

> **I caught him by the bottom of his legs and lowered him headfirst over a garbage barrel full of trays, smashed beets, spattered milk, and strings of chop suey. "I'm gonna throw you away, Dominick. . . ."**

Apparently much of our best writing and talking comes naturally, sometimes physiologically, affected by nervous tension, blood pressure, or self-hypnotizing concentration upon a thought or feeling. Remembering a stirring event, we experience again part of its excitement, which affects our nervous system, and in turn, the centers of language in our bodies. And so we write with rhythms that belong to that event, with words that sound out feeling and thought. Then the words are coming to us like a sudden freshet that develops when the snow melts. It's a happening we can't and shouldn't completely control, lest we shut off all the flow.

RESPONDING TO WRITERS

In the seminars, people gain confidence through free writing. They find words coming to them. They gain more confidence when they see the response of their peers to those words. They themselves respond to the writing of others. And they build their own standards for good writing. They have seen what works.

But the process isn't always easy. It requires writers to stand behind their writing as listeners test it. Being new to the experience, listeners often are afraid to say a piece of writing has failed to move them, and why. Yet as a paper is being read aloud, they're always responding unconsciously. They grunt approval, sigh in empathy, tense in their chairs during a suspenseful story, or emit sounds signifying disgust, fear, or agreement. At times they become dazed and tune out, heads nodding toward sleep, and the author must face failure.

When the listeners perceive a point, they usually laugh. A "har-har" follows an obvious gag. A chuckle appreciates a well-delivered insight. A building, and eventually exploding, laugh testifies to a rousing presentation of a piece of life. Some of the most profound renderings of experience—which Shakespeare's Gloucester in *King Lear* called "seeing feelingly"—often draw forth no more than lowered eyes or the slightest shaking of a head. But they are reactions and can be read by those in the seminar circle.

Both the writing and responding are complex. To do them well, we must act unconsciously at that moment; but to extend our ability to do them well—to move it toward habit—we need to be conscious of what we've done, and what kind of writing has moved the audience. When we're living at our highest capabilities, experiencing life to the fullest, we're alternating between unconscious and conscious behavior. At our most exciting and powerful moments these two forces come together and fuse. The perfect model for this relationship is the Moebius Strip, or Loop, which was conceived by a German astronomer and topologist in the middle of the nineteenth century.

You can make a Moebius Loop by cutting a strip of paper, say one-half inch wide, down the length of a typing sheet, giving it a twist, and taping its ends together so it looks like this:

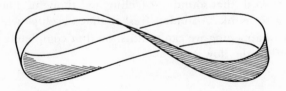

If you place your pencil point on the strip and draw the paper through its length, holding the pencil there, you'll find that without turning to the other side of the strip your pencil has marked both sides and met its beginning. You'll realize that August Moebius created a one-sided loop. The two sides flow into each other.

Print UNCONSCIOUS on one side and CONSCIOUS behind it on the other side, and you'll have a model of human behavior. The two ways differ but come together as one. They need each other. Together they can work wonders. Lest you think I'm providing you with Superman's power, I must say that no one has discovered something like a light switch that will turn on the unconscious powers whenever we want them. We can say roughly when they usually appear: We're highly motivated, concentrating on one finely focused intention, performing in a field where we're experienced and knowledgeable, and not distracted by a multitude of instructions or directions from outside. In the act, we forget the first, conscious self and discover that a second self is doing things beautifully. The second self takes over so that writing seems to be simply putting down what a voice within us is saying.

In the program that this book outlines, you'll find it easier to get on the Moebius Loop than ever before in school, for you'll be at first encouraged to write freely (employing your unconscious) and then to act as an editor (employing your conscious). You'll be allowed to tell stories of your own experiences and those of other people you've known, a basic need for all of us. This course is a first step. It will show what language powers reside in you, and how to extend them. But you must write and respond to others' writing and learn to use their responses to your writing. It's a course to run, not a couch to lie on. As the writer and radio interviewer Studs Terkel says, "Take it easy, but take it."

chapter 1
the
poison
fish

ONE DAY a college student stopped a professor in the hall and said, "I have this terrible instructor who says I can't write. Therefore I shouldn't teach English. He really grinds me. In another class I've been reading James Joyce, so I wrote this little comment on the instructor in Joyce's style. Do you think I should submit it to *The Review?*"

The professor looked at the lines she had written about her instructor:

> . . . the stridents in his glass lisdyke him immersely. Day each that we tumble into the glass he sez to mee, "Eets too badly that you someday fright preach Engfish."

and he knew the student had found a name for the phony, pretentious language of the schools—Engfish.

Most English teachers have been trained to correct students' writing, not to read it; so they put down those bloody correction marks in the margins. When the students see them, they think they mean that teachers don't care what students write, only how they punctuate and spell. So students give them Engfish. The teachers call the assignments by their traditional name—*themes*. No one outside school ever writes anything called *themes*. They're teachers' exercises, not really a kind of communication. On the first assignment in a college class, a student begins his theme like this:

> I went downtown today for the first time. When I got there I was completely astonished by the hustle and the bustle that was going on. My first impression of the downtown area was quite impressive.

Beautiful Engfish. The writer said not simply that he was astonished, but completely astonished, as if the word *astonished* had no force of its own. The student reported (*pretended* would be a truer word) to have observed hustle and bustle, and then explained in true Engfish that the hustle and bustle was going on. He managed to work in the academic word *area,* and finished by saying the impression was impressive.

> *But wise men pierce this rotten diction*
> *and fasten words again to visible things.*
> RALPH WALDO EMERSON

Teachers don't want Engfish, but they get it. Discouraged, they often try a different tack. Ask the students to write about sports; then maybe they'll drop Engfish because they care about what they're saying. One starts a theme like this:

> The co-captains of the respective teams are going out to the middle of the field for the toss of the coin.

Engfish again. Only two teams play in a football game and there could be no reason in that sentence for using the word *respective*. But it was the sort of word the writer thought Engfish teachers wanted.

With all that fish smell permeating the room, teachers feel queasy. They try other ways of getting rid of Engfish. They ask students to keep personal journals. Maybe if they talk about themselves they'll find their natural voices. The next day one woman turns in a journal containing this entry:

> It is hard to realize just how much you miss someone until you are away from this person. It seems that the time spent away from this person is wasted. You seem to wait and wait till you can see this person again. Then when the time comes, it passes far too quickly.

Another kind of Engfish—not fancy, academic language, but simple everyday words that say nothing because they keep all the woman's experience private. Anyone else reading that entry would forget it instantly because neither the writer nor the person written about comes alive. A year later the sentence would mean almost nothing even to the writer.

Teachers become fed up with writing like that. They don't see that most of the signals in the school are telling students to write Engfish. Even the textbook begins with an Engfish sentence, and surely it should be a model of writing for students. Its first sentence is:

> If you are a student who desires assistance in order to write
> effectively and fluently, then this textbook is written for
> you.

Pure Engfish undefiled, a tongue never spoken outside the walls. No student would stop another on campus and say, "I desire assistance in locating Sangren Hall," or "Will you show me the most effective way to write this paper?" Naturally the student thinks the textbook is a model of the language teachers want, so she gives that language to them.

Students thoroughly trained in Engfish are hard put to find their natural voices in the classroom. They've left them out in the hall. Much earlier in life, though, they occasionally have written sharply and truly, as this third-grader did:

> I can play huhwayun music on my gettar. It is like when
> grandma took a sick spell. Now she waz shut up tight as
> a jar with a lid on. She gave a scream. When she gave that
> scream it was high. But it got lower and lower. Huhwayun
> music sounds something like when she was getting lower.

From that passage a reader learns what "huhwayun" music sounds like.

> *Man's maturity: to have regained the*
> *seriousness that he had as a child at play.*
> FRIEDRICH NIETZSCHE

The difference between the college students' writing and the third-grade child's is simple: One is dead, the other alive. In the child's comments the words speak to each other—*high* speaks to *lower*. And the ideas and things speak to each other—the Hawaiian guitar is like grandmother, and when she was sick she was like a jar with a lid on. The whole passage speaks to the reader. It's not pretentious. It's not phony. It's not private. In the Engfish paragraphs of the student themes the words almost never speak to each other, and when they do, they say only "Blah."

College students were once third-graders and occasionally wrote like that. Where did they lose that skill? Why?

They spend many hours in school mastering Engfish. The fact that the teacher and the textbook sometimes employ Engfish suggests to them that it's the official language of the school. They're learning a language that prevents them from working toward truths, and so they slide into telling lies.

In this empty circle, teachers and students wander around boring each other. But there is a way out.

He told the truth in order to see.

GENE BARO

chapter 2
writing
freely

TELLING TRUTHS

ALL GOOD writers speak in honest voices
and tell the truth. For example, here's Eudora Welty in her novel
Delta Wedding writing about India, a girl of nine, watching her
Uncle George make up with his wife after a quarrel:

> Just now they kissed, with India coming up close on her
> toes to see if she could tell yet what there was about a kiss.

Asked what makes students write badly, Eudora Welty once said:

> The trouble with bad student writing is the trouble with
> all bad writing. It is not serious, and it does not tell the
> truth.

This is the first requirement for good writing: truth; not *the* truth
(whoever knows surely what that is?), but some kind of truth—a connection between the things written about, the words used in the
writing, and the author's experience in a world she knows well—whether
in fact or dream or imagination.

Part of growing up is learning to tell lies, big and little, sophisti-
cated and crude, conscious and unconscious. The good writer differs
from the bad one in constantly trying to shake the habit. She holds herself to the highest standard of truth telling. Often she emulates chil-

dren, who tell the truth so easily, partly because they do not sense how truth will shock their elders.

A seventh-grade boy once wrote:

> I'd like to be a car. You get to go all over and get to go through mud puddles without getting yelled at . . . that's what I'd like to be.

The style of this passage is not distinguished. *Get* is here not a key word and yet it's employed three times. The writer switches confusingly from *I* to *you*. The language of the passage is not exciting. No memorable pictures are projected. Yet the statement strikes with force because the boy speaks truly: his shoes and the tires of the car do become muddy. He gets yelled at by his parents and the car does not. The comparison surprises. Its candor draws a smile from the reader.

> *I never think I have hit it hard unless it rebounds.*
>
> SAMUEL JOHNSON

Any person trying to write honestly and accurately soon finds he has already learned a hundred ways of writing falsely. As a child he spoke and wrote honestly most of the time, but when he reaches fifteen, honesty and truth come harder. The pressures on his ego are greater. He reaches for impressive language; often it's pretentious and phony. He imitates the style of adults, who are often bad writers themselves. They ask questions. So he asks questions in his writing: "Did you ever think what might have happened to South Africa if the Boer War had not been fought?" A false question. The writer knows most—if not all—of his readers have not thought of this possibility. However well meant—a false question. In class this person is anxious to impress the teacher, so he begins his paper by saying:

> The automobile is a mechanism fascinating to everyone in all its diverse manifestations and in every conceivable kind of situation or circumstance.

His first remark is simply untrue. Cars do not fascinate everyone.

In this paper the writer has placed his vocabulary on exhibit (*mechanism, diverse, manifestations, conceivable, situation, circumstance*) rather than put it to work. An honest writer makes every word pull its weight. In this writer's opening sentence, the words *kind of* are not working at all. They could be dropped with no loss. What does he mean by "all the diverse manifestations" of a car? Cars don't occur in manifestations but in models. If the cars he's referring to are custom-made and not strictly speaking "models," then he should say he's writing about hybrid cars. At the opening of his paper, his reader has no inkling that he's talking about home-made cars. And nothing could be more untrue than the thought conveyed by the last phrase—that everyone finds cars fascinating "in every conceivable kind of situation or circumstance." When the valves need regrinding at 17,000 miles at a cost of $125.00, even the car lover finds his loved one repulsive.

Compare this writer's pretentious and untrue statement about cars with this account:

Thundering down a Northern Michigan highway at night I am separated from the rest of the world. The windows of the car are all rolled down and the wind makes a deep rumbling as the car rises and falls with the dips in the pavement. The white center lines come out of the darkness ahead into the beams of the headlights only to disappear again under the front edge of the hood. The lights also pick up trees, fenceposts, and an occasional deer or raccoon standing by the roadside, but like the white lines they come into view only for a few seconds and then are lost in the blackness behind me. The only signs I have that any world exists outside the range of the headlights are the continuous cheerping and buzzing of the crickets and the smells from farms and sulphur pits I pass. But the rushing wind soon clears out these odors, leaving me by myself again to listen to the quickly passing crickets I will never see. The faint green lights and the red bar on the dashboard tell me I'm plunging ahead at 90 m.p.h.; I put more pressure on the pedal under my foot; the bar moves up to 100 . . . 110. The lines flash by faster and the roar of the wind drowns out the noise of the crickets and the night. I am flying through. I can feel the vibrations of the road through the steering wheel. I turn the wheel slightly for the gradual curve ahead and then back again for the long straightaway. I press the pedal to the floor and at the same time reach down to touch the buttons on my left that will roll up the windows for more speed; the bar reads 115 . . . 120, buried. With the windows up, the only sound is the high-pitched moan from the engine as it labors to keep the rest of the machine hurtling blindly ahead like a runaway express train. Only I have the power to control it. I flick on the brights to advance my scope of vision and the white lines

come out of the black further up ahead, yet because of the
speed, they're out of sight even faster than before. I am
detached from the rest of the world as it blurs past. I am
alone.

HENRY HALL JAMES

This boy may have been driving at an immorally high speed—even
for a relatively uninhabited region—but he was writing morally,
because he was staying true to the feel of his experience. Writing this
way requires a quick jump in the car and a zooming away before one
remembers all the driving habits he has picked up watching bad
older drivers. Try writing for truth.

> *Never say that you feel a thing unless*
> *you feel it distinctly; and if you do not*
> *feel it distinctly, say at once that you do*
> *not as yet quite know your own mind.*

SAMUEL BUTLER

WRITING FREELY WITHOUT FOCUS

WRITING ONE: Write for ten minutes as fast as you can, never
stopping to ponder a thought. Put down whatever comes to your
mind. If nothing comes, write, "Nothing comes to my mind" until you
get started. Or look in front of you or out the window and begin
describing whatever you see. Let yourself wander to any subject,
feeling, or idea, but keep writing. When ten minutes is up, you should
have filled a large notebook-sized page. Remember you're hitting
practice shots. If what you write is bad or dull, no one will object.

Save all the writing which you produce while reading this book.
Keep it in a manila filing folder so you can go back to it to revise
it or look for paragraphs or pages that may be combined or expanded
into stronger work. As time passes, you'll see your words differently
and sometimes learn from them without doing further work.

Here's what one student wrote in ten minutes:

> **Electrical storm, the greatest show on earth and all for**
> **free. It looks like arc welding, the helium arc on a torch.**
> **Long day cooped up in dark, dirty factory welding gas**
> **tanks, tanks for trucks, buses, tractors. Twenty-seven in**
> **every hour day after day. Hot sparks, blinding flashes. Like**
> **the time a tank had been cleaned with gasoline and the**
> **fumes not removed. Just one impression was the result, not**
> **heat or light or sound—all of them rolled into one impact**

when the torch set off the fumes. No real damage, just a
lot of smoke and twisted metal. There was an electrical
storm the night before I was to quit the job. It's strange
how much more difficult it was to get up that morning
dreading every hour of work. An interesting couple kissing
with real passion in front of 23 people in a small room off
the Union lounge. At any rate the electrical storm had
knocked out the transformer and there wasn't any work
that day. It didn't bother me, but what of the regular workers who the loss of a day's pay could mean the missing of a
rent or car payment? Terror is a rare thing in American
life, that is the fear of actual physical harm, but that last
day at work I saw real fear in someone. All the workers
were standing in the yard waiting to see if they were going
to work that day and a truck driver brought in a load of
steel. He thought we were on strike, and industrial workers are not well-known for the kindness they meet strike
breakers with. And the driver had a lot to lose—his truck
and perhaps a few teeth.

No Engfish in that writing. No phoniness or pretension. Apparently
the writer put down words so fast he used his own natural language
without thinking of his expression. He got a lot said in a short space,
and at times wrote skillfully, as when he rendered exactly the effect
of the explosion:

Just one impression was the result, not heat or light or
sound—all of them rolled into one impact when the torch
set off the fumes.

Like any human being who wants to communicate, he recorded facts
that speak: a couple kissing in front of 23 people, a day without work
might mean a worker missed a rent or car payment. Telling facts as
true as those led him to a strong and surprising generalization: "Terror
is a rare thing in American life."

But overall, the paper is a jerky piece of writing. The writer frequently changes subject without warning and hints that he realizes
he's doing this by beginning one sentence with the phrase: "At any
rate." He begins the paper talking about an unidentified storm, is reminded of welding, diverted by a couple kissing nearby, jogged by the
memory of a storm that affected his work in a factory, and led to
discuss the attitudes of industrial workers toward strike-breaking. He
makes connections between some of these subjects and fails to do so
with others. Apparently he doesn't develop the description of the

storm that he begins with. He doesn't present a full picture of the kissing couple or the reaction or lack of reaction from the 23 people sitting nearby.

It's not a fully realized bit of writing, but it's honest and at moments strikes its own sparks and sounds its small explosions. The student who dashed off this paper can write, no doubt about that. And he got rid of his Engfish on the first try. He's on his way.

Another student in the same class turned in this paper for her first free writing:

> Everyone wants to feel useful to someone, anyone. They want to feel they are doing something to help, even in a minor way. If you don't feel useful you become depressed. You feel without. No friends, nothing to look forward to. There seems a loss of ambition and concentration. The world seems against, you find unimportant matters to brood over.
>
> Whenever everything seems at its worst, you find a person who is worse off than you. Guilt runs through every pore, your petty worries become unimportant to you. The world seems much happier now.

The writer of that passage was trying for Great Thoughts instead of for truth. Her language comes out flabby and her great thoughts obvious and tired, with none of the surprise of the statement "Terror is a rare thing in American life." She doesn't really care what her words say, or she never would have written

> Whenever everything seems at its worst, you find a person who is worse off than you.

The fact is that when everything seems at its worst for some of us, we sometimes find a person better off than we are and we feel even worse.

In contrast, here's another person feeling bad about the world seeming against her, only she's trying to be true—to the world out there—the facts of it, to what someone actually said to her, and to her own feelings, not to what she thinks the teacher wants.

> Everyone around here is having an awful time getting along with me. I'm being positively intolerable. Mom is trying really hard not to say anything in the wrong tone of voice, so that I feel kind of—what's that old-fashioned word, *ashamed* of myself. One day I'm in a great mood, and you could yell at me all you wanted without making me mad or hurt. The next day (or the next hour for that

matter) you could say "Good morning," then yawn, and I'd burst into tears. I suppose that is not awfully abnormal (at least that's what Mom says—in her psychological tone, "It's just a phase. You'll grow out of it.") By the way, that makes me mad, too. I don't like to have my life summed up in a series of phases. It seems like she's saying, "You can't help acting like an idiot. It comes natural at this age. But don't worry, you'll outgrow it. It'll pass."

A good part of the time, writers must sense their readers out there. In a way they become their own readers while they write. They talk to a reader and hear that talk themselves. When you acquire that knack, readers will come along with you.

Behind that terrible piece of Engfish beginning "Everyone wants to feel useful to someone" may lie some good stories. But the writer never gave the reader a *Once*. She never began to describe the day on which she found a person worse off than her, much less showed the reader that person. The girl who said, "Everyone around here is having an awful time getting along with me," didn't get down to a *Once* either except when she quoted what Mom must have said once, or—more accurately—many times. If she had, she probably would have produced a long valuable story. The writer who thinks of a *Once* is almost sure to get going and say something that counts for her and her reader.

A professor received these paragraphs from identical twins in her class.

1

I have not had a bad day like that one for a long time. I guess this Christmas season was just too much. I feel like I have evolved from a cocoon now. I can see the light again. Things seem so funny when you see them, and it is like trying to look through cardboard. You are missing something.

2

The first day we got in the wrong math section. Wrong room—300 instead of 309. Then Tuesday we got stuck in the snow in the driveway, and we missed the math class. Got there in time to say good-bye to the instructor. See you Thursday.

The first writer never got down to revealing the day, only the feelings she had as a result of it. Her metaphor about trying to look through cardboard is good, but the day is nothing at all because she refused to *once* it even once. The second writer let the reader know what happened, once, twice, and three times, and her paragraph swings a little.

When you write freely whatever comes into your mind, remember that memory or thought is now coming to you as a *once* and it probably is based on many *onces* you need to put down for yourself and your reader.

WRITING TWO: Write three or more of these absolutely free writings. Choose times when no one will disturb you, before breakfast or late at night perhaps. Go beyond ten minutes if the river keeps flowing. But don't expect anything. You're just warming up. Maybe none of your ten-minute writings will produce an interesting sentence. Don't worry. Write. And don't think about punctuation or grammar or style. Put down one word as a sentence if you wish. Maybe your writing will be completely uninteresting to others. As long as you're trying to write honestly and you're writing fast and steadily to fill up a page or two without stopping, you're writing freely.

WRITING FREELY WITH FOCUS

Free, or "shotgun" writing (as teacher John Bennett at Central High School, Kalamazoo, Michigan, calls it) involves no pressure. If the writer goofs he hasn't failed, but simply filled a page that can be thrown away.

WRITING THREE: Now try free writing with more purpose. Stay on one subject for fifteen or twenty minutes as the writer did when she said that everyone thought she was being positively intolerable. But if you find that subject takes your mind off to another related subject, let yourself go to that. The one necessity in such shotgunning is that you keep writing freely and quickly.

> *Thought is an infection. In the case of certain thoughts it becomes an epidemic.*
>
> WALLACE STEVENS

Here is a focused free writing:

I was walking down the hill to the valley. Then all of a sudden, the girl in front of me took a flip. Ha! Ha! If I didn't know better, I would have thought that she was on the gymnastic team. I took no more than two steps. Wham! There I lay. Ha! Ha!

Reminds me of a time back home when my friends and
I went to Garbage Hill. A great place to go tobogganing.
It was our first time there and we didn't know what the hill
was like. Dark out, the sky was clear, and the night cold.
At the bottom and about 150 feet out were the woods. We
couldn't understand why people avoided them.

We started at the top of the hill, an almost straight drop.
I didn't think that we would be able to make it. Have you
ever been on a vibrating machine? What a way to lose
weight, or a few other things. Hit a mound toward the bottom of the hill. The toboggan flew through the air, along
with a couple of my friends. There were just two of us left.
We landed and shot. Everything became blurry. The woods
came up fast. Whizzing past trees. Splash! There we sat, up
to our heads in water.

This writing is so honest it reveals the writer twice making a fool of
himself. He puts the reader there by *once-ing* both incidents.

Not every strong communication employs the secret of once. If
writers are faithful to their feelings and true to the world they have
experienced or imagined, they sometimes can write generalizations that
carry the punch of particular facts, as did this student in a free writing:

When I was a kid I was fat. It's no fun to be fat. I used
to try to be jolly, but that's hard to do when you don't have
a damn thing to be jolly about. How can you laugh after
you spill your lunch tray all over the cafeteria floor? Or,
even worse, score the winning point in a tense intramural
game at the wrong basket. I couldn't run fast, which left
out sports, and wasn't jolly enough to raise myself in the
social strata, so I became—I guess it was inevitable—a
nothing.

But really, it's kind of fun to be nothing. You sit around
with your nothing friends and laugh at the cool kids as they
try to keep up their image. I didn't have to try, which
relieved a lot of pressure, and was content in my nothing
world, a never-never land between social life and death. It's
easier my way, since I can think about other things that
are important to a kid—like grades. Every little kid has to
get good grades if he's a nothing, since there's little else
to do.

This peace was short-lived, because I started to emerge
from my ugly duckling shell, and the cool ones recognized

that I had potential. So I became one of the cool kids being laughed at by the nothings. But at least now they applaud when I spill my lunch tray all over the cafeteria floor—the applause makes it cool.

Don't fool yourself into believing that the little papers printed here were written by persons trying to sound impressive. These writers were writing as fast as they could for truth, and these papers represent only the moments when they hit the target. Often they missed. When you sit down to write freely you must write as fast as you can. You're being asked to move far away from Engfish and that fearful nervous act of trying to say what teachers said or what they want you to say. Speak for yourself here. If what you say is too personal or confessional, don't turn it in to the instructor, or ask to have your name kept secret. Consider this free writing.

The black row shifted again. Not all together like an "about face," but one after another, in a chain reaction. Without raising his hand, one black boy addressed the white girl, "Listen baby, you just don't know what happened. We know. It wasn't no blind pig that set off them riots." Chorus—"Yeah, we know."

The girl's fat face had two almost completely round red blotches on it, but she continued, "Well, if you all know, then why don't you tell us—tell me?"

He slouched down in his chair, half closed his eyes and flicked his hanging wrist. "You don't wanna know. That's all."

This paper reports an uncomfortable truth. It's not pleasant to think that some black and white persons feel such hostility toward each other, but the writer puts down her truth. It is more apt to move people to action than Engfishy pleas for kindness and love.

There must be no gap between expression and meaning, between real and declared aims . . . It means not saying or thinking, "I didn't mean to hurt your feelings," when there really existed a desire to hurt. It means not saying "luncheon" or "home" for the purpose of appearing upper-class or well-educa-

ted. It means not using the passive mood
to contribute to no one in particular
opinions that one is unwilling to call
one's own.

DONALD HALL

Telling our truths is hard. We all slip easily into deception—both of ourselves and others. But a continuing effort to tell truth when writing can become an exciting habit, and often one truth breeds another. On both the lowest and highest plane, try to be honest. For example, one student wrote,

> **I just wish the city would plow the sidewalks. They do where I—well, where my folks live . . .**

She remembered she no longer lived at home but in an apartment and couldn't validly say the city plowed the snow at her place. The point she made is small and perhaps trivial, but the habit she was developing was large and valuable. If she had occasion to rewrite the account in which those sentences occurred, she would restate the fact and not call attention to the correction:

> I just wish the city would plow the sidewalks outside our apartment. They do where my folks live.

In the next focused free writing, the effort to tell truth paid off more significantly.

> **In a few minutes Mom and Dad are going out to eat. She's got on a long-sleeved yellow dress, black fish-net nylons and black heels. When she doesn't notice, Dad looks at her. Then he rests his head on the back of the red chair and closes his eyes.**
>
> **Last night Bob brought me home at twelve o'clock. We had been wrestling and playing tag on the grass in back of Sangren. We were still laughing when he let me out of the car. I pinched his buns and then he messed up my hair. We gave each other a noisy kiss under our five-watt porch light, and he left.**
>
> **Mom and Dad were still up. I was relieved because I thought we might have wakened them. I started to go upstairs when Dad asked me to wait. I put my books down and sat at the desk. Mom's face was tight and her freckles were little red spots. Dad kept puffing on his pipe. He began. "Your mother and I have decided to get a divorce.**

But even though I'm leaving, remember you're still my
daughter and you always will be."

Then he started to cry. Mom and I were crying too. I
ran over and put my arms around him. His tears felt hot
on my neck. Then he said, "Go to your mother, she feels
bad, too."

He left tonight—to his little apartment on Copper Street.
Mom helped him move, and she cried when she saw it.
The bedroom is lavender with a purple bedspread. The
furniture looks like Antique Barn. A big crack runs up and
down the door. When he left, he took a lamp, four glasses,
and an ash tray.

> *. . . what is always provocative in a work*
> *of art: roughness of surface. While . . .*
> *[these writings] pass under our eyes they*
> *are full of dents and grooves and lumps*
> *and spikes which draw from us little*
> *cries of approval and disapproval.*
>
> E. M. FORSTER

You may wonder how these students could produce such complete
writings in a quick rush. Actually several of the accounts ran longer,
and their wasted words and irrelevant parts were dropped. One or two
papers came off the writer's pen just as they are presented here, but
that is a rare happening even for professional writers.

> *. . . I sometimes begin a drawing with no*
> *preconceived problem to solve, with only*
> *the desire to use pencil on paper and*
> *make lines, tones and shapes with no*
> *conscious aim; but as my mind takes in*
> *what is so produced a point arrives*
> *where some idea becomes conscious and*
> *crystallizes, and then a control and order-*
> *ing begins to take place.*
>
> HENRY MOORE, SCULPTOR

WRITING FOUR: Write freely for twenty or thirty minutes about
something or somebody you knew. Let yourself record the lumps
and grooves, the dents and spikes.

chapter 3
what
is
good
writing?

HERE'S a poem written by a college woman.

Around the driveway
and down our side of the block
my father's hand was on the back fender
and he was running behind and beside
giving me safe speed
so I could concentrate on steering.
Just coasting
I avoided the big trees,
maneuvered around people on the sidewalk
and began to see the cracks in pavement ahead.
He said
I was doing fine.
But the pedals came up from behind
reminding my legs they were long enough
and nudged my heels to cooperate
to push my own weight
down and around

27

unmercifully faster
laughingly
leaving him behind.
I turned a corner
and for a moment looked back
at him on the front porch
wearing an undershirt and uncertainty.
Too soon
way on the far side of some block
I try to keep my balance.

LOIS BERG

The poem speaks the girl's affection for her father without hearts and flowers. It puts the reader on a real bicycle that is moving over a real street with Father's hand on the rear fender. It doesn't take the reader down the road of life guided by some mysterious spirit. The narrator doesn't kid herself about Father. He encouraged her, but was no shining knight, rather a man wearing an undershirt and uncertainty. She'll have a hard time keeping her balance without him, but she knows she'll have to ride on her own someday—everyday. This is good writing: it doesn't waste words, it shows that the writer knows what she's talking about—the pedals come up from behind—its facts speak more than their literal significance.

There is no wing like meaning.

WALLACE STEVENS

Any kind of writing improves as it approaches the skills with which Miss Berg wrote her poem. For example, economy. People who must write directions for opening and storing a jar of peanut butter improve as writers if they learn to say more with fewer words. The writer for the Sears Roebuck catalog improves as she learns to dramatize more fully the product in use—to put the reader there, seeing and feeling what he will buy. Here's a good piece of writing from the *Sears Spring Through Summer Catalog*, 1966:

Dropped in mid-summer from a helicopter when loaded with 25 pounds of sand . . . also dropped when frozen at 20° below zero . . . IT BOUNCED. But Sears new exclusive Trash Can simply wouldn't break! (and because it's all heavy-weight plastic, there was *no noisy metallic clang*).

Sears Best . . . because of these important reasons:

Because Handy Bottom Grips plus side handles and lid handle for easy portability. No hand-cutting bail handle here.

Because friction-fit Top stays on without twisting, fits snugly without getting stuck.

Because No Seams. Holds water, won't leak. The utility area stays cleaner . . . won't be as likely to attract pests.

Because Stands Boiling Water, "boiling" hot sun . . . "boiling" hot concrete. Made to withstand the weather.

Treated with SANI-GARD to retard odor and bacteria . . . Won't "pick up" odors . . . resists the growth of fungi, mildew and bacteria that cause them.

In some senses, Lois Berg's bicycle poem can't be compared with an advertisement for a trash can; its intention is different, its achievement greater. But the Sears writer comes closer to creating good literature than many ad writers. She doesn't shoot off a roman candle of unsupported adjectives—Magnificent! Unheard-of! Stupendous! Instead she tells clearly how the can was tested for durability. Like Lois Berg she makes the reader believe, because the details she presents suggest that she knows what she's talking about.

Writing a sports report, "Orioles' 16 Hits Rout Yanks, 9-4," for *The New York Times*, August 11, 1966, Joseph Durso shows that like a poet he knows how to make his words speak to each other as well as to the reader:

The barrage consisted of these consecutive elements: a triple to left by Russ Snyder (leading the Yankees to draw their infield in), a single past the infield by Frank Robinson, a single past the infield by Brooks Robinson and a home run past everybody by Powell.

"Past the infield . . . past the infield . . . past everybody." The Sears writer said "Because friction-fit Top stays on . . . Because No Seams . . . Because Stands Boiling Water . . ."

Steve Smith begins his column "Sport" in *Car and Driver*, September, 1966, with this paragraph:

After completing our six-car comparison road test (elsewhere in this issue), we started back to the city on the Long Island Expressway, known variously as the L.I. Distressway, and the world's longest parking lot. It was a quiet Tuesday afternoon, so we weren't expecting much traffic. Soon, however, the three westbound lanes reached the saturation point, slowed to a crawl and then to a stop.

Temperatures and tempers rose. Some of the traffic bled off onto the two-lane parallel service road, allowing about half-a-mile of progress before clotting. Somebody had the bright idea of trying three abreast, and traffic telescoped another few hundred yards. In desperation, drivers veered off the roadway onto the center mall and the outside verge, becoming trapped by cars that had pulled off to let radiators cool. Finally, those that were able inched north and south the width of the island, then turned east. Within three hours, every major artery into the city was hopelessly snarled. Nothing moved. The System had broken down once again.

Mr. Smith cites two humorous names for the Long Island Expressway, employs sound beautifully in ending his sentence "slowed to a crawl and then to a stop" and makes the words *bled* and *clot* speak to each other in a metaphor. Like Miss Berg he seldom uses dull and empty verbs like *have, make, is,* and *come.* Instead he says *telescoped, veered, trapped, pulled off, inched, snarled,* and *broken down.*

In *The Field Book of Ponds and Streams* (G. P. Putnam's Sons, 1930), Anne Haven Morgan writes:

Mayfly nymphs are of many shapes and sizes; some have flattened heads and bodies and their sprawling legs are held akimbo as in *Heptagenia.* Active runners, like *Calliboetis,* are set high on spindling legs, while the little creeper, *Leptophlebia,* almost drags its low slung body.

Like Miss Berg, Dr. Morgan employs adjectives that aren't vague and inert, but precise and active: *flattened, sprawling, spindling, low slung.*

Guidebooks are usually crammed with fact but written without flavor. *The New York Guidebook* edited by John A. Kouwenhoven (Dell Publishing Company, 1964) includes a chapter by Jean Shepherd, who writes:

After midnight you can fuel up for your stroll at Riker's Corner House on the northeast corner of Sixth and 57th. By day it is filled with quick-lunch office types, but after midnight (it's an all-night, seven-day-a-week operation) there's as motley a crew as you can find this side of an average painting by Hieronymus Bosch. Good guys and bad guys, reverends and chicks, all assembled for a plate of scrambled eggs with onions, cr a slab of chocolate cream pie. There are no tables, only a horseshoe-shaped counter, which is served from somewhere in the kitchen by an end-less belt on a high podium in the center. At Christmas-time the podium is covered with elves, brownies, and a tiny electric train that I once saw derail and crash into seven banana splits. The applause was deafening. In the spring, this same treadmill is decorated with plastic daffodils and rubber tulips, and so each succeeding season is celebrated amid the hamburgers. It's the only way some of the cus-tomers can tell what time of year it is. Many of them have not seen the sun since they were kids.

Before you start east on 57th, look up Sixth Avenue. Two blocks north you will see the dark mass of Central Park, unfortunately an excellent place to stay out of after dark. There are romantics who will disagree with this. But there are equally large numbers of experienced patrolmen and unfortunates who have been mugged, who will tell you the truth.

Like all good writers Mr. Shepherd chooses from his experience what surprises him and will surprise his reader, and he delivers it in sentences that hammer the surprise: ". . . a tiny electric train that I once saw derail and crash into seven banana splits." He knows the strategy of using unexpected words together: "each succeeding season is celebrated amid the hamburgers." And he's not willing to gloss over truth to make Central Park at night seem romantic to tourists.

Writing is good not because of who writes it or where it appears. Shakespeare and William Faulkner wrote badly at times, and good publishers have marketed bad work. Writing is good because of what it says, how it opens up a world of ideas or fact for readers. And how accurately and memorably it speaks, a voice issuing from a human being who is fascinating, surprising, illuminating. But still a human being and a writer who doesn't always strike sparks.

> . . . failure . . . is the poet's only real business. The one hope is for a better and better failure . . .
>
> JOHN CIARDI

Most good writing is clear, vigorous, honest, alive, sensuous, appro-priate, unsentimental, rhythmic, without pretension, fresh, meta-phorical, evocative in sound, economical, authoritative, surprising, memorable, and light. If you set out to collect examples of good

writing you'll be surprised to find how many writers you admire
are humorous or light. *Hamlet*, a story of decadence and tragedy, is
at the same time one of the lightest plays ever written. Mark Van
Doren, a professor at Columbia University who encouraged many
young persons in America to keep writing until they became successful
authors, used to say in his literature classes that a great work of art
possesses a quality of lightness. It's never like a ponderous public
building that looks as if it's going to sink into the ground. Lightness
can be achieved in many ways—by varying style; by continually lifting
the reader with genuine, rather than trick, surprises; by not taking
oneself too seriously for the circumstances. For example, directions for
cooking needn't be boring and deadly: Irma S. Rombauer and Marion
Rombauer Becker take space in *The Joy of Cooking* to put some joy
into their opening discussion of salads:

> I remember the final scene of a medieval Maeterlinck play.
> The stage is strewed with those dead or dying. The sweet
> young heroine whimpers, "I am not happy here." Then the
> head of the house, or what remains of it, an ancient noble,
> asks quaveringly, "Will there be a salad for supper?"

This in a cookbook. Here's a college teacher's dittoed instructions
for her students:

> Trippers will meet at 7:15 (Kalamazoo time) in front of
> the Union. The bus will leave promptly at 7:30 a.m. There
> will be no watering stops between Kalamazoo and Chicago,
> so I strongly recommend that you all eat something vaguely
> resembling breakfast before we start—something substan-
> tial and comforting like a Hershey bar.
>   At 11:15 (Chicago time) we will go en masse to the
> Berghoff for lunch. The Berghoff is a marvelous old Ger-
> man place where the food is good and the prices are low. I
> think that the $1.50 lunch will make you all feel genial and
> broad-minded about Chicago, the museum, and modern art.
>   After lunch everyone is on his own in the museum.
> Museum fatigue is a very real phenomenon and I caution
> you to use some restraint in your viewing, taking the 20th
> century first and whatever else you can manage after that.

The teacher who wrote these directions didn't strain to be funny;
she simply let her own voice take over instead of the voice of doom
we often take on when we feel ourselves in a position of authority.

If you feel you can never write as well as John Steinbeck, Charles Dickens, or the writers quoted in this chapter, you may be right. But you can write as well as you spoke at your brilliant best when you were five years old, and you can write as well as some of the catalog or guide book writers presented in this chapter—if you find a voice that rings true to you and you learn to record the surprises of the world faithfully. The free writing by beginning writers quoted in the preceding chapters displays many of the characteristics of good writing discussed here; for example:

Opposition between facts that creates tension: . . . his little apartment . . . The bedroom is lavender with a purple bedspread.

Surprising happening, told with appropriate sound effect: We landed and shot. Everything became blurry. The woods came up fast. Whizzing past trees. Splash! There we sat, up to our heads in water.

Author speaking in authentic voice: I used to try to be jolly, but that's hard to do when you don't have a damn thing to be jolly about.

Character speaking in authentic voice: "Well, if you all know, then why don't you tell us—tell me?"

Economical use of words: The next day (or the next hour for that matter) you could say "Good morning," then yawn, and I'd burst into tears.

Apt metaphor: Electrical storm . . . like arc welding, the helium arc on a torch.

Surprising expression: And the driver had a lot to lose—his truck and perhaps a few teeth.

Strong verbs: He slouched down in his chair, half closed his eyes and flicked his hanging wrist.

Strong repetition: But really it's kind of fun to be nothing. You sit around with your nothing friends . . . content in my nothing world . . . .

The persons who produced these free writings may need to master additional skills, but they have already written many sentences that ring true and stay in the reader's ear.

> *The best writing, both prose and poetry, as Shakespeare pre-eminently shows, makes use, with condensation and selection, of playful, impassioned, imaginative talk.*
>
> **SIDNEY COX**

You may wonder how I can be so sure what good writing is. Not everyone likes the same authors or reporters. When you sit in the circle of writers and responders discussed in Chapter 9 of this book, you'll devise your own standards. They'll differ somewhat from those of others in your circle and in other circles, but probably not on certain fundamentals. Those who have worked in the circle have studied the reactions of the members as they listened to writings being read aloud. From the expressions on faces, grunts of approval, sighs, actions signifying boredom, and spoken comments, they slowly came to believe that most good writings gain their power in these ways:

1. They don't waste words.
2. They speak in an authentic voice.
3. They put readers there, make them believe.
4. They cause things to happen for them as they happened for the writer (or narrator).
5. They create oppositions which pay off in surprise.
6. They build.
7. They ask something of readers.
8. They reward them with meaning.

chapter 4
tightening

GOOD WRITERS meet their readers only at
their best. If you should read the sentences in their wastebaskets, you
would find them full of bad starts and complete misses. When you
write, you can discard your bad tries and forget them.

Benjamin Franklin, who helped Thomas Jefferson write the
Declaration of Independence—a skillfully revised document—once told
this anecdote to Mr. Jefferson:

> When I was a journeyman printer, one of my companions,
> an apprentice Hatter, having served out his time, was about
> to open a shop for himself. His first concern was to have a
> handsome signboard, with a proper inscription. He com-
> posed it in these words: "John Thompson, Hatter, makes
> and sells hats for ready money." with a figure of a hat
> subjoined. But he thought he would submit it to his friends
> for their amendments. The first he shewed it to thought the
> word "hatter" tautologous, because followed by the words
> "makes hats" which shew he was a hatter. It was struck out.
> The next observed that the word "makes" might as well be
> omitted, because his customers would not care who made
> the hats. If good and to their mind, they would buy, by
> whomsoever made. He struck it out. A third said he thought
> the words "for ready money" were useless as it was not the
> custom of the place to sell on credit. Every one who pur-
> chased expected to pay. They were parted with, and the
> inscription now stood "John Thompson sells hats." *"Sells*

35

hats" says his next friend? Why nobody will expect you to give them away. What then is the use of that word? It was stricken out and "hats" followed it, the rather, as there was one painted on the board. So his inscription was reduced ultimately to "John Thompson" with the figure of a hat subjoined.

You can cut out the unnecessary words in your writing in this way. The principle is simple: don't repeat words or ideas unless they strengthen what you want to say. "Hatter . . . makes hats" repeats *hat* to no avail. Don't tell your reader that "Mr. Smith is a man who—." The words *Mr. Smith* reveal that Smith is a man. Don't say "Lincoln School is a *school* that I really like." Look at what happens when a writer cuts out weak repetitions:

Original. He looked at Mike. Mike was his brother.

Tightened. He looked at his brother Mike.

Original. The beginning of the play shows Richard as a confident and strong man while the end shows him as a desolate and weak man.

Tightened. The beginning of the play shows Richard confident and strong; the end shows him desolate and weak.

Before you get carried away with cutting out weak repetition, remember that strong repetition is the heart of all good writing, in fact the heart of all good music making, hurdle racing, hammering, walking, or courting. Repetitions set up pattern. Only with pattern can you achieve emphasis and variety. Da-da-da, da-da-da, da-da-dum. That *dum* is smart because it comes after all those *da's*. It picks up its power as you wait through all those *da's* for something to happen. Repeat and vary. That's the secret of achieving significant form in all art and communication.

This book will demonstrate how the repeat-and-vary pattern strengthens writing in many ways, but for the present, consider only how to omit those repetitions in your writing which aren't working powerfully, which get in the readers' way rather than drive them down your road. If you can learn to say in a few words all you want to say, with precision and fullness, you'll delight yourself and your reader. We all love a person who says a great deal in a few words. Most of us feel that life will be too short; so we praise the person who can hammer the nail with only three blows. We don't want to hear:

> In order that the ruling organization of a country that is
> committed to a democratic organization organized to give

the people a voice in its procedures, and thinks of their well-being, shall not become disorganized and come to an end in these times . . .

And we don't want to hear:

That government of the people and government by the people and government for the people shall not perish from the earth.

That's so much government that we can't hear the people. We want to hear

. . . that government of the people, by the people, for the people, shall not perish from the earth.

That statement repeats *people,* not *government.* The man who wrote those words respected people and knew his *repeat-and-vary* principle. Further examples of how to repeat words powerfully will be presented in Chapter 12.

REVISING ONE: In your WRITING ONE and WRITING TWO papers, lightly circle all repeated words. Then consider each one. Do you want to retain it? If you want to omit it, draw brackets in pencil around it so that after you show the revision to others and give it time to cool off, you can restore an omitted word easily if you choose. Thomas Jefferson used brackets to recommend omissions to others, and most editors today follow him.

> *Life is the elimination of what is dead.*
> WALLACE STEVENS

The words *which, who,* and *that* often clutter up sentences. Good writers remove excessive Whooery, Whichery, or Thatery.

1. Mr. Rendew, Alice's father, [was a man who] actually liked to have his lawnmower go wrong so he could tinker with its motor.
2. George [is the type of man who] always shines his shoes before going downtown.
3. [The people that] I would like to tell you about [are] Father and Mother.

Other words, for example *all* and *what,* often fail to add meaning to a sentence and need cutting.

1. [All] I wish [is that] he would admit that passion has a respectable place in our lives.

2. [What I mean to say is that] no child should beat his mother.

The careless use of the word *thing* is more serious and damaging.

Original. The thing that enrages me is mosquitoes inside my open shirt collar.

Revision. Mosquitoes inside my open shirt collar enrage me.

3. [The] first [thing] I'd like to say [is] . . .

Original. Of all the things in the world I can't stand, boiled hot dogs are the worst.

Revision. I can't stand boiled hot dogs.

Why do schools turn out students so masterly in word wastery? Simple. Knowledge consists to some extent in naming and ordering things. So schools teach categorizing—how to place things in classes, species, etc. (Note that the word *things* is used twice in the two preceding sentences, but meaningfully, not emptily. These two uses of *things* are necessary and justifiable.)

Thus educated persons become addicted to such categorizing words as:

type	situation	phase	factor
kind	area	aspect	one

Often the words are not pulling their weight in a sentence.

Original. The first level of the poem gives the situation of a dull sergeant speaking to a group of new recruits.

Revision. The first level of the poem presents a dull sergeant speaking to a group of recruits.

1. The Queen realized that her life was not [a] carefree and spotless [one].
2. He was a typical [type of] fraternity man.

When a writer must categorize and generalize, these words are valuable, but often they are abominations.

Namery, another sickness, is the habit of naming things which do not need naming. Consider this passage:

Juliet and Rosalind are women who fall in love. This is one of the few similarities between these two characters. They are different in age, with Juliet being an impetuous adolescent and Rosalind being a mature adult. This difference is illustrated by the manner in which each character falls

> **in love. Juliet rushes into romance and gets married as quickly as possible while Rosalind makes sure of her love for Orlando—a much more rational and logical choice than Juliet's.**

This paragraph is devastated by Namery. The author says that Juliet and Rosalind fall in love and then unnecessarily says these acts are similar. He says the two are different in age and then later says one is an adolescent and the other an adult. He wastes completely the sentence:

> This difference is illustrated by the manner in which each character falls in love.

because the next sentence shows the difference specifically. The paragraph could be cut in half without losing essential meaning:

> One of the few similarities between Juliet and Rosalind is that they both fall in love; but Juliet rushes into romance while Rosalind makes sure of her love for Orlando. Juliet is an impetuous adolescent, Rosalind a mature adult.

Essentially Namery is a failure to recognize that one's audience may possess brains. The writer says:

> George came in with a new idea. It was a thought that had never struck his boss.

Readers don't need to be told that an idea is a thought. All they need is

> George came in with an idea that had never struck his boss.

In schools, Namery usually involves a special vocabulary.

> The causes of the basic difficulties in the area of mathematics are manifold. Fractions present the student with an entirely new set of assumptions.

The introductory sentence stupefies the reader with its dull buzzing. The writer should have said:

> Fractions are hard to learn because they present students with new assumptions.

Too often writers introduce everything to their audience: "Now we are going to look at large cities and then we are going to compare them with small towns," they say, when all they mean to do is compare Chicago, Illinois, with Bad Axe, Michigan.

REVISING TWO: Take one of your free writings you like best and tighten it by removing all Whooery, Whichery, Thatery, and Namery.

When you examine your own writing for weak repetition, you may not be able to see it. You need a way of looking for it. Ask yourself where you have said something twice without meaning to. The following passage from a student paper shows weak repetition of both words and ideas. Try cutting it in about half.

> **Hands, did you ever notice how many different kinds of men's hands there are? I first began to notice hands when I found that all men's hands were not as large as my Dad's hands. They were large, strong, and forceful, yet always gentle like the man. His hand encompasses mine even now when he takes it gently yet firmly, as though providing it with a cover of protection against the outside world. But he has always been like that, strong and protective, yet gentle. When those hands hold a baby, the baby stops crying and is quiet as though calmed by their strength and gentleness. When those hands take a pencil and draw an idea, the lines are firm and confident. Other men seem to respond when they shake his hand to the friendliness and strength behind the handshake.**

The assertions in that passage are simple and unsurprising. They don't need a lot of repetition to be clear to the reader.

REVISING THREE: Look over two of your past writings for meanings unnecessarily repeated. For example:

Valerie scrutinized my face [carefully].

The word *scrutinize* means to examine carefully.

Original. Richard has a consistently bad habit of not listening to what people are saying to him unless he's sure it will please him.

Revision. Richard consistently fails to listen to people unless he's sure they'll please him.

The word *habit* means a consistent or frequent action. Because *consistently* is used, *habit* can be eliminated.

The ground felt [peculiar. It was] soft as clouds.

If the ground was soft as clouds, it must have felt peculiar, and the writer need not make the opening comment. In the revision, she hits readers with surprise. She doesn't waste a word telling them that a surprise is coming. Note how the following verbose statement is brought alive by simple tightening:

Original. I see a man whose face is hidden by shadow except where the sun reveals it.

Revision. I see the sun-lit half of a man's face.

You may properly think of wasting words as a form of dishonesty. No writers mean to do it; but when they do it, they risk losing both the reader's attention and trust.

> *A young author is tempted to leave any-thing he has written through fear of not having enough to say if he goes cutting out too freely. But it is easier to be long than short.*
>
> SAMUEL BUTLER

If you stand right fronting and face to face to a fact, you will see the sun glimmer on both its surfaces, as if it were a cimeter [scimitar], and feel its sweet edge dividing you through the heart and marrow.

HENRY THOREAU

chapter 5
telling
facts

TELLING FACTS are lying all around you every minute of your life. Through free writing you've already seen they're available to you without asking. So let them come to you. If occasionally they won't, look for them, run them down.

Instead of saying,

> I found my trip to see my fiancé was marvelous. Being with him was even more thrilling than I thought it would be. I think it's real love.

give the reader the fact that drove you to that generalization,

> **He had a two-week leave after Basic, so I flew to Jersey and we stayed with his parents on the Shore. It was great being with him—even when his whole family watched us watch television.**

Instead of trying to express how great, how small, how wonderful, how sad something is, establish its size or intensity with facts. This is the natural way to write. A college junior living on a large campus one day realized something about her home town. Instead of saying,

> I had never realized how awfully small my home town is— really small!

she gave the facts that led her to that realization.

I hadn't realized how small my home town actually is until I received my absentee voter application from the township clerk today. He enclosed a note with the proper forms:

> Theo—Fill in balance of form & return in envelope provided.
>> Be seeing you—
>>> (signed) Graydon

Now the meaning in *awfully small* is precisely established. The writer didn't have to organize a treasure hunt to find these telling facts. They had come to her in an envelope and all she had to do was open them to her reader.

Not all facts speak powerfully. Some add up only to boredom. In that bad textbook you studied all the provisions of the treaties and all the principal rivers, but the facts never bunched together and spoke to you.

> *"It's something very like learning geography,"* thought Alice, *as she stood on tiptoe in hopes of being able to see a little farther. "Principal rivers—there are none. Principal mountains—I'm on the only one, but I don't think it's got any name."*
>
> LEWIS CARROLL

As a writer you can't help feel that all your facts belong together because they all belong to you, but your readers have no such glue working for them. They may not know you at all, and they don't know why one of your facts should appear beside another unless you make its relationship apparent. The world of things and ideas out there is no file drawer. It makes sense for us, reduces itself to something comprehensible, only as we look at it with an idea or feeling that sorts and selects. So writers are under a fierce obligation to choose those facts that seem to them and will seem to their readers to belong on the same page.

> *. . . only what fits is allowed.*
>
> NORMAN PODHORETZ

Professional writers make three or four drafts of their work to get rid of the facts that don't belong. In going through the program of this book, if you don't rewrite almost every paper that seems valu-

able to you and others, you won't give your thoughts and feelings the
presentation they deserve. Few good pieces of writing have been published that weren't cut and revised and added to.

Consider what might be cut from this story to ensure that everything
that remains is fitting.

FIRST DRAFT

**Sitting in the Student Union watching the bus boys do their
work brought to my mind memories of when Sandy and I
were on Mackinaw Island last summer. The bus boy went
around dumping ashtrays into his bucket, picking up trays
with large assortments of trash, and stashing them under
his cart.**

**On the island the only mode of transportation is man's
greatest invention, the horse. What caught my eye were the
similar facial expressions on the bus boy in the Student
Union and the boy who toted the wheelbarrow and shovel
behind the horse carriages on the island.**

**Sandy and I stopped and talked with that unfortunate
fellow. We were quite lost, and needed directions, but who
would ever think of asking a manure gatherer how to get to
a certain fort on the other side of the island? Embarrassing,
but we were lost. It was his expression which jolted me,
though. An unsure expression, his mouth and eyes abstractly forming a question mark. Imagine. A job shoveling
horse dung. Tourists with their Brownie Instamatic cam-
eras and their insolent children asking about the boy with
the wheelbarrow would be this young boy's biggest enemy.
He was in view of the whole world. He's no different from
anyone else, yet his job sets him apart.**

**He was embarrassed as I, at first; but after bulling
around for a few minutes, I knew that he was just like me,
except he knew where he was. My embarrassment was like
that of someone foreign to a large city asking a bum on
Skid Row to get to such and such a street. Not quite as
drastic, but on the same psychological level. But his expression—so lost, so uneasy, and I was the one who was lost.**

That paper was written freely in fifteen minutes. When the writer and
an editor worked it over until only the facts that spoke to each other
and to the writer's main intention remained, it was considerably
shorter. First, they decided that mentioning Sandy was unnecessary and
confusing. She may have been fascinating and have said or done things

that bore upon the author's relationship to the manure gatherer; but as she was presented, she didn't fit. She hadn't been made a working part of the story, and unless she were, she would have to depart. Second, they found many little facts and expressions in the story which were repetitive or weak, including the forced, unnecessary statement that the horse is "man's greatest invention." Here's the result of their revising:

SECOND DRAFT

The busboy in the Union went around dumping ashtrays into his bucket and stashing huge assortments of dishes and trays under his cart. His expression reminded me of a boy I saw on Mackinaw Island last summer, who toted a wheelbarrow and shovel behind the horse carriages.

I was lost and asked him, a manure gatherer, directions to a fort on the other side of the island. His expression jolted me: an unsure look, his mouth and eyes abstractly forming a question mark.

Imagine. A job shoveling horse dung! Tourists with their Kodak Instamatics and insolent children asking about the guy with the wheelbarrow.

We were both embarrassed. I felt like someone foreign to a large city asking directions of a bum on Skid Row; he expected me to be like the Instamatic People.

He was no different from me, except he knew where he was.

A fundamental in writing is to reach for a fact instead of trying to be lucky with a Great Idea. When you have to mention anything in order to tell a story or make a point, force yourself to put down the name of that thing if it has a name, or to show it in its particular setting or doing its thing particularly. Don't say you pushed the throttle and the motorbike did its thing. Give the name of that thing and the sound and feel or smell, or whatever you can.

Once a writer finds a telling fact and puts it down, it often pulls from the depths other telling facts. Once a university senior admitted that what she had written about her father was vague and unsatisfactory. Her professor told her to get some facts down, so they would begin suggesting other facts. She did. Here's the result:

Everytime I try to speak of my father I find words like *gentle*, *sweet*, *funny*, or *shy* popping up, and they are useless, meaningless. "Tell what your father *did*, what he *said*," you say, and I am stuck. How do I make a story from the things my father did?

I will tell you what he did.

My father walked to the far side of our pasture, found a cow with her newborn calf, and carried the calf home in his arms.

My father was rarely seen without at least two small children on or around him. He gave them horseback rides, told them funny stories, and lifted them atop a cow named Blackie, who didn't mind being used for a horse—his own children—until one by one all six of them grew too old for that sort of nonsense, then the young nieces and nephews, and next, last, the neighbor's children.

My dad followed me upstairs after he punished me once and said he was sorry and rubbed my back until I didn't cry anymore.

He raised and cared for twenty-five pure-bred Jersey cows, and he sang while he worked away his life and was poorer than any other farmer in the county.

My dad made a huge bowl of popcorn and spent countless hours reading Agatha Christie murder mysteries in bed as he munched.

Because he was an incurable dreamer, he straightened out the family's financial crises only on paper, by selling cows which in reality he could not bear to lose because he loved them.

When he was forty-seven years old my dad found out that he had a very serious heart condition, and he never went across the road to the barn again, but sat silent before the pot-bellied stove in our kitchen and puffed on a pipe. Every day he made tea and dry jokes for his wife and children and visitors.

When he felt stronger, he was sent to be rehabilitated in Waterloo, Iowa. On a bitter, cold day in January, 1959, he died in his sleep. He did not live to see his cows taken away that morning by the man who had bought them.

WRITING FIVE: Put down a telling fact about something that counts for you—an experience, idea, or feeling. Then wait to see if other facts are coming along behind it. If they are, start writing a story or extended comment without explaining or discussing anything except through telling facts. If you find the flow of facts has stopped, quit writing sentences and wait for a fact to arise. When it appears, write it down quickly as on a grocery list, then jot down others if they appear. After you have a sizeable list, begin writing again.

chapter 6
fabulous realities

MOST OF US go through each day looking for what we saw yesterday and we find it, to our half-realized disappointment. But people who daily expect to encounter fabulous realities run smack into them again and again. They keep their minds open for their eyes.

Asked to expect surprise, a number of students explored their nearby worlds for fabulous realities. Here are some they found:

1. I was speeding along the highway when I saw a small yellow sign.

    SLOW
    MEN
    WORKING

    It was followed by a larger one in black and white, reading

    YOUR HIGHWAY DOLLARS
    AT WORK

2. At a football game yesterday at Waldo Stadium a blind man sat next to me listening to his radio.

3. I stood in the checkout lane behind a boy who looked about sixteen. He waited for the clerk to begin ringing up his package

of Pall Malls, then reached out and added five packs of bubble gum.

4. Ever since Rennie found out that Jane, his co-worker, doesn't like him, he tries to upset her when they are together. I asked him why he did this. He said, "I hate intolerant people."

5. At the Allegan County Fair I approached the cotton candy stand and told the girl I wanted pink. After she gave it to me she turned to get my change and I noticed a piece of cotton in her ear.

6. Today I found a dead bird in the gutter with its mangled wing held in place by "Magic Transparent Tape."

7. A drunk teenager trying to cross West Main at Michigan assisted by a little old lady.

8. I excitedly opened my only two valentines from males. They were just alike.

9. A girl with a deep V in her blouse holding her books over it.

10. The instructor in Social Conflict said, "Man has aggressive tendencies and is less efficient in controlling them than other animals." A fly landed on his notes. With deadly accuracy he splattered it over the white paper.

11. A small boy, obviously lost, walked up to a security guard at Hudson's department store, and asked, "Did you see a lady walk by here without me?"

12. A pregnant woman carrying a globe of the world in front of her up a steep sidewalk in the city.

13. In the middle of a heated argument with me, my wife goes to the refrigerator, gets a bottle of ginger ale, fills two glasses, gives me one, and continues the argument.

Each statement surprises. It's not fairly surprising, but absolutely surprising, because it's unique. A robin sitting in the April snow in Illinois or Massachusetts wouldn't qualify as a fabulous reality. In those states a late short snow often occurs after robins have arrived.

Tension is necessary to make a fabulous reality. Two things that don't belong together touch in some way. And their touching creates waves of further suggestion that aren't stated. In the middle of the young man's argument, his wife interrupts him, but not to put him down, rather to make him more comfortable. The argument is heated; she gives him a cold drink.

> *When I went to those great cities I saw*
> *wonders I had never seen in Ireland. But*
> *when I came back to Ireland I found all*

the wonders there waiting for me. You
see they had been there all the time;
but my eyes had never been opened to
them. I did not know what my own
house was like, because I had never been
outside it.

BERNARD SHAW [*Keegan speaking*]

COLLECTING ONE: This weekend keep a piece of paper or note-book in your pocket or pocketbook and jot down five fabulous reali-ties you see. When you have a chance, write them in sentences. Keep revising them until you have built up to the surprise rather than given it away weakly. Note that most of the above fabulous realities (1) place the happening in a particular setting, (2) put the reader there through telling details, (3) make the action happen for the reader as it hap-pened for the writer, (4) don't waste words, (5) don't explain, but present facts and force the reader to find the surprise, (6) put the kicker at the end.

The following passage suffers because of Explainery:

> **Last week I saw two guys walking down Western Avenue carrying on a conversation ten feet apart. I even walked between them. Interpersonal relationships are growing less personal, but this was too much almost to believe. One of them, I suppose, had determined to assert himself, keep his pace, and have the other come up to him. The other prob-ably determined the opposite, so they walked along making fools of themselves.**

That's a beautiful comment on life and contains all the elements necessary to a fabulous reality, but it needs better telling. Here's a possible rewriting:

> Last week I saw two guys walking down Western Avenue carrying on a conversation ten feet apart. As one quickened his pace, so did the other. Even when I walked between them, they kept up their conversation. Interpersonal rela-tionships are growing less personal.

In that passage the last sentence violates the rule for fabulous realities of not explaining the point. But an editor might urge the writer to use it there because its sociological language contrasts with the ridiculous but down-to-earth behavior of the two boys and so creates another kind of tension and surprise. You may find one of your fabulous realities gains by such a plain and outright judgment at the end, but usually these short charged statements lose too much of their electricity when judgments or explanations are given.

Note how the facts in this fabulous reality do all the telling by themselves.

> **A pimply-faced, dirty, barefooted, greasy, string-haired girl smoking a cigarette and eating a peanut butter and jelly sandwich riding a crowded elevator at the University of Michigan while reading How to Win Friends and Influence People.**

COLLECTING TWO: Collect five or more additional fabulous realities. Don't be easily satisfied. Tension. Punch at the end. Uniqueness. Implications or suggestions that spread beyond the statement.

The looking and discovering involved in producing fabulous realities isn't a trick and not an exercise. It's the way good writers see. Because their eyes aren't tired, their readers turn their pages with surprise. In *People of the Abyss,* a book about the city of London, Jack London wrote:

> From the slimy spittle-drenched sidewalk, they were picking up bits of orange peel, apple skin, and grape stems, and they were eating them. The pits of green gage plums they cracked between their teeth for the kernels inside. They picked up stray crumbs of bread the size of peas, apple cores so black and dirty one would not take them to be apple cores, and these things these two men took into their mouths, and chewed them, and swallowed them; and this, between six and seven o'clock in the evening of August 20, year of our Lord 1902, in the heart of the greatest, wealthiest, and most powerful empire the world has ever seen.

Note that Jack London is here not just telling an unusual incident but is writing toward an idea—that the great English capital city didn't save its citizens from degrading poverty. Surprising realities suffuse good essays and articles as they do good stories. One of the reasons students in schools seldom write powerful themes or essays is that they mistakenly think good nonfiction writing is abstract and dull. Actually, the best writers of nonfiction (articles, essays, autobiography, history, etc.) continually surprise their readers with fabulous realities.

When you read accounts others have written of surprising realities like Jack London's, you may feel they were lucky but you were never blessed. But reality is often fabulous for anyone who remains awake.

> *He [Thoreau] knew how to sit immovable, a part of the rock he rested on, until the bird, the reptile, the fish, which had retired from him, should come back and resume its habits, nay, moved by curiosity, should come to him and watch him.*
>
> RALPH WALDO EMERSON

The unfamiliar frequently appears amazing, as does the familiar when it's scrutinized more closely than usual.

WRITING SIX: Some of the fabulous realities you discover may require more setting and development than others. Jack London needed more than two or three lines to build the surprise and meaning of his observation of men eating garbage in London. Here's such an Extended Fabulous Reality written by a young woman:

> **I was walking down the sidewalk, picking colored leaves out of scattered piles along the curb when a group of elephant-shouldered boys in football uniforms turned into the street, cussing, shouting, and glaring ahead of them as if looking for someone to kick.**
>
> **I stood back against a tree to let them pass, and the tallest boy slowed down, stopped and picked something up. Turning and walking back toward me, he reached out and set it carefully in my hand. It was a tiny pale yellow leaf, with no breaks in it anywhere.**
>
> JANN H. CAIN

Often we encounter memorable surprises that are too short to be stated in the classic pared-down form of a fabulous reality but not long enough to constitute a publishable short story or article. Don't allow those moments to pass unrecorded. Write them down, tighten and polish them. Maybe you can find a way to present them with others like a string of fat beads. Maybe your teacher will publish yours and those of other students on a bulletin board or in a broadsheet.

The following little story depends as much for its surprise upon the feelings of the writer as upon the details of the account. In it, the ordinarily weak word *very* is used to help signal the surprise.

GOLDEN LEAVES

We drove slowly along a leaf-filled road. Cars passed and made the leaves flutter behind them. A soft crackling sound. We wanted to drink in enough of fall to last us through the winter.

To my right I saw a girl. She was fat and very ugly. Some distance behind her was a bright red pick-up truck. It was old but appropriate. The girl was smiling.

She stood in a small valley surrounded by huge trees. Golden leaves were up to her knees. She was putting away a badminton net for the winter. It had been tied to trees. She had loosened one end and was carefully folding it, walking slowly toward the other. A soft wind came up and dropped more leaves around her. She brushed one away that landed in her hair. As she walked, she kicked piles of leaves. Her house was to her right. It was big, white, and fit in the country. A spotted dog ran out to join her. He barked playfully at her feet.

She was laughing and very beautiful.

MINDY STILES

Record two extended fabulous realities. If you search for surprising moments in the past, they'll come to you. Don't force. Don't try for side-splitting gags. Don't retell someone else's trite story. Simply put down an event. As you can see, it may involve the ordinary—an ugly girl, a yellow leaf—but told as a reality, as it happened, it grows and develops into surprise.

chapter 7
through
facts
to realities

HERE'S A PASSAGE that might be called
Bad Edgar Allan Poe:

> Perhaps the most unusual incident of my childhood occur-
> red in the living room of my own suburban home. The
> mantelpiece in that room was an eight-by-one-foot block of
> solid sandstone which protruded substantially out from the
> formation of lesser blocks which supported it. I was seated
> on the floor directly under the mantelpiece moderately
> absorbed in a book, when a harsh crack and a heavy grating
> sound tore my gaze upward. The mantelpiece was falling.
> Falling on me . . . I lunged. The movement was probably
> born more of instinct than logic, but it saved me certain in-
> jury. The huge sandstone mass missed me completely, but
> one of the smaller blocks dragged down with it fell with
> painful impact on my left forearm. I was quite lucky, or so I
> was told.

In that passage, the writer keeps nudging the reader and saying between the lines, "Isn't this a horrifying experience? Right now you're
supposed to be thrilled and frozen in fear." The nudges are in the adjectives and adverbs: *most unusual* incident, protruded *substantially*
(are most protrusions unsubstantial?), *moderately* absorbed (please
man, look up the word *absorbed*) , *harsh* crack (do cracks sound soft
and sweet ever?), *painful* impact. The writer won't let the facts speak.

53

He's like a mother telling you her little boy is a great story teller and interrupting him to improve upon his story.

This account of the falling of a mantelpiece, like most poor writing, is heavy in style where it should be heavy in fact. The falling of a mantelpiece upon a child is a weighty matter, but here the writing is ponderous, not the blow from the mantelpiece. It's dishonest writing. Note the last sentence:

I was quite lucky, or so I was told.

You're not sure? You had to be told? Probably the writer began writing the account with the same dishonest attitude. He was going to impress people with a near tragedy. When a writer messes around with little truths in this way, he can't go through the facts to larger truths. But if he keeps faith with himself and what he's writing about, he makes a small experience illuminate the nature of similar or parallel experiences the reader has had. For example:

> With one foot rested on a bag of cement and his chin lean-ing on the back of his hand, which was cupped over the end of a long-handled shovel, Steve watched me while I filled the cement mixer with shovelful after shovelful of gravel. As his blue eyes followed every movement I made, he twitched his bicep and kept saying, "I sure hope you can wheel cement. You said you could."
>
> Without answering, I began the mixer, and turned on the water. The drum inside rotated slowly, throwing the dry gravel and powdery cement together with a stream of water. Within minutes the solution had been thoroughly mixed and small, wet globs of cement were being spit out of the mixer as the cement inside slapped back and forth.
>
> Steve relaxed his bicep and motioned for me to position the wheelbarrow in closer to the mixer. After I was ready, he poured the cement into the wheelbarrow. Cement is thick but very loose, and moving it in a wheelbarrow is difficult. The momentum of the solution is in the direction it goes.
>
> I crouched down, picking up the handles, and eased forward. I felt every pound shift as half the mass of mud sloshed forward, the other half to the right. I took about five steps, moving each foot deliberately from one posi-tion to the next, as if a weighted yoke was balancing on my shoulders. After the fifth step I found myself struggling

with 400 pounds of cement and the next moment there lay an unplotted sidewalk and an overturned wheelbarrow in front of me. Steve, trying to control the twitch in his bicep, jeered, "I thought you said you could run a wheel-barrow!"

MICHAEL PARRISH

In that piece of writing, the cement moves and the writer gets to the wet facts and the feeling of things going out of control in the hands of a novice. The writer put down such telling facts that they said more than he expected them to. He wrote essentials and produced essences.

WRITING SEVEN: Choose an experience that affected you strongly and write down its telling facts as truthfully as you can. Try to go right through those facts until you feel inside the experience as physically as you feel the sweaty warmth of your body inside a thick unbreathing raincoat on a hot summer day.

Here's a girl doing that in what might be called a little case-history:

At 10:30 Wednesday morning—a few trucks every once in a while on I94 and one or two cars. Joe made me put my seatbelt on before he went to sleep in the back seat. My stomach was a little tense. I was constantly aware that I was driving someone else's car at an unwavering 65. It was like flying.

As I approached a slower-moving blue Galaxie, I put my turn signal on, glided over into the left lane before I came too close to him, never losing or gaining speed. I put my turn signal on after checking in my rearview mirror and glided back into the right hand lane still going 65. I was coming up to a cream colored Plymouth trailing a semi. I glanced in my side view mirror, turned my head slightly to check my blind spot—it was clear—and pulled into the left lane again. As I was practically alongside the old lady in the Plymouth, she started to move in my direction.

I was going to give her the horn and reached for the chrome half-circle. It wasn't there. Of course not, this wasn't my car. I didn't want to use the power brakes because I wasn't used to them and at 65 I was afraid I'd put both Joe in the back seat, and me, through the windshield. I was sure she wouldn't hit me. And she'd see me before she got much closer. I heard a small clank and the highway, trees, hills, and cars were spinning like a rotating

moving picture was being played around the windshield. I
felt a lurch and the picture had abruptly changed. I was
looking straight down the hood of Joe's car onto the ground,
thinking I was going to die. Only the words existed in my
head—"I'm going to die." The car bounced back down,
not turning over, and stopped. I turned around to see what
happened to Joe. He wasn't sleeping any more, but sitting
straight up. Leaning forward, clutching the back of my
seat, he was all right. The numbness left my body and was
replaced by a sense of people milling around the car and
opening the door next to me. I looked at Joe and started
to cry.

NANCY HUNTER

In that account the writer didn't give the old line about a car accident: "everything happened so fast it was a blur, and when I began
to understand what had occurred . . ." but let facts, recounted one after
another, show the instantaneousness and yet the clarity of the action
for her. That paradoxical combination is one of the essences of most
accidents.

The factual narratives in this chapter all tell what the writers did
and felt. They are written about them and from their viewpoint.
Here's a short account telling facts about *someone else's* experience and
going through the facts to the essence:

Two men are moving sod with a wheelbarrow on the lawn
outside Waldo Library. They take turns hauling the dirt
from the truck to the area for the new seedlings. When it's
one man's turn, the other walks behind a respectful distance, but doesn't touch the wheelbarrow even when it
stalls on a rock on the steep grade. He stands off a few
paces while the hauler dumps the load awkwardly, scrap-
ing with a shovel in one hand while tipping the wheelbarrow with the other hand and his knee. After all the dirt
is out, the second man steps forward and rakes the sod into
place. They then reverse jobs and repeat the operation.

What the observer of that little charade found by going through the
facts were the essentials of not working very hard.

A beginning writer should simply tell us what he or she knows. A
case-history of how she carried her papers on the route one morning,
of how he prepares for school in a family of seven in a house with one
bathroom, of how she got ready to play her first game of varsity basket-

ball. A day, a week, an hour—in which a writer takes readers through a process. It can be a story of someone or something else in action, going through an interval of time.

WRITING CASE-HISTORIES

You don't have to be a professional writer to tell a case-history with authority and power. You only have to know your journey intimately and carry some attitude toward it that enables you to select details that keep the history alive and significant—something more than a bad list of names and dates. Michihiko Hachiya, a medical doctor in Japan, was wounded on August 6, 1945, by the first nuclear explosion directed against human beings. The next morning he awoke to groans of patients and a new Hiroshima. He told the story of his experiences, a simple case-history of what happened to him then.

> Dr. Katsube looked me over and after feeling my pulse, said: "You received many wounds, but they all missed vital spots."
>
> He then described them and told me how they had been treated. I was surprised to learn that my shoulder had been severely cut but relieved at his optimism for my recovery.
>
> "How many patients are in the hospital?" I asked Dr. Koyama.
>
> "About a hundred and fifty," he replied. "Quite a few have died, but there are still so many that there is no place to put one's foot down. They are packed in everywhere, even the toilets."
>
> •   •   •
>
> Downstairs, I ran into Mr. Hirohata sitting on a bench and sat down beside him. Mr. Hirohata had been employed in the Telephone Bureau and was at work in the building when the explosion occurred. Despite the fact that he was less than four hundred meters from the hypocenter, Mr. Hirohata escaped injury.
>
> "How did you avoid injury when nearly everyone around you was killed or hurt?" I asked.
>
> "The thick concrete wall of the building protected me," answered Mr. Hirohata, "but people standing near the windows were killed instantly or died later from burns or cuts. The night shift was just leaving and the day shift coming

on when the explosion occurred. Forty or more were killed near the entrance. About fifteen employees in the construction department, stripped to the waist, were outside taking gymnastics. They died instantly.

"Doctor, a human being who has been roasted becomes quite small, doesn't he? Those people all looked like little boys after the explosion. Is there any reason why my hair should be falling out and I feel so weak? I'm worried, doctor, because I have been told that I would die and this has already happened to some people I know who didn't seem to be hurt at all by the *pika*."

"Mr. Hirohata, I don't believe you need worry about yourself," I answered, trying to be reassuring, "Like so many others, you've been through a dreadful experience, and on top of that have tried to work night and day here at the Bureau. What else could one expect? You must go home, stay absolutely quiet in bed, and get all the good nourishing food you can."

This excerpt from a 233-page book shows that Dr. Hachiya wrote down his experience in incidents and conversations as they came to him. He called the book *Hiroshima Diary: The Journal of a Japanese Physician, August 6—September 30, 1945*. He told what he did, what others did, whom he saw, what they said to each other. Writers of case-histories try to put the reader there, right in the process, the place, the action. If they see a woman riding a bicycle with a broken red reflector on its rear bumper, they don't write: "I saw a woman riding a damaged bicycle," but "I saw a woman riding a bicycle with a broken red reflector on its rear bumper."

If you record the details of a process or experience and then write them into a case-history, in one sense you're an authority. You may not know more about that process or experience than some others, but your written record commands respect by its truth to particular fact. Here's a case-history written by a student:

THROUGH THE GATES

When I walked through the gates of McLean Steel everybody from the afternoon shift was watching me. They stared as if they could sense I was a new worker. As I walked I glanced to my left and saw a short fat man looking at me. He was clean and chewing a cigar between his crummy smile. I looked to the right and saw a kid about my age sitting on the curb. His clothes and face were dirty and he looked worn out. He wasn't smiling. I seemed to be on a long endless walk, but finally I reached the labor hut. This was the second initiation point, but the workers' stares didn't bother me because I had already seen the kinds of looks they were giving me. I wasn't surprised to find a lot of laborers were college kids working for the summer.

At exactly midnight our foreman for the week came into the hut with a job list. It didn't take long to find out how important seniority was in bidding for jobs. As it turned out, the lowest workers on the list, eight other college kids and I, had to work in the rust-furnace basement—a job no one else wanted. The basement was full of leaking hot water pipes which had rusted, and together with the heat gave the basement its name.

I went outside, grabbed a shovel, and followed the others. We went down flights of stairs to a basement full of many rooms. The heat was tremendous and soon everyone was in their T-shirts. It felt like we were being pushed into a large oven. The rooms were filled with mud, sand, slime, and bricks, as well as rocks which had hardened into large piles. Covering the basement floor were about six inches of muddy water.

Our foreman showed up and told us our job was to clean out about three-fourths of the rooms in the basement. We were supposed to place the debris on a conveyor. We all looked around and then at each other, and no one moved until the foreman yelled, "Are you guys waiting for an invitation? Get the hell to work!"

We divided the jobs so that two men worked with picks on the piles, four men shoveled, two men rolled the wheelbarrows, and the last man worked the conveyor. We switched jobs periodically so as to make the work even. I was sweating just standing still. The stagnant odor of the water made me sick. The rooms were small, so we worked under cramped conditions. Mike was swinging a pick and had to lean against a wall to get at the pile he was supposed to work. Hot water was leaking down the wall from the pipes above and hitting him. Leaning against the wall was the only way to get the job done. Somebody had to do it and since it was his turn, he didn't complain. Everybody else was doing their job. Bruce wore out his gloves, so everyone took turns going without gloves. The blisters came easier, but unnoticed after a while.

We worked at a good pace for three hours, until lunch time, which was at three in the morning. When I walked outside, a cool breeze gave me the chills. I just stood there, taking deep breaths, letting the air soak through all the bones in my body. Everybody sat on a curb looking out through a fence onto a street. It felt like being in prison. Nobody said much, and if they did, nobody listened. I took off my helmet and lay on some grass looking up at the stars. It was funny how good the calm night and stars made me feel. After twenty minutes I started back to the basement. I looked up and felt I was heading from heaven to purgatory.

When everybody reached the basement we decided to finish the job early. For two hours we strained and shoveled as fast as we could to get the job done. The heat soaked up what energy everyone had left and we were all exhausted. We found a long bench and sat down, waiting for quitting time. After a few minutes the foreman came back and told us to finish the rest of the basement, and left. No one moved: half of the guys didn't hear him because they were sleeping. When he came back, he kicked everyone awake and gave us a speech which was supposed to make us jump to our feet.

"Do you want your jobs?" he brightly asked. No one answered. "Then get up and start working and if I see anyone sitting down again, you're fired."

We started cleaning the rest of the rooms. The piles seemed larger, shovels were heavier, and wheelbarrows harder to push. Blisters didn't go unnoticed and backs started aching like hundreds of needles were sticking to our skins. When I was rolling one of the wheelbarrows to the conveyor, it tipped over. I bent to pick up some rocks and noticed him standing above the basement making sure the work got done, waiting for someone to relax. His smile made me feel like he was Satan laughing at all the suckers he had working for him in Hell.

Well, we got the job done and I got out of that hole and sat on a curb waiting to check out. Morning workers would glance at me when they walked by. I didn't smile.

At eight in the morning I finally checked out and walking to my car wasn't surprised to hear, "Hey Joe, I'll meet you at the bar in ten minutes."

I think I could have gone for a drink then.

MARIO ROVEDA

Writing case-histories is one of the best means of learning the secret of once. You can begin at a natural beginning—when you punched the time clock and started work or when the first act in a process was carried out. Then you can keep on telling the incident through time, as it happened. To give your reader the full experience, you may have to take facts from several different days' experience and put them together so they appear to belong to only one day. That's not necessarily presenting the case falsely, if you're trying to show what the whole experience has meant to you. Only if you distort the truth of fact and feeling are you lying as a writer; for example, if you tell of working at a Dairy Queen stand in a small town where business was almost always slow and you collect facts from only the unusually busy days like the town's Centennial celebration you'd be misrepresenting the ongoing fact of your work. But if the Centennial day impressed you, you might make your story a case-history of what a busy day was like in an ordinarily unbusy town. Whatever your decision, it will be a liberating one if you swing at some truths that counted for you.

Here's a case-history of a girl's love affair with a car.

FIRST CAR

I had driven my first car somewhere between 1,000 and 1,500 miles, and a little slip of white paper in the glove compartment told me it was time for an oil change and grease job. So I pulled into a Shell station and asked if I could make an appointment. I was told to come back two days later at 5:00 and they would have time to do it. On that day I drove in and hauled out that piece of paper that told me what I was supposed to know about keeping my car running.

"How many cans of oil does this car hold?" I asked, saying *cans* instead of *quarts*, *pints*, or *gallons*, so I wouldn't seem like I was totally ignorant.

"It depends on what size can you use." He blew it, but saved me by adding, "It'll hold four of those over there in the window."

I smiled as if to say, "Of course," then like my dad had told me (and written on the piece of paper) I told him how to add the oil.

"OK," I said, "put in one quart less than it will hold and add a can of CD_2."

"I never heard of CD_2" he retorted. This made me feel superior because here I, just a car-stupid girl, knew about something he didn't.

"How about a can of STP?" he asked. He had to explain that it was an "additive" (which left a big question in my mind, but I kept my mouth shut).

"All right, if you're sure it's the same thing," I answered, knowing he couldn't possibly say it was if he didn't know what CD_2 was. "Put in one quart less than it will hold," I repeated, "and add a can of STP."

"Look, little Miss Wisconsin," he boomed—I guess he noticed my license plates—"STP *mixes* with the oil. It doesn't increase the oil level."

"But my dad said—" (I pouted, looking at my little white sheet of salvation). He didn't let me finish.

"That may be true if it's with that other stuff, not with this," he said, shoving a can of STP through the window of the car.

So I relented, figuring he must know more than I did, even if he hadn't ever heard of CD_2.

A few days later, I pulled in and a new guy came over to the car.

"Oh, so you're the girl from Wisconsin! What did your dad tell you to do now, put gas in it?"

Right then it became clear that I never could get excited about that car. It never would be mine. It belonged to the garage mechanic, the fuel pump, the oil can, and to the one thing that made it possible to get these—the credit card, which was in my dad's name. Even the charge card belongs to the oil company, really, so I'm just taking that car into its owners to care for, and who am I to tell someone what to do with what belongs to them?

DARCY CUDLIP

WRITING EIGHT: Write a case-history. Put the reader there through telling facts and try to go through them to some essentials of what you are writing about.

To do this you must know intimately and deeply what you are writing about. Either choose an experience or process you have gone through many times, or sit down before a happening and take notes on it as it happens.

REVISING FOUR: When you've finished your first draft of the case-history, put it aside for a day. Then read it aloud to see whether any leading idea or feeling emerges. If you find one stirring a little, consider cutting out those parts that don't touch this idea or feeling, and adding more details that strengthen it.

If you care about what you write, and know or observe it closely, you'll reveal to your readers things they don't know. Stay awake when you observe. If you or other human beings are in action, the chances are high that you'll be recording some fabulous realities.

A professional caution: Consider changing real names in your case-history to fictional names. What if your work becomes published, or passed around locally? What you consider an unbiased report of how Mrs. Smithweather, the science teacher, swore at John Saunders in lab may not strike Mrs. Smithweather in that way. If you had money, she might properly sue you for libel. Some real names you must keep in your writing or its point may be lost, but inspect all names and weigh the need to change them. Samuel Butler wrote a long book which became the classic English story of a rebellious son and a tyrannical, self-righteous father. Butler's real father was a sadist to him, but he refused to publish this book until after his father had died. And then it came out as a novel, with Butler's father carrying a fictional name. Butler himself died before *The Way of All Flesh* was published and he never knew that he had written one of the finest novels in the English language. The least you can do is protect Mrs. Smithweather and yourself by changing names.

But to have a full kit of auditory pat-
terns curved to real emotions we do need
to listen. We need to listen, with inside
matching on our own part, to those
whose phrases fit their inner state. We
are lucky if we listen less to lecturers and
experts, more to farmers, mechanics,
truck drivers . . . laundresses, and child-
ren out of school.

SIDNEY COX

chapter 8
people
talking

"WHAT?" said John.
"What'd you say?" said Mary.
"I said *what*."

A pretty nothing conversation, but it probably caught you, held you,
and perhaps brought a slight smile to your face. The moment a writer
presents a person saying something and the reader realizes another
person is around to hear it, a small tension builds in the reader until
he finds out what the response is.

Think of using conversation in your writing. It's a way of adding
opposition and suspense. Most persons who haven't written much dialogue think it's difficult to produce. On the contrary, it's easy for most
beginning writers. They've heard conversation all their lives—listened
to more words than they've read.

Conversation gives force to writing and cuts down on Explainery.
In a dialogue the writer doesn't constantly say how the speakers feel as
they respond to each other. Frequently they say the opposite of what
they feel. The reader has to figure out whether one man's words are
striking sparks with the others' or cooling them or making no contact
at all.

64

When you write conversation, try for truth to the feeling and ideas expressed by persons in real situations. Try also for the true sound of each speaker's language–languages. Every person speaks a native language that belongs to her country. She also speaks a dialect, which belongs to a region of the country. She speaks jargons or argots which belong to a group of persons she associates with at play or work—the gang from 14th Street or the workers at the Aerospace Company. And she speaks an idiolect, or personal language, which is hers alone. It's spiced by a word or two she made up herself, or an original grammatical construction she fell into at age four and never climbed out of.

You can tell quickly when a written conversation is phony. Engfish conversation, for example. The supermarket cashier is saying "Oh, it's been delightful to have you as our customer today, Miss Watkins," or the bank manager is saying, "OK, Watkins. You write the check properly, we give you the bread."

Here's a college dialogue:

1

(Women's residence hall. Girl sitting at study desk. Enter Jean, friend from down the hall.)

Jean: Hi, Lin!

Lin: Hi, Jean: (Phone rings.) Just a minute. (She rises and walks to phone and picks up receiver.) Hello.

Tom: Hi, Lin. Whatcha doin'?

Lin: Oh, hi, Tom! I'm writing a paper for Teaching and Learning.

Tom: Huh?

Jean (turns and starts to leave room): Talk ta ya later, Lin. Tell Tom I said hi.

Lin (nodding to Jean): Writing a paper for Teaching and Learning. Jean said hi.

Tom: What's it about?

Lin: Just a paper on teaching.

Tom: Who's there with ya?

Lin: Nobody:

Tom: What the hell'd I hear then?

Lin: Jean just left.

Tom: Thought ya said nobody was there!

Lin (sarcastically): Huh?

Tom: Forget it! (Pause.) How many guys in your classes this semester?

Lin: Two.

Tom: Two? Come on, how many are there?

Lin: Two!

Tom: O.K. How many in your other class?

Lin: One.

Tom: Huh?

Lin: Yeh! Not many guys in elementary ed.

Tom: God, quit lyin' ta me!

Lin: I'm not lying, Tom!

Tom: Hell, come on, I know ya.

Lin: After three and a half years, you sure don't act like you do!

Tom: God, don't start preachin', this is costin' me money! (Pause.)

Lin: Okay. Goodbye! (Pause.)

Tom: Yeh. Bye.

Lin: Tom? I love you.

Tom: Can't hear ya, the damn fans are runnin'.

Lin: Tom, come on!

Tom (quickly): Yeh, I lub ya. Bye. (Click)

Lin: Sonofabitch!

That's a conversation. Two persons exchanging words, listening to each other, responding. Like most good writers, the author of that dialogue wrote out of close knowledge. If she were writing of diplomats or plumbers—making them talk—she might have made a mess of their conversation because she couldn't use her ear.

In the following dialogue, a mother uses her ear to remember how she and her boy talk to each other. The responses are quick and frank. You can tell that this mother knows her child but that he's not her peer.

2

(3:30 and my 7-year-old was arriving home from school.)

Hi, David, how are you?

OK, I guess. Didn't have a good day at school, though.

Oh? What happened?

Nobody likes me. John wouldn't let me play on his football team at recess.

Um, wonder why. You always have before. Did you say or do something to make him mad?

(Taking off his jacket and dropping it on the floor), Nope. He just said, "Brown, you can't play today."

Didn't you ask why?

If I had, he would have said, " 'Cause you're too stupid."
Nobody likes me.

David, you know that isn't true.

Yes it is. Mrs. Strand wouldn't ask me a question either.

Well David, I know everyone in the class can't be asked a
question every day. There just isn't enough time.

(Looking up at me in a disgusted way), Mom, there are
32 kids in my class. Everyone else was asked a question.

Oh good grief, David, everyone?

Well, almost. She doesn't like me, either. You don't even
like me, do you, Mom? You just yelled at me.

David, why don't you go in your room and play awhile?

(He gives me a big grin.) OK, Mom.

In informal conversation, persons seldom give speeches to each
other, or lectures. Part of the truth of Dialogue 1 comes from the
short answers given by the speakers. But sometimes a speech will erupt
into a little sermon. The writer presenting it must be sure it's lively
or that its dullness sharpens the whole dialogue or he'll bore his
reader as the speechifier often bores his listeners. In the following dialogue, a woman suddenly gives a lecture to her roommates.

3

Barbie: Why don't you think he came?

Ann: I dunno.

Barbie: Maybe because we didn't really seem to click last
time we were together. Remember, I told you about it? He
was in a super good mood, and I was kind of depressed
because of all that work I had to do. Do you think that
could be it?

Ann: Maybe.

Barbie: I wish I just knew for sure. I hate guessing. I'm
sure I'd feel a whole lot better if I knew the reason.

Ann: What difference would it make?

Barbie: Well, at least I'd know. I wouldn't have to go
through all these tortuous guessing games, would I? It
would either be a good reason that I would accept and
forgive him for, and everything would be all right. Or else
it would be just an excuse and everything would be over.
But I'd know one way or the other. Don't you see that at
all?

Ann: He still didn't come, did he?

Barbie: God, Ann, aren't you the least bit sensitive? Or even curious? After all, Ben is a pretty big part of my life. He's the only boy I'm dating now and I see him practically every weekend. You know it's pretty hard to just meet boys anywhere. It's so much easier if you're at a party with a date. You meet a thousand guys that way. And they think you must have something to be there in the first place. They sure feel different about asking a girl out that they've met at a party before, and just picking someone up in the Union. I really don't understand you. Sometimes you don't seem to know anything about the way things are. You didn't even seem to care when Michael started living with some other girl all of a sudden. You never said a word to me about it. I thought you would feel something after a year and a half. I wish I knew what to do. At least you're usually sensible. Do you think I should call him?

Ann: I don't know if you'll understand this or not, Barbie, but *I don't care what you do!*

Because conversations are inherently dramatic they're often more persuasive than lectures or sermons or editorials. Here's a conversation that makes a point about the writer's attitude toward a patriotic ritual in a school. The reader is expected to recognize the point from what's said in the dialogue.

4

(Fifth-grade class, 9:00 A.M.)

Mike: Will you please stand to say the pledge.

Class: I pledge allegiance to the flag of the United States of America, and to the republic for which it stands, one nation, under God——

Teacher: Excuse me, class. Mike, why aren't you saying the pledge with us? You're the pledge leader. That's an important job.

Mike (hesitating): It doesn't make sense. Our nation isn't run by God.

Teacher: Now, Mike, we all know that we say the pledge so that we can feel we all belong to one nation, and we're working to make that nation great. Now you wouldn't want us to think you aren't proud of our country, would you?

Mike: No—I guess not.

Teacher: Let's start again.

(The pledge is said the second time.)

Teacher: All right, let's all get our handwriting books and begin working on page 9. (Pause.) Mike, did you hear me? You're going to have to shape up. That's twice I've had to speak to you today, and in only ten minutes!

(Mike looks down at his feet as everyone stares at him, and mutters): See, God's not running my nation.

In the following dialogue a subtle tension is built without any stage directions or explanations by the writer.

5

(Open house on Sunday in the dorm.)

How do you like my room?

Who are those guys on the wall?

Just some friends. One of them is Jack. Guess which?

That.

Nope. That. I'll take him away. I'll replace them all when I get your picture.

You don't have to.

I know, but I want to. Do you want to see my photo album?

Sure.

Sit down. Oh, thanks for the roses again, see.

I see, they were long, that's good. Is that the card? What did it say?

Tom.

Let me see. Hey, I said to write more.

Here's a pen, write some more.

"To Renée with love." I don't sign my name that way.

Do it again there.

When was this taken? I don't like you with short hair. Don't cut it.

Why not?

Because I don't want you to.

O.K.

Who's that guy?

Jack.

Where was it?

In our back yard.

With a flower in hand.

I like it, it was our senior party. Let me take your picture. Don't get up! Come on.

Come on where? I don't like it.

Well, I do. Take that rose and hold it.

Do you always ask guys to hold flowers?

No, just special people.

How about Jack? Special people, eh?

That's all over. Take it now. Not in your mouth. Tom,
stay still.

I hate this.

You gave it to me.

In the above small drama you probably sensed the tight, nervous,
half-joking sound of a conversation between persons testing each
other's romantic feeling. A delicate probing, yet revealed in the
sparest dialogue.

> *I notice particularly the cadence of*
> *their voices, the sort of phrases they'll*
> *use, and that's what I'm all the time try-*
> *ing to hear in my head, how people*
> *word things—because everybody speaks*
> *an entirely different language . . .*
>
> FRANK O'CONNOR

WRITING NINE: Write two short dialogues that carry truth that
counts for you and voices that you believe speak truly and individually.

WRITING TEN: Now write down an experience or a person and
use dialogue to inject life and tension into the paper. Maybe you
already have done a free writing that can be extended and strengthened with conversation. Note how the dialogue in the following
paper gives validity to its happenings. The children have their way
of talking, the bus driver has his, and neither talking sounds like
the writer writing.

6

I do not enjoy riding in cars. My somewhat sane mind
becomes lost, and instinct takes over. Every driver on the
road, including the one driving me, must be a maniac.

Buses are different, however. On the campus route, it
doesn't matter where I sit. It's always so crowded you can't
see where you're going. The bus driver reigns supreme.
You put yourself in his hands and suddenly Linus's blanket

envelops you. Perhaps I should have said buses *were* different, though.

Yesterday my last class ended. I was wary. All of a sudden here comes the bus. Calling up some unknown energy reserve, I dashed to the corner; hair, purse, and earrings flapping. The all-knowing bus driver stopped. He was taking some grade schoolers home and said he had to go to the trailer parks behind Wayside before going to the East Campus. "Do you mind?" God, no. I just wanted to sit down.

The kids were running up and down and sticking their heads out the windows. In general, doing all the cute tricks that kids do to drive you nuts. I graciously bestowed my benevolent adult smile upon them. After making the stops at the trailer courts, there were still six kids left on the bus. The all-knowing bus driver said, "Where you kids go? You should have gotten off already."

Kid: Well, the bus picked us up this morning.

Bus Driver: Not my bus. Where do you live?

Kid: In those new apartments.

Bus Driver: What ones?

Kid: Those new ones by the old ones.

Bus Driver: What old ones?

Kid: By the railroad tracks.

Bus Driver: My bus isn't supposed to go to any new ones.

Kid: The bus picked us up this morning.

Bus Driver: Not my bus.

Meanwhile, we're going down Stadium Drive. The oldest girl, about eight or nine, starts directing the bus driver and we realize that the new ones are the new married apartments.

Girl: Turn in this driveway.

Bus Driver: My bus isn't supposed to go here. Nobody told me.

Kid: This is where the bus picked us up this morning.

Bus Driver: Not my bus. Is there a place to turn around?

Kid: Stop here. That's where we live.

Bus Driver: Where am I supposed to turn around?

Girl: Go around that curve, and there's a place.

The kids are disposed of. Soon now I'll be home. Around the curve we go. It looks like this road goes back to the main one. Uh, oh. Here comes a pickup, telling us to stop.

And there ahead, the road stops. It's not complete. Out stomps the pickup man.

Pickup: You can't get through there.

Bus Driver: Where can I turn around? Those kids said I could turn around.

Pickup: You can't bring that bus in here.

Bus Driver: Where the — am I supposed to turn around?

The pickup man stomps off, having preserved law and order. Now it's only the bus driver and me against this narrow road, perhaps wide enough for a car to turn around. But a bus? The bus driver is doing the things you do to a bus to make it go in reverse. And I realize I'm the only passenger. There are windows and more windows and I have a perfect view. In front is the unfinished road, to the right, a steep ditch, to the left, cliffs of apartments, and they're all panting. I'm sitting in the front, on one of those sideways seats that hold four people. *Reverse,* grrrind, I slam to the left. *Forward,* grrrind. I slam to the right. *Brakes,* pow! I fibrillate. Back and forth. Stop, go. Grrrind, pow! We almost go over into the ditch. We just miss colliding with a cliff. Then—ahhh—we've done it. We've turned around. The bus driver says he hopes it didn't disturb me. I stutter and gag on the tongue in my throat and just titter nervously. But I'm almost home. He stops, I grab onto the pole by the door and try to remember how to make my feet move. As I get down, he says, "If you hadn't been in the bus, I would have driven it in the ditch and let them bastards worry about it. Nobody told me I was supposed to take those kids there."

I watched the bus drive away on wheels of clay.

KATHLEEN BOLINGER

From now on when you write anything, consider whether dialogue may help your cause.

chapter 9
the
helping
circle

ALMOST EVERY GOOD WRITER has learned
to write in circles. First, she writes for herself and then reads aloud her
writing and listens. It sounds different, as if it had made a circle and
become someone else's writing. She can judge it better.

Second, she reads it to a friend or member of the family. Now it
sounds different from the way it did when she read it to herself. She
begins to sense how the writing may come across to another person who
didn't share the experiences and feelings she wrote about. The listener
doesn't have to say anything, but simply be there—and the writing becomes an object apart from the writer. She's objective about it.

A writer can ask the listener to comment on the writing she has read
to him. But if he's the only one responding, that requirement presses
hard. What if he didn't like it? wasn't moved by it? or couldn't follow
it? He hates to say anything that may hurt the writer. That's why—

73

especially in the beginning—you'll gain from having a group of people, rather than one person, listen to your writing. In class listening to a paper, individuals don't feel the pressure of having to respond if they're unsure of their feelings. They know others are present who will probably speak up. But sitting with you, the writer, a single listener knows he must say something when you finish reading.

In class he comments on a paper knowing that others may see it differently. His judgment is open to disagreement; he's not the sole authority passing sentence on the defendant. And the differing opinions which arise in a class make the comments easier for the writer to take. She can carry them home and later decide which to use or ignore.

So the circle—at times frightening to every writer—is her third best resource. First, her own experience (including thoughts, feelings, and knowledge she picks up from others). Second, her skills as a writer. And third, the help the circle gives her to sharpen and hone those skills.

In the beginning the writer feels unsure. She should be encouraged. The group agrees to comment on parts or aspects of her initial free writings that they like. If they find none, they say nothing. That's not a lie, but a decision not to talk. If they like anything—a word, phrase, ending, idea—they speak up. Perhaps the writing places them in an event fully enough to evoke a similar feeling they thought no one else had experienced. They acknowledge that. After three or four meetings, when enough free writing has been examined for everyone, or almost everyone, to hear praise from the circle, the prohibition against negative comments may be dropped.

> *Think of and look at your work as though it were done by your enemy. If you look at it to admire it you are lost. . . . If we look at it to see where it is wrong, we shall see this and make it righter. If we look at it to see where it is right, we shall see this and shall not make it righter. We cannot see it both wrong and right at the same time.*
>
> SAMUEL BUTLER

Now imagine yourself in the circle. No one calls on you. You speak if you have strong feelings. Truthfully. The moment you or others in the circle make a phony comment to please the writer or teacher, or to show off your knowledge, the power of the circle dissipates.

As you're listening to the paper read aloud, study your reactions. At the end, check in on your feelings, as if you were connecting the jack plug for the earphone to your radio. Then report what you found. You don't have to say something you think the teacher expects to hear, something profound. You don't have to use literary terms. The writer doesn't care about them. She wants to know whether she has scored with you, made you believe, moved you enough that you may remember her writing tomorrow or next month. If you don't know why you liked or disliked it, she still would be pleased to know it moved you. She doesn't have to hear the reasons. She'd like to, but she'll take what she can get. Perhaps another in the circle will help you see why you liked the piece and thus will help you and the writer.

Imagine that the following piece of writing by one of the members of your circle has just been read aloud. What are your responses?

GOOD GIRL

I hated my parents. They were so unfair. I was a junior— 17 years old—and I still had a 12:00 curfew. Worse than that, they'd never let me go out with my boyfriend. They were *really* against going steady. I could go out with Jeff *once* every two weeks *IF* I went out with someone else in the meantime. No matter how many "A"s I got, or how many times I went to Church—no matter how many times I reminded them that I DIDN'T SMOKE OR DRINK OR HANG AROUND WITH THE WRONG CROWD—they still didn't trust me.

"We know you're a good girl, Linda, but it's the good girls that get in trouble."

Well, I loved Jeff and I didn't want to go out with anyone else. So when the Valentine's Dance came, I knew I had to be there with Jeff. Since it fell on one of our "off" weekends, we decided that we'd double with Rick and Mary. That way Rick could pick me up.

I spent at least ten minutes in my room convincing myself that Rick was my date. After all, he was going to drive me there and drive me home. That made him my "date." Then I went out to face the judge.

"Dad, can I go to the Valentine's Dance this weekend?" No response.

"Dad! Can I go to the Valentine's Dance this weekend?" Slowly, slowly, a head rose from the newspaper. His eyes went right through me, trying to psych me out.

"With who?"

"Rick. Rick Henderson."

He looked inquisitively at Mom, then she answered me.

"Why, he's the good-looking boy, isn't he?"

"Yeah. I guess so."

"What night is the dance?"

"Friday."

"I don't see why you shouldn't go. He's a nice young man."

"Thanks Mom."

Immediately I slumped into the easy chair trying to hide. I kept my eyes glued on the TV, looking engrossed. I wanted to avoid any suspicion or further questioning. The subject was dropped.

Rick picked me up at 8:30 sharp. Mom was really impressed when he handed me the box of candy Jeff had bought me.

"Now don't forget—I want you home by midnight," my father barked.

"Have a good time, but be good," my mother chirped.

And we were out the door. It was as if I had just passed a final exam. I felt instant relief.

Jeff loved to dance as much as I did. Our favorite was the Jerk, but we spent most of the night learning the Boog-a-Loo. "Shimmy to the left, shimmy to the right. Glide left, glide right." Over and over and over again. We sweated so much from trying so hard that our faces stuck together during the slow dance.

"Uh—I'd better go wipe my face off." Jeff always got embarrassed about stuff like that.

"OK, Jeff, I want to comb my hair anyway."

So we parted company at the john doors. Inside, Susan was stooped against the corner. Her eyes were puffed and red. Her mouth was covered by a sopping, rumpled Kleenex. Her boyfriend was there with another girl that night and Susan had had enough. She was going to break up with him. Joan, her best friend, stood by coaching her. "Give him the note! Give him the note, Susan! Then he'll be sorry."

I had to stay with Susan until Joan delivered the note and came back to tell us what he said. By the time I got out of the john, it was time to go home.

It was 11:30 by the time we left, so that gave us fifteen minutes to go parking. That was always the most fun of the night. I would never go all the way—and Jeff said he respected me so much that he'd never ask me to. So we just experimented a lot. We never did anything wrong—except French kissing. The priest told us that was a mortal sin, but we took care of that by going to confession.

After fifteen minutes of steaming up the windows, we stopped and Mary and I switched seats. I kept my face pressed hard against the cold window so the flush on my face would dissolve and my lips wouldn't be so swollen.

Now was the worst part. When we reached my corner I knew my dad was still up. I could see the TV light in the window. I always wished we could skip this part of the night. I was petrified. If Dad found out—

"Rick, quick! Dim your lights!" The blue Ford convertible crawled until we were two doors from my house. Then Rick slipped into neutral and slid. As we inched to the driveway, I ordered Jeff and Mary to hunch down on the floor. I whispered my final instructions over the seat.

"Now don't move till you're out of the driveway again, OK?"

"All right, but you better hurry. I don't like it down here!"

"Shhh! He's gonna hear!"

We oooozed the car doors open, very, very carefully. And left them open so Dad wouldn't hear them slam.

Not one word was uttered all the way to the porch. I reached for the door, but before I could touch it my father's face was plastered in front of me, right where the door knocker should have been.

Here's the way a circle responded to "Good Girl."

"I thought it was great," said Bette. And the writer felt wonderful. She wanted to go home and write another story and earn more praise.

"Yeah," said Alicia, "that's the way it was in high school. Only it was my mother, and she sat in the dark waiting for me."

"I liked the mother saying, 'You're a good girl, but it's the good girls who get in trouble.' Just like parents," said Jane. And the writer knew she had hit truth.

"I thought it was very good," said Jim, "but the opening was bad. Seems like it went on forever before the story got started." The writer began to feel poor.

"Oh, I didn't think so," said Jeanne. "Maybe it was a little slow at the beginning, but I think the whole thing moved along and kept my interest." The writer began to recover.

The teacher said: "What do you think about that? Let's look at the opening again." And he read it—a long paragraph.

"Yeah, don't tell us you hate your parents. The story shows that. I'd like to see the whole first paragraph chucked," said Jim.

"Oh no," said Judy, "You have to have that part there. 'I could go out with Jeff once every two weeks if I went out with someone else in the meantime.' That explains a lot that comes later."

"Yeah, maybe so," said Jim.

"And there's another part," said Mike. "This kooky part here about Susan in the john. It takes away—all of that stuff—from the main story, which is about Jeff and the writer. And the story is pretty long anyway."

"I don't think so," said Melanie. "That's good stuff, I think, and it's real. Girls do have moments like that in the john. And it's about a boy-friend and so it makes another little story within the story—about boy-friends and girlfriends."

"Maybe so," said Mike, "but I think it has to be cut out. It just doesn't accomplish enough to be allowed to interrupt the main story."

"Ah, come on," said Ben. "You can't take everything out of the story. It's not your story, you know. Maybe the writer thinks it's important."

The writer is forced to become more objective about her story; she now knows that there are two ways of looking at it. It may be both strong and weak in its present form. The teacher ends the discussion by saying, "It's up to the writer now."

"Well," said Jennie. "If you made her cut that out, she'd have to cut out the part about Jeff being embarrassed to say he has to go to the john, and I like that."

"Oh, not necessarily. I think that could stay," said Jane.

"We don't have to decide that here, either," said the teacher. "The writer has been alerted. She can make her mind up later. Any further suggestions for improvement?"

"Couple of things," said Tim. "I marked them on the ditto. Let's see—some Explainery, paragraph four. 'That made him my "date"' is un-necessary. Reader gets that. And in the paragraph after all the dialogue 'looking engrossed' isn't necessary after we've been told her eyes were glued on TV."

"Yeah," said Jennie, "and 'eyes glued' is a cliché. Just say, 'I kept my eyes on the TV.' And you don't need to say 'I wanted to avoid any suspicion or further questioning' because the reader knows that's why she's looking so hard at TV."

"And two more I marked," said Tim. " 'I felt instant relief.' The reader knows that. And toward the end: 'Now was the worst part.' That's a giveaway. And 'I was petrified. If Dad found out—' Omit that."

"In the fourth paragraph," said the teacher, " 'I spent at least ten minutes . . .' 'At least' is one of those phrases that almost never scores.

Could drop it and still make the point ten minutes was a long time."

Mike said, "I agree that 'Now was the worst part' is a giveaway, but I think the whole paragraph could be made better. It's the order of things, I guess. 'I knew my dad was still up' comes before she sees the TV light in the window."

"How about rewriting it this way?" said Sue: " 'When we reached my corner I could see the TV light in the window. Dad was still up. I always wished we could skip this part of the night.' And that's the whole paragraph. The rest is left out."

Murmurs of approval from several people in the class.

"And if the car doors are ooooozed open—I like that—then it must have been done 'very, very carefully,' " said Sue. "So maybe drop the 'very, very carefully.' "

"It's a good ending," said John. "Really great."

"Yeah," said Mindy. "And that reminds me, there's a bad *really* in there somewhere that ought to go."

That was the end of comment on "Good Girl." From this account you may conclude that everyone in the class responded to the paper. Not so. There were twenty-two students and only fifteen spoke up. The other seven may have remained silent for a number of reasons. Some may have been shy. Others may have felt uncertain about the story. Others may have had something to say but decided it wasn't striking enough to be valuable. And still others may have had things to say but decided to keep still because they felt they had talked too much in recent days. In the circle you're not required to comment on every paper. You're not being challenged to talk all the time, but rather encouraged to speak what you feel when you're strongly moved.

Maybe more could be added to this paper, or more dropped. The persons in the circle can make suggestions, but they should never feel responsible for the final rewriting of any work presented to them. That's the author's job.

> *A writer is unfair to himself when he is unable to be hard on himself.*
>
> MARIANNE MOORE

That helping session was carried out by a group that had worked together for two-thirds of a semester. In first sessions they were awkward and sometimes inexpert editors because they didn't know enough about writing. Listening to people respond to papers over the months, they learned what strategies score.

Often those in the circle didn't find themselves in close agreement on a paper. Here, for example, is a free writing done late in the semester. When it was read aloud a division occurred.

WHILE WATCHING THE DARK FOR YOU

> You're not getting out so easily. I'm gonna beat the hell out of that darn thing inside you, and make you stick it out in this place with me. How can you pull this rap on me? Are you trying to ditch me? Do I have to spend all my Saturday nights beating your back to ease the pressure, or driving you to the hospital so they can pump their needles into you, when they say you aren't reacting to anything? It would have been a hell of a lot easier if they had taken it all out when they hacked you up. How long can my overused words soothe you into a restless sleep? Who will I watch the dark for when you won't need me? How many nights do I have to sit by the phone until you call so I can breathe again? How much "us" is left? Misdeal! Get a new dealer! I can't hold out in this game much longer.
>
> You turn in your sleep and pull me closer. No, there's no one out here but me.
>
> I curse my parents for christening me "the strong"; you, for letting me love you; and my teacher, as my bare feet hit the cold tiles, and I pick up a pen to write.

Upon hearing that piece of writing, the circle split into two camps. One could be represented by Jim, who said, "Boy, that leaves me cold. I don't have the slightest idea what's going on. What's happening? How did this person get hacked up? Who's the dealer? What's being dealt? That's what I call 'private writing.'"

The other camp was led by Jennie, who said, "I thought it was good. I liked the feel of it. I sense a lot of feeling there and the paper just rushes along for me. I see this contrast between the writer hating the sick person for making her—is the writer a she? They're sleeping together—for making her work so hard to help him—or her, I don't know, really—and the feeling of love at the same time."

"O.K.," said Jim. "But that's not writing when you refuse to tell the reader what happened, who these people are, and why it's such a misdeal from somebody—"

"It's a misdeal from God, or fate," said Jennie. "That's obvious. I don't want to be told everything. I want something left up to me, and I get a great feeling from this writing. Maybe it could be expanded—it's only a free writing. But I don't want it thrown away."

The argument went on until it was clear that about half the responders valued the paper and half wanted it abandoned. The writer walked back to her room thinking she was a failure. True, many had admired things about the writing, but she remembered the negative remarks. As a listener in the circle, consider not only what your remarks say about a paper but what they'll do over the long run to help the writer. If she hasn't scored yet with the class, you probably should refrain from pointing out a great many weaknesses in her paper. If several of her writings have been well received in the circle, you can allow yourself more negative comments. A supposedly helpful remark this week may be damaging, although two weeks from now it may be useful. Wait until a writer can use your suggestion.

> *He [Ezra Pound] was a marvelous critic because he didn't try to turn you into an imitation of himself. He tried to see what you were trying to do.*
>
> T. S. ELIOT

But whatever, don't forget that if most of the comments have been negative, the writer is apt to leave the room thinking her paper a failure despite those two or three assertions that it was great.

As the semester goes along, you'll develop an increasing sense of what's fair, good, and great writing. You may decide that all of the papers read in one class meeting are strong, but one is deeper and more complex, surprises readers more than the others, and takes them into waters new to them. The best writing teaches readers to see better. I feel the following story, "Our Father," goes farther down than "Good Girl."

OUR FATHER

If it wasn't for memories of the past I would probably run out of my existence and head straight for a snow bank and throw myself into it and never come out. Memories sustain me. Especially of my father. They offer solace. I don't have many of him—only seven years' worth.

Dad had ulcers so we had to eat crummy food sometimes. Like mashed potatoes covered with soft-boiled eggs. Every time I took a mouthful I wanted to throw up. Mom said they were good for me. But I didn't have ulcers.

I had to sit at the table until I ate them. After two hours, the eggs were sticky and the potatoes were hard and clumpy

and I gagged every time I tried to eat them. Dad would get upset and I would cry and go to my room where I hid behind a big yellow chair. Whenever Dad got mad I hid behind that chair. He always came to look for me. First he searched the dresser drawers, wondering out loud where I could be. I would giggle and he'd look under the bed and in the closet. Finally he'd discover me peering through the yellow chair.

Dad took me shopping a lot. Once when we went to buy leggings I saw a dress I liked. It was white with black lines and a black rose below the collar. I wore the dress at my seventh birthday party. Dad was in the hospital for the last time then. I was mad at Mom because she spent most of the day with him.

I got to see Dad just before he died. That's when they let underaged children into the rooms. I'll never forget what he looked like. He had tubes up his nose and weighed only eighty pounds. He wanted to kiss me. But I was afraid. I wouldn't let him. So he kissed a brand-new Tiny Tears doll and gave it to me. But Christ, I don't know where it is today. It must be packed away in the basement. It must be.

I remember seeing Dad at the funeral home. Every few minutes I said to Mom, "Let's go see Daddy." Some people think it's stupid to expose dead bodies. But that's one more memory I have of Dad. And I wasn't afraid of him then.

"Our Father, who art in heaven . . ."

In the circle this story succeeded with almost all the listeners, but they still tried to help the author. Several said the first paragraph might be cut out.

One said, "But you need the phrase 'seven years' to tell that the writer was seven when she had this experience."

"No," said another listener, "later it says 'at my seventh birthday party.' "

One listener suggested cutting out the sentences "It must be packed away in the basement. It must be." so that the paper ended this way:

. . . I wouldn't let him. So he kissed a brand-new Tiny Tears doll and gave it to me. But Christ, I don't know where it is today.

"Our Father, who art in heaven . . ."

But another said she couldn't give up the next-to-last paragraph about exposing dead bodies. An argument began, and for understandable reasons. No decision in editing is harder to make than one to delete a strong portion of a writing. The argument was resolved when one listener recommended that the next-to-last paragraph be placed at the beginning of the paper so the rest of the story functioned as a flashback.

Another listener advised dropping the last sentence, and a second debate arose about deleting a strong passage.

The warmest argument arose at the end of the hour. "I don't like the use of the word *Christ*," said Karen. "Especially when the paper ends with a part of the Lord's Prayer."

"Oh come on," said Larry. "The writer is speaking to you in this story. That's her voice. She's really moved. That's what she would say."

"Maybe so," said Karen, "but—no, I don't think so. She's not speaking here, she's writing."

"I know that. But she's talking directly to the reader there, spilling out her feelings. People swear when they are deeply moved, don't they?"

Another debate that didn't have to be decided by the people in the circle. They had done their job—responded. The writer could make the decision on her own.

In the circle, as time goes on, you'll find yourself expecting more and more of other writers and yourself. Probably you'll become tougher about accepting sentimental writing, which triggers readers into tears or pity without giving them the factual basis for such response. "Our Father" doesn't do that, but the following excerpts from another paper do:

THE LAST TIME

I was on my way to the vet's, with that tiny little bundle in my arms. Its poor little eyes looked up at me pleadingly, as if to say, "Don't let them put me away." I knew I had to do it. They would eventually take my dear doggie away from me. I couldn't bear the thought. . . When I left the vet's office that night I knew I was a murderer.

It's hard to tell that writer her story was dangerously sentimental. One way is to suggest some wise cuts, but just taking out *dear* and *poor little eyes* won't do the job in this story. It needs to be entirely rewritten.

In the second story, if you have not for-gotten, huntsmen wound an elk, she has

*the look of a human being, and no one
has the heart to kill her. Not a bad subject, but dangerous in this respect, that it
is hard to avoid sentimentality; the piece
has to be written in the style of a police
report, without words that arouse pity,
and should begin like this: "On such and
such a date huntsmen wounded a young
elk in the Daraganov forest." But should
you moisten the language with a tear, you
will deprive the subject of its sternness
and of everything deserving attention. . . .*

ANTON CHEKHOV

As a listener in the circle you may aid such a writer by reminding her
of another story that has been read in class which took up matters of
great emotion without being sentimental. "Our Father" is an example,
and so is the following story which speaks with hard telling facts. It
carries a heavy load of emotion but the weight keeps moving forward;
it never shifts sideways into sentimentality and pulls the story off the
road.

BERNY

I work in the kitchen at the State Hospital. Berny is a patient there. Each night, except when he forgets, which isn't
often, he helps me by mopping in the dining room and dish
room as I go about doing my other chores.

Berny stands about five feet seven with gray curly hair
combed straight back, and big dark blue eyes. His face looks
like it's been chiseled out of stone, with skin stretched tight
over bone, his Adam's apple jutting out and muscles showing
like cords in his neck.

As soon as everyone is through eating, Berny will slowly
walk up to me, hands in pockets, asking in a dead tone, with
glazed unblinking eyes, "Time to mop up, John?" My name
isn't John, but that's what Berny calls me, so it's all right.
I'd look at him real close, reach my hand out and say in a
fervent tone, "How the hell ya doing, Berny? Ya sure are
looking good."

He'd reach out his thin hand in an exaggerated way and
say with a wrinkled brow, "Fine, John."

"Well good," I reply smiling. "Let's go get the bucket." I'd usually check on him a couple of times as he mopped the dining room, walking in as he zealously worked. "How's it coming, Berny?"

"Fine. Fine, John."

"Sure is looking good." And it did. Berny did an immaculate job.

Sometimes he'd forget he had to mop the dish room and would start on his way to dump the bucket. Usually I'd catch him just as he was dumping it. "Berny, ya gotta mop the dish room yet," I'd say very gently because sometimes he'd get down on himself because he forgot.

Then after he'd finished the dish room and I'd finished my chores, we'd walk back to the mop room, I dumping the water and he putting away the mop. And quite often he'd turn to me in a daze and ask, "Is today Sunday, John?"

"No Berny, today is Thursday," I'd softly answer.

"Oh. Well, is the store open? I need a pack of cigarettes."

"Ya it is, Berny," I'd say, putting my hand on his back. "Come on to the locker room and I'll get you some money."

"All right. I'd appreciate it," he'd say with renewed enthusiasm. Then he'd follow me to the locker room and I'd hand him the money and shake hands with him.

"There ya go, Berny."

He'd make a big circle motion with his arm as he reached to shake. I'd smile. "Thanks for working, Berny."

He'd reply strongly, "I appreciate working. I love to work." And he'd start dancing down the hall.

"Well, good, Berny."

"I'm going to the Regent Roof and the Ramona Gardens on 454 Adams Street in Grand Rapids, Michigan." And he'd dance farther down the hall.

"We'll see you tomorrow, Berny."

"I appreciate working."

After hearing that story, the circle unanimously called it powerful. The only suggestion was to check the tense of verbs throughout. All those *would's* and *I'd's* lessened the immediacy of the story. Maybe the author could say:

Again and again we went through the same little drama.

"Is today Sunday, John?"

"No, Berny, today is Thursday," I answered softly.

And at the end the writer could say "And he started dancing down the hall . . . And he danced farther down the hall." The "would style" of narration is full of traps. Maybe Berny often did the same things, but it's unlikely that each time he mentioned dancing he gave the address of the Ramona Gardens.

In responding to "Berny," one listener said, "It's the dancing at the end that got to me. This poor half-there guy mopping the floor suddenly starts dancing in the mental hospital and he's happy. The dance becomes such a symbol in that terrible place."

A good observation. The story communicates on several levels, including the symbolic. It's saying things beyond the first level of what's factually happening. So the reader gets twice as much for her money. That's what the best writers do—like Shakespeare and Tennessee Williams and Jonathan Swift. They give you more than you paid for. At times all of us are capable of writing like that; often we do it without realizing what's happening.

As a member of the circle, you're a party to a contract. Others will help you. You must speak up and help them. If only a few members respond and the others remain silent, there is no circle. If one person dominates, soon others will not listen to him, no matter how wise his comments. This group can become literally a circle of energy. You have probably seldom experienced a relationship like this in which a group of people are praising your work and helping you make it better —or saying it's weak and helping you make it better. Over the weeks and months that helping spirit builds. It can give you the confidence to do what you've never done before, if you'll take part in the circle. When everyone is responding to others' writing, then the writing and responding improve.

If you don't keep up in your writing, but continue to comment on others' work, they'll eventually resent your remarks. They'll think: "You're not pulling your weight here. What right have you to tell me what's wrong with my writing?" If you write powerfully and consistently and receive praise from the circle but refuse to helps others, they'll resent you for two reasons: "You're not being fair, and as a powerful writer you're especially qualified to help the rest of us."

The most surprising outcome of work in the circle is that your remarks about other persons' writing strengthen your own. When you comment on how a paper might end better or why its metaphors are strong, you're printing that thought on your brain more sharply than when you simply experience it. Speaking it forth under the pressure of the group makes it yours, perhaps forever. One day writing a metaphor or an ending, you'll think of what you once said in the circle, and your help to another person will become help to you.

SOME REMINDERS TO CIRCLERS:

1. Avoid beginning comments about a writing with small points. First, let the writer know your large reaction, especially if it's positive. Then later in the discussion bring up the small suggestion; for example, to cut a word or change a phrase.

2. If you're the leader in the circle, don't let an argument drag on about a point that has been discussed fully. You can say, "Well, John has now been given several alternatives. He can take them home and decide which one he wants to use in rewriting his work, or he can turn down all of them." The circle is not a debating society but a gathering of helpers.

3. If you find yourself talking too much or too little, remember that the most helpful responder presents his best thought—the one most apt to surprise and be useful. He resists the impulse to make obvious comments.

4. If you feel reluctant to talk. think of your responsibility to others. Responsibility—ability to respond. There's no other you in the world. No other person with the same set of past experiences. Only you can say what you feel and think, what *your* response to a writing was. That's what every serious writer is looking for: the effect of his writing upon individuals. You can't say anything wrong to him if you truthfully report your response to his work. And you may help him a lot.

5. Occasionally close your eyes while listening to a writing being read. But only in a circle whose members already know that listeners are apt to do that on purpose, not because they're bored.

6. As a responder you can sometimes draw out another responder who's reluctant to speak fully his feelings. "You said the story was too cute. Can you say more about why you felt that way?"

COLLECTING THREE: Lest this chapter should remain too general, here's a specific matter that every responder and writer should ponder [Good echo of sound—*responder, ponder?* No. And now that I look at that sentence closely, I see that the command "every responder and writer should ponder" is insulting to my readers. Sounds like Mother dressing the kids for church. And I don't need the comment about the chapter perhaps remaining too general. Just give the facts, Macrorie, without the lecture. So I'll start again]:

You can help people in the circle find worn-out expressions in their writing. You don't need to pounce on them gleefully and scornfully. You can simply say calmly, "And I found several clichés—Line 5, 'in the final analysis'; last paragraph, 'with tender loving care.'" And the writer can remove them later if she sees fit.

Copy in your journal a dozen or more clichés you find in print and in the writing of your classmates. Here are some examples, along with fresh expressions which possess their own unique truth. Some of the latter were written by junior-high students:

CLICHÉS	FRESH EXPRESSIONS
1. out of the clear blue sky	1. That man is hairless as a window.
2. cold shivers up my back	
3. eyes glued	2. If this kid was a dog, he looks like he's been chasing parked cars and punched his nose in.
4. down in the dumps	
5. racked our brains	
6. broke my heart	3. Her mouth looks like she has been eating red candy and got it all over.
7. lump in my throat	
8. safe and sound	
9. well aware	4. His eyes look like you picked them up from a kid's marble game, big and brown.
10. one and only	
11. last but not least	
12. not a care in the world	5. It was quiet in the woods and smelled of hot pine trees.
13. heavy as a rock	
14. light as a feather	6. His wooden leg was lying on the bedroom floor by the side of his bed, on the rug, like a faithful dog.
15. hit the nail on the head	
16. sharp as a tack	
17. alive and well	
18. in no time flat	7. I watched her trace the path of the blood [on a medical chart] and felt my heart pumping.
19. a complete disaster	
20. reckless abandon	
21. not a care in the world	8. All the colors outside are muted as if someone forgot to dust off the trees and grass.
22. remember only too well	
23. rude awakening	
24. deeply disturbed	9. I turned my head to the side, resting it on his shoulder and could feel his warm Listerine breath on the back of my neck.
25. grim tragedy	
26. not too good	
27. pay dearly	

chapter 10
oppositions

STRONG WRITERS bring together oppositions of one kind or another. Kitchen language and elevated language, long and short sentences, fast and slow rhythms. And what they choose to present from life—whether it be object, act, or idea—is frequently the negative and the positive, one thing and its opposite, two ideas that antagonize each other. The result is tension. And the surprise that comes from new combinations. And news.

When you wonder whether you ever think anything worth communicating to others in writing, you need only look at what you've written and ask whether it contains tension and surprise. Put the following short papers to that test:

> This university is the first university I have attended. The university itself is not bad, but the dorms leave something to be desired. I cannot see why the students in the dorms waste so much time fooling around when they can use this time profitably studying.
>
> I'll be here approximately two years. I am going to make those two years the most profitable years of my life and education.
>
> My course of study is that of Food Distribution. I plan and hope to become a supermarket manager for the Brinner Food Company located in Detroit, Michigan.

> I am going to try extremely hard this semester, as a fresh-
> man, to build my grades as high as possible. This is not
> just to show everyone I can do the work, or for personal
> satisfaction, but to build my self-confidence in myself. I
> plan to have both a profitable and enjoyable stay here at
> the university.

About all that can be said of that paper is "Ugh." The incoming
freshman is sure he's going to study hard and be a good boy. No
surprise. Nothing within his paper *speaks to anything else in the
paper*. No tension as there is in this paper:

> During my student teaching in summer school, my critic
> and I would occasionally take the class to the library. The
> first time we went, I was sitting with a confused ninth-
> grade boy trying to explain to him how to do a summary.
> The fat authoritarian librarian stomped over to us and
> whispered at me through clenched teeth, "Either you shut
> your mouth, young lady, or take your books and get out of
> here. You haven't stopped that mouth for ten minutes.
> This is a library, not a place to flirt."

Here the opposition comes up strong because the writer expects the
reader to get the point on his own. (Incidentally, the word *authoritarian* above is Explainery and should be removed. The librarian's
ugly language, faithfully presented, does the job, needs no help from
an adjective.)

Most professional writing sets up oppositions that build tension
and pay off in surprises. William Hazlitt, who died in 1830, is still
read today because his sentences are pungent and biting. He called
one of his essays "On the Ignorance of the Learned" (opposition already in the title), and built tension in this way:

> The book-worm wraps himself up in his web of verbal gen-
> eralities, and sees only the glimmering shadows of things re-
> flected from the minds of others. Nature *puts him out*. The
> impressions of real objects, stripped of the disguises of words
> and voluminous roundabout descriptions, are blows that
> stagger him; and he turns from the bustle, the noise, and
> glare, and whirling motion of the world about him (which
> he has not an eye to follow in its fantastic changes, nor an
> understanding to reduce to fixed principles), to the quiet
> monotony of the dead languages, and the less startling and
> more intelligible combinations of the letters of the alphabet.

A beginning writer often says, "But I can't do anything as difficult as that." He can. He already does. In conversation he frequently puts together exciting oppositions—they are what impel him home to his roommate or spouse to tell the news. When writing, a person who has no pertinent news to tell should simply record a fact that interests her. Then she'll have something to oppose. A something must be caught by the mind before anything can arise to oppose it. Here's an entry in a high school girl's journal.

> Daddy sat in the big chair by the windows, his eyes fierce on *The Scientific American,* and I wormed in next to him, as I always did, knees tucked up in my flannel nightie. He squeezed me almost too tightly. "I'll warm ya up." And pushed a kiss in my hair.
>
> I asked him about the stars—I don't remember what, and he began talking: of star life and distance and spectrums. "They have found that there is a dividing line of red light, which separates the spectrum, and depending on which side of the planet this line is towards . . ."
>
> Such comfort in his enjoyment of explanation, and my mind drifted out the window and lived on planets. His honey-words dripped over me but I didn't really hear them, and they became slower and rougher and they stopped. His head dropped back and his mouth, open, breathed heavily as I looked up.
>
> "Daddy, Daddy, wake up."
>
> "Huh . . . huh? Oh, what was I talking about?"
>
> And I snuggled in again.

The writer has put down a scene. Nothing surprising—that Father sits down with a magazine and Daughter in nightie snuggles up with him. The language and thought are simple and appropriate for a little girl with Daddy. But then ". . . star life and distance and spectrums." An opposition arises.

Then harmony again: Daddy is happy talking astronomy and Daughter happy snuggling. Opposition: he likes to talk about stars but goes to sleep while doing it. Opposition: she doesn't understand the talk but stays awake. Opposition: The little girl has to tell the father to wake up. Opposition: Having waked him, she snuggles in again and as waker assumes the sleep position.

When the writer began her little paper she probably didn't know how many oppositions were going to arise in the story. In a way, such oppositions create themselves for a writer, but the writer who's not ready for surprises won't be given all of them. It's O.K. to snuggle while Daddy is reading, but if you're going to find him sleeping you have to remain awake yourself.

The most available and obvious truths are frequently closed to us because we're not open to possible surprise, to seeing the opposite of the common. One day when Henry Thoreau was describing as precisely as possible how a squirrel runs, he asked himself about the opposite—how the squirrel walks. And as he observed squirrels more and more, he came to the conclusion squirrels never walk. A surprising truth. One day in a Shakespeare class students were trying to decide why they didn't like *Richard II* as much as the other plays they had read. Richard was an effeminate man thrust into kingship who kept turning on and off about whether he wanted to be king. One student said that the play contained almost no humor. A simple observation, but one that told a great deal about this play by a writer who customarily introduced humor into the most pressured tragedies. Richard is a fascinating man, but a man and a play without humor are apt to place second in popularity contests. To see what's there but invisible, to see what's not there but expected, requires that persons are willing to oppose their habitual opinions and expectations.

> *He who knows only his own side of the case, knows little of that.*
>
> JOHN STUART MILL

Make it a habit to look for oppositions. You'll find suddenly that you're wiser than you thought. Do it automatically. If you find yourself putting down *hot,* consider the possibility of *cold* in the same circumstances; if *simple,* then *complex;* if *loving,* then *hating;* etc. The habit will prevent you from oversimplifying people and processes and ideas. If you're trying to draw a portrait of a person you know and find yourself putting down good traits, ask if he has any bad. Or vice versa. Note how the writer of this journal entry did that.

> **I'm not bragging or anything like that, but the fact is I live in a dorm. I also have the weirdest wall-mate. We share the bathroom. Everyone calls him The Farmer. He lives on a farm, no doubt—carries with him the old habits and customs of the ancient farm hand. He's only showered three times since school started back in September. No, I'm**

not lying, only three times. Now you might be wondering, "How does he know he's only taken three showers?" Well, when most people take a shower it's a commonplace event, but with him I call it a major overhaul. He showers, washes his hair, brushes his teeth, and finally takes off his gold-spotted shirt and puts on his green-spotted one. So whenever he changes shirts, the floor knows he's taken a shower.

It also takes him about an hour in the shower. One day in the Big Three, I was beginning to think he forgot where his body parts were. But the really weird thing is he always talks about crabs. When he comes out of the shower he yells, "Well, those crabs are gone for a while."

Sometimes you forget about his odor and dirt, like when he offers you some of his mother's home-made cookies. They're not so bad if you drink a lot of water. The Farmer usually shares whatever he has, so most of the time we overlook his bad traits.

But when his caustic body aroma strikes you, it's like a spike in your heart; you've got to get rid of it. Right now everyone is on his back to clean up, partly because he stinks, but also because he's really a good guy. Like I always say, "If you look at a car with a corroded body, it doesn't mean the engine's bad."

In that paper the writer has found oppositions. Now he needs to say more about the good side of The Farmer, let the reader see him in action positively.

When mothers write of their children, they often brag insufferably until the reader doubts all their assertions because the kid simply couldn't be that good. In the following small portrait of a daughter, the writer sees oppositions and thus finds lively truths.

Karen is twelve, the not-quite, almost, nearly stage. One minute she teases for nylons. "But Mother, all the girls wear them!" The next she insists on a unicycle for Christmas.

She wants a horse for her birthday. Convincing her father wasn't difficult. When she puts her arms around him and tosses that long blonde hair, he'd get her an elephant if she asked.

Her bed is never made before 4 P.M. and her clothes are always in piles around her room. She doesn't throw them

there. They seem to come off by some witchcraft. She's always surprised to see them down there on the floor.

It takes her fifteen minutes to clear six cups and saucers
from the dining room table and she is the only one I know
who sits on the kitchen counter while drying dishes.

When urged to "Please get those dishes done," she re-
plies, "O.K., Mother, dear," in her half-laughing, half-cares-
sing, half-child and half-adult way.

WRITING ELEVEN: Write two 10–15 minute free writings (putting
down the words as fast as you can and aiming to fill at least a full
page) in which you begin with something and move to an opposition.
Keep going, don't stop to reflect long. It makes no difference whether
you write more about the first thing or the second, just so they oppose
each other. Perhaps they'll seem strong oppositions as you begin and
almost identical twins when you finish. No matter. Be open for surprises.

You don't need to write about persons. Maybe a place interests you
and sets up oppositions for you, or one place opposes another as it did
for the person who wrote this description.

I often go to the library to the row of study rooms on the
second floor. I have no favorite, they all seem identical,
although I know they're not. I choose the first empty room.

One wall is completely taken up by a wooden door with a
window in it. On an old label on the glass someone has
scribbled "Help."

The writer of this paper now continues with more physical details about
the room. Probably they'll begin to bore you. When you write, remember that description gets boring fast unless shown through some human
action or brought alive by oppositions and surprises. The next lines
from this paper are enclosed in brackets to suggest that they might be
left out in a second draft.

[The wall opposite the door contains a long window looking out onto shelf after shelf of books and other tables
where other people are studying. The two remaining walls
are unbroken except for a heat register and an electric
socket. The floor is paved with black linoleum tiles freckled
white, the ceiling with white acoustical tiles dotted black.]

The air vent in the ceiling is surrounded by rings of dirty
stains. The yellow walls have been scratched, scuffed, and
scribbled on by countless occupants. Some have tried to

immortalize themselves: "Steve loves Linda." "Call Betty, 381-8596." "D.W. + J.B." Others are anonymously clever— "G. Houle was here." or philosophical—"Why, why, why?" or sceptic—"Repent sinners." Even the table top is scored with idle carving: "Kiss me," "Mel 1965," "Sigma Phi Epsilon." These writings seem pathetically disembodied, detached from the people who wrote them. Their attempt to make the bare wall and table more personal only advertises impersonality and coldness. The room belongs to no one. Any person can enter, leave his initials, his scuff mark, his cigarette butts, and never return . . .

Now the writer sets up her opposition—the library room against her dorm room:

> Sometimes I stay in my dorm room to study. It seems less severe than library study rooms, but it's not. The smell is of hair spray and unwashed feet. Room 348 is larger than most dorm rooms because four girls live here. But the jumble of furniture and possessions makes it always crowded. Besides the regulation university desks and chairs, we've added a rocker, a record player, a crowded bookcase, and an orange rug now faded by lint and dust. The window sill looks like a continuation of the desk next to it. Mugs, bottles, pencilholders, pictures, a clock, a Kleenex box, books, papers, and a football pom-pom flow from one onto the other, and the bookshelf at the end of the desk is piled with bright colored volumes. When the brown window curtains are opened, the view is of another red-brick dorm.
>
> The personal touches that a library study room lacks are only temporary here. Nothing will remain of my roommates and me when we leave, except a few more scratches on the desks and tape marks on the walls. But the four of us in 348 don't often think of the depressing impermanence around us, of the unknown girls who have lived here before us, and who will live here after, trying to cover a dormitory room with home. Instead we listen to the music coming faintly down the hall. Sometimes we say a few words to each other about the day's happenings, but my roommates seem as far from me as the people who sit outside the windows of my study room in the library. They walk past my life silently. I see them for one minute or one year, but in time I won't see them at all. And I won't miss them. I like them now, but then I won't care.

The habit of seeing oppositions within one thing or person or between things and persons marks the intelligent man, even the wise or profound man. Shakespeare became famous in large part because he created characters who were round instead of flat. There was room in them for fascinating oppositions. Shylock was a cruel moneylender and a harsh father, but he gave one of the greatest of all speeches against racial or religious discrimination. Today it could have been expressed point by point by any of our leading black militants.

> He hath disgraced me, and hindered me half a million; laughed at my losses, mocked at my gains, scorned my nation, thwarted my bargains, cooled my friends, heated mine enemies; and what's his reason? I am a Jew. Hath not a Jew eyes? Hath not a Jew hands, organs, dimensions, senses, affections, passions? fed with the same food, hurt with the same weapons, subject to the same diseases, healed by the same means, warmed and cooled by the same winter and summer, as a Christian is? If you prick us, do we not bleed? if you tickle us, do we not laugh? if you poison us, do we not die? and if you wrong us, shall we not revenge? if we are like you in the rest, we will resemble you in that. If a Jew wrong a Christian, what is his humility? Revenge. If a Christian wrong a Jew, what should his sufferance be by Christian example? Why, revenge. The villainy you teach me, I will execute; and it shall go hard but I will better the instruction.

Those words from a man who had often appeared unfeeling come as a surprise to the reader of *The Merchant of Venice*. The whole speech is based on an opposition—Jew to Christian, says Shylock, supposedly different, but actually the same in their humanity. Note how easily Shakespeare sets up opposing words: *warmed—cooled, Christian example*—the reader expects a positive virtue to follow, but he gets— *revenge*.

Nothing mysterious about the fundamental of presenting oppositions. Because Shakespeare uses it brilliantly doesn't mean you can't use it in your way. If it becomes habitual to you, occasionally you'll slide into statement as strong as Shakespeare's. For example, you may think of something as ordinary and yet inspired as Shylock's "if you tickle us, do we not laugh?" which comes on the reader so surprisingly in the midst of that train of dignified and solemn comparison.

A college freshman once was writing idly in her journal in the laundry room of a dormitory and put down these words:

> I leaned against the washer and as it began its cycle, my
> entire body pulsated with it. It was as if I were holding my
> heart in my hand, and I was terribly excited. Then sud-
> denly the washer stopped.

She made the jump between the throb of the washing machine and the
throb of her heart. Oppositions frequently gain in power from being
different not only in content or idea but in tone or level as well. We
think of a washing machine as lowly and mechanical and a human
heart exalted and pulsing.

The passages of student writing printed in this book are almost all
short, of such length that they would not be published in most magazines or anthologies. They're short for two reasons; the first is that
long examples would make the book fat, the second is that beginning
writers usually think they can't sustain powerfully a long piece of writing, and so they seldom try. They can—you can, if you go about the
job the way professional writers do.

They use every possible method. Collect materials and evidence in
notebooks. Make tape recordings of what people say. Take pictures to
aid their memory. Consult books and magazines. They put to use many
of the strategies presented in this book—sometimes four or five in one
effort.

Here's a long story about two boys. Right away you may have
thought: "Two—probably in opposition." Yes, in both opposition and
harmony. It's a big story made up of a lot of little stories. Words and
acts speak to each other constantly and remind the writer of others he
may have forgotten. It's a story of a large opposition and how the writer
came to understand its meaning and value.

* * *

NOT ANOTHER WORD

Richard Thurman

Because I was one of the bigger, healthier boys in the class—and
also one of the biggest, smoothest liars, and thus apt to set an inspiring
example for the others—Miss Devron would often begin the morning's
inquisition with me. "Paul Adam," she would say, beaming down

upon me, "would you be kind enough to tell us what you had for breakfast this morning?"

Even in the third grade, we were perceptive enough to sense that Miss Devron's inquiries into our daily breakfast menus sprang from something deeper than a mere interest in keeping us healthy. One look at her size and you knew what supreme importance food had in her life, and since we were her children—those she would never have herself, because of age, temperament, and general appearance—she apparently found it necessary to feel her way into our souls by following a glass of fruit juice and an egg and a slice of ham down our throats each morning. It wasn't just her zeal to know us personally through the food we ate that made us guard against her with a series of outrageous lies; she also wanted to know our families—their general way of life, their social and economic status in our small Utah town, and whether or not they lived in accordance with the Mormon doctrines, which were as inseparable from our lives as the mountain air we breathed. And she had a nasty way of pointing out any deviation from her set of standards by interrupting the stream of breakfast reports. "Hominy grits!" I remember her saying on one of the first mornings we were in her class. "Did you hear, class? Ronald Adair had hominy grits for breakfast."

She smiled her closed smile of wisdom and commiseration at Ronald, and placed the index finger of her left hand like a hot dog between her second and third chins while waggling her free hand scoldingly in his direction. "It's a lucky thing for you, young man, that your parents somehow had the energy to come out West, where you can get a new start in life," she said. "It's food like hominy grits that has kept the South backward so long. Out *here* we eat bacon and ham-and-eggs and hot cereal and fresh fruit juices and good buttered toast with jam. You're very lucky, young man! My, yes."

With such tactics she soon taught us to lie, and regardless of what each of us had eaten at home, there in Miss Devron's class we began to share a breakfast as monotonous as it was sumptuous. It was only a variation in quantity that crept into our diets from the first student's report to the last, for if one egg and a modest piece of ham were enough to start Miss Devron's fingers strolling contentedly over the terraces of her chins, it took considerably more than this to keep them happy and moving by the time the class was half through its recital, and by the time the last student's turn came, Miss Devron's wolfish appetite responded to nothing less than a gorge. Lila Willig was the last student on our class list. She looked as if she were made from five laths, and in the hectic flush of her unhealthiness—perhaps caused by near-starvation at home—she would sometimes get a little hysterical and report that she had eaten twenty-five eggs and a whole ham. I'm sure now that this was not because of any native waggishness in Lila, but we thought it was then, and we always laughed until Miss Devron had to pound the desk with her ruler.

"Now, stop that foolishness, Lila," she would say briskly. "Tell the class right out how many eggs you had for breakfast."

"Five," Lila would say, nervously scratching her frizzled yellow curls until they stood out like coiled wires. She could have said nothing else. The boy in front of her had just reported a breakfast of five eggs; anything less from Lila would have been picked up by Miss Devron as an example of parental neglect.

"That's better," the teacher would say, her fingers resuming their stroll. "And as I look over your faces this morning, class, I can already see the differences that good eating habits can make in one's life. How much brighter your eyes! How much stronger your backs!"

We simpered back at her, only vaguely and uneasily aware that she was a tyrant who was flattening our individuality with the weight of her righteous self-assurance. In less than a month under her, we were reduced to a spineless group of sycophantic ham, egg, and cereal eaters, with only Lila's occasional lapses to show us what a dull mold we had been crushed into. And then our integrity was rescued in an unexpected way.

The new boy who turned up in our class a month after the opening of school certainly looked like no hero. He was smaller than most of us, and while all of us boys were proudly wearing corduroy knickers, he still wore the short pants we scorned, and in the sharp air of that October morning his thin legs were mottled with a network of blue. We welcomed this pathetic figure with a fine generosity of spirit. "Where you from?" one of us asked him as we walked up to where he was standing, at the edge of the playground.

"New York."

"New York!" we said, and I now had an explanation of why he was such a puny-looking little rat. From the handful of Western movies and cowboy books I had already absorbed, I knew the kind of magic that enters into a man's blood when he is born west of the Mississippi River. His eye is clearer, his nerves are truer, his gait is more tireless, his aim is steadier, and in the very heart of his manliness there is a dimension that effete Easterners know nothing about. All this I knew as I looked down at the new boy's skinny blue legs.

"New York, eh?" I said menacingly, moving up to him until I could have rested my chin on top of his head.

"That's right," he said, lounging against the top rail of the play-ground fence and casually lifting one foot to rest it on the lower rail.

I eyed him with a steely coldness I had learned from a story about a man who had built the Union Pacific Railroad across the plains and who could drive a spike into a tie with two hammer blows. I put my fingers into my belt, just above where my six-shooters should have been. "Who's your old man voting for?" I asked. "Al Smith or Hoover?"

"Al Smith."

"Well, then, I guess I'll have to beat you up."

Perhaps nowadays, what with the broadened horizons brought on by the Second World War, Korea, UNESCO, and the stress on social-adjustment patterns in modern education, a new student from, say, Siam or Afghanistan can take his place unobtrusively in an American schoolroom. I don't know. But I do know that in my part of America in 1928 a new student had to fight his way into school, particularly if he had come to us from more than five blocks away. It will be under-stood, then, that I had no unusual political precocity or passion at the age of eight, and that this difference in our fathers' political views was only a pretext for me to beat up the new boy, who had offended every one of us by coming all the way from New York, with his short pants and blue skin.

We sized each other up for a second. Then he shrugged his thin shoulders and said "O.K.," and the quickness with which he squared away for battle gave me a little turn. We circled around each other, with everyone urging me to get in there and show him what was what. But just then the bell rang, and I felt a surge of relief that was just a bit disconcerting to anyone born as far west as I had been.

"I'll finish with you later," I said.

"O.K.," he said, with that same unnerving readiness.

Something more immediate than our father's political inclinations operated to bring us closer together that morning. Miss Devron put the new boy in the empty seat just in front of me, and I spent the first few minutes of class watching his blue neck turn pink in the warm room, while the pupils drearily went through their recital of breakfasts eaten that morning.

"And now the new boy, Robert Bloom," said Miss Devron, smiling down at him. "What did you have this morning?"

He had been listening carefully to what was going on, and once, when he turned his profile to me, I could see that he was enjoying himself. The rest of the pupils had answered from their seats, but he stood up in the aisle. He stood at attention like a soldier.

"I had a cup of coffee and a snail, Ma'am."

There was a stony quiet for a second, and then the dazzling irreverence of what he had said burst through us with shock waves of pure delight. Miss Devron pounded on the desk with the ruler, and her red chins trembled in front of her like molten lava. "Class!" she cried. "Class, we'll have order here! Come to order. Come to order this instant!"

But she was trying to calm down a madhouse.

"A cup of coffee and a snail, please!" somebody shouted.

"Give me a worm with mine!" somebody yelled back.

And on we went, up that enticing road of suggestibility, until we were eating snakes on muffins. The special delight, of course, was the coffee. *There* was the alluring evil and joy of what he had said, because most of us in that room, including Miss Devron, were Mormons, who felt, in a way beyond reason, that murder was no more than a high-spirited lark compared to drinking coffee or smoking. It wasn't until Miss Devron and her ruler and the powers of light finally triumphed over the dark joy in us that we began to realize the outrageousness of what he had said. We slunk back from debauchery to righteousness under Miss Devron's glowering eye, and finally he was left standing there, all alone before the glare of our joint indignation.

"We should never laugh at those who don't know better, class," Miss Devron began, in a carefully controlled voice. "We must share our knowledge with those less fortunate, and help them to know the truth. Robert comes from a part of the country where they don't know about health. Now then, Robert, that can't be all you had for breakfast, can it?" She looked at him with the pity, the heart-spoken prayer, and the tenderness of a missionary meeting with a cannibal for the first time.

"No, Ma'am," he said. "I had two cups of coffee."

The tight breath gathered in our throats again, but Miss Devron was in control now, and aside from a few blown cheeks and red faces there was no sign that we were not with her in spirit.

"Now, class," she continued, "I want to ask Robert's pardon for what I'm about to do, but I think we can all learn a great deal from what he has told us and from what we can see. Very soon now Robert will be as big and strong as any of you, because he will soon be eating the right foods. But look at him now. See how small he is? *This* is what comes from not eating the right foods and from drinking coffee."

We looked him over, almost seeming to pass him from desk to desk, as if he were a mounted disease-carrying bug we were studying. But what a happy, smiling bug! To judge from his face, he considered the attention we gave him an unexpectedly hearty welcome to his new school.

"I don't think it's the coffee, Ma'am," he suddenly added. "My dad says I steal too many of his cigarettes."

During the next couple of minutes, Miss Devron could have fired salvos of cannon shells over our heads without getting our attention. We were like an oppressed people hailing with insane joy the coming of a revolutionary leader. Even the girls in the room were caught up in the exultation of our victory. All the cigars, cigarettes, or drinking straws filled with grains of coffee that any of us had smoked in secret, all our uneasy past abandonments to appetite, curiosity, and lawlessness were suddenly recalled and made more glorious by Robert's cheerful confession. We worshipped him instantly, and at the end of the day a lot of us walked with him, proud to be seen with such a man. We were walking along with him, swearing, talking about smoking, and making faces at the girls on the other side of the street, when he stopped and tapped me on the arm.

"How about this place?" he said, pointing to a strip of grass between two houses.

"What do you mean?" I asked.

"Your old man's voting for Hoover, isn't he?"

"Sure, but . . ."

"Well, let's fight."

I wanted no part of the fight now, but Robert insisted. He proceeded to support his political views with a ferocity I couldn't seem to match, and it wasn't until he hit me a hard one in the eye that I brought any personal enthusiasm to the fight. From then on, my size and strength started getting the better of him, but no one in the group around us was shouting for me. Those who had been beside me that morning were now yelling for Robert to kill me, and I must say that he did his best. But I finally knocked him down and sat on top of him, and kept his shoulders pinned to the grass until he admitted that Hoover would win the election. When he was up again, he expressed some strong reservations about his opinion, but the election a few days later proved I was right, and, with our political differences out of the way, we became the best of friends.

For the next two or three weeks, Miss Devron tried her best to change Robert's breakfast habits, or at least to get him to lie a little in the interests of classroom harmony. But his incorruptible honesty soon inspired the rest of us to tell what we had really had for breakfast. Variety returned to the menu, and Miss Devron's discovery that some of the larger, healthier children, like me, frequently ate what tasted good for breakfast, instead of simply what was good for them, seemed to undermine her spirit. She acknowledged defeat one morning when she opened class by reading aloud to us from a book of dog stories by Albert Payson Terhune. Subsequently, she read to us whenever there were spare minutes in the day, and the breakfast lists were forgotten. From that time on, she was one of our favorite teachers.

My first idea about Robert's father was that he was a sailor in the United States Navy. Robert showed me pictures of him in a sailor suit—pictures in which he was leaning against a palm tree; laughing, with his arm around two girls; pulling a rope; scrubbing the deck of a ship; or standing on his hands, with a distant and smoking volcano framed between his spread legs. Then I learned that he was no longer in the Navy but was selling something—"selling something out on the road," as Robert described it. With only that imagination-tickling description, I developed the permanent expectation of turning a corner in the city someday and seeing Robert's father selling something right in the middle of the road. What he would be selling I couldn't imagine, nor had I a clear idea of how he would be doing it. Salesmen were never allowed in my own neighborhood, and the only prototype of Mr. Bloom I could conjure up was a man I had seen at the circus the year before. He had been standing outside one of the tents—a man with a dark face and a croaking voice, who kept urging us to come in, trying to scoop us up over his shoulder and into the dark tent with a dipping swing of his straw hat. "Selling, selling, selling!" my mother had said to my father. "It's plain disgusting." And so the man with the straw hat became Mr. Bloom, and I always had the feeling that Robert's house, too, was somehow disgusting. But it was also the most exciting house I had ever been in.

The excitement would hit me as soon as I entered the front door—usually in the form of Robert's dog, an overgrown mongrel lummox called Buddy. I think he was mostly a police dog, but any remnants of purebred respectability had worn thin through long association with the underworld of back alleys and garbage cans, and through personal vice, for the dog was a hopeless drunkard. At least once a week, Robert and I would take a bottle of beer from his refrigerator (and how thrilling it was for me to be in a house containing anything so illegal and wicked as a bottle of beer!) and pour some of it out into a saucer for the dog. He would go at it with a ravenous thirst, frothing the beer with slaps from his scooping tongue until the white suds were all over the floor and his muzzle. He looked as if he were mad, and soon he would act mad. He would lurch around the house, bumping into chairs and tables, and endangering ashtrays and bric-a-brac in his weaving course. I would hold him by the collar at one end of the living room while Robert called him from the other end, and negotiating those fifteen feet of open rug held for him all the peril and adventure of a walk on a slippery deck in a typhoon. Once he made it to safety, he would sit down, brace himself against a chair, and look at us triumphantly. We would never get him drunk when Robert's mother was around, of course. That was the one thing I ever saw her really angry about. But she was a person of such unquenchable joy and good cheer that even the sight of Buddy drunk that one time didn't keep her angry for long.

She came home from town unexpectedly that day. Buddy's flank had just crashed into a floor lamp and Robert was juggling it back to equilibrium when his mother walked in the front door.

"Robert, have you got that dog drunk again?" she asked, after one look.

"Yes, Mom."

His truthfulness, both at school and at home, always amazed me. For me the truth was usually a fearful thing; my telling it often seemed to hurt my father or my mother, or someone else. But Robert was dauntless before it.

"I've *told* you not to, Robert," Mrs. Bloom said. "You know I have. Poor Buddy! Just look at him. That's no way to treat a dog."

We all looked at him, and I, at least, was conscience-stricken at what we had done. But none of us could remain remorseful for long. Deep in his cups, Buddy had misgauged the size and slipperiness of the low black leather hassock in front of the rocking chair, and though he managed to plant one haunch on it, it kept sliding off. He would edge it back momentarily, his happy face conveying to all of us his certainty that he was seated there four-square and in perfect dignity. I don't know what there was about him—perhaps a certain slack-jawed serenity—but we all started laughing helplessly at the same time. Robert's mother threw herself onto the couch, and Robert and I rolled on the floor in our laughter, while Buddy watched us out of one open eye.

She recovered enough after a time to continue her scolding, but she couldn't get more than a few words out without looking at

Buddy, and then she would laugh again. Finally, she gave us some cookies and milk, and poured out a big saucerful of thick cream for Buddy, which she said would sober him faster than anything else. While Robert was drinking his milk at the kitchen table, she came up behind him and slipped her arms under his and clasped her hands on his chest. She kissed him on his neck and on his cheek and up into his hair, and all this time he went on eating his cookies and drinking his milk. I hardly dared to look at them, but I *had* to see the way she kissed him. She was a young woman, with long, dark hair, and black eyes that opened very suddenly at times, then closed very slowly, the lids seeming to take great pleasure in their long trip back down. The nails of her fingers, clasped on Robert's chest, were buffed to a high polish, and her lips were full and red, and looked wonderfully soft against Robert's cheek. I was the fifth, and youngest, child in my family, and I had only been pecked at gingerly by thin lips pulled tight against clenched teeth, and now I could almost feel that cushioned touch of Robert's mother's kiss on my own cheek. I had no name for the feeling it gave me. I was simply fascinated.

She straightened up, put her hand to the back of her hair, and walked to the refrigerator again. "Boys, boys, boys!" she said, "Little devils, all of you. Little heartless devils, getting dogs drunk, pulling girls' hair, fighting, swearing. You're no good, any of you." As she said it, she dug two big scoops of applesauce out of a bowl and slapped them into two dishes.

"So why do I like you so much?" she said to me as she leaned over the table to put a dish in front of me. She was wearing the kind of low dress she usually wore, but I didn't dare look away from her face. I just looked at her smile, and that was everywhere. Then she leaned over and kissed my forehead.

By the time I left for home, Buddy was on his feet and feeling well enough to walk to the corner with Robert and me.

"I like your mother," I said.

"Ah, she's all right," he said, leveling his toe at a rock and kicking it out into the street.

"You bet she's all right. I'd like to marry her when I grow up."

"She's already married."

"I know she is. My gosh, don't I know that? I just said I'd like to, that's all."

We stood on the corner and kicked a few more rocks into the street. And then we were just standing there. Suddenly there was between us a strip of that infinite desolation that surrounds and crisscrosses life, which children must face without the comfort of philosophy or the retreat of memory.

Robert slapped the dog on the side as hard as he could. "Come on, you," he said to him, and I stood and watched them run down the street. I wondered why he never seemed to like the dog except when we got him drunk. I would have given anything for him, but it had been made clear to me at home long before that our yard was too beautiful to be ruined by a "dirty dog."

Besides Buddy, and Robert's mother, with whom I fell more and more in love as I sampled her cakes, home-canned fruit, dill pickles, candy, sandwiches, and lemonade, there were other charms at Robert's house that made my own seem intolerably dreary. Although it was nearly Christmas and I had known Robert for more than two months, I still hadn't met his father, and yet I had come to feel that I knew him as well as my own, or even better. My father's actual physical arrival at home, after a day spent seeing patients in his office or operating at the hospital or attending a church meeting, was the main thing that impressed his existence upon me. He was so neat, so disciplined in his habits, and so completely without vices, eccentricities, or hobbies that he carried himself completely with him wherever he went. But Robert's father lay scattered about the house in the form of pipes, fishing equipment, shotguns, whiskey bottles locked in a glass-front cabinet, a tennis racket, a set of rusty golf clubs, and a three-foot-long Chinese beheading sword, with a dragon engraved on the length of the blade and a dull, pewtery stain on the bright steel, which Robert said was blood. His father had brought the sword home from China when he was in the Navy, and it hung, with its handle wrapped in cords of scarlet silk, above the bed that he and Robert's mother slept in. I was so taken by the sword at the time that I thought anyone would die of pride to have it hanging above his bed, but I now see what a generous concession to his male taste it was for her to have it there. I remember the room as delicately feminine in decor, but it was his room, too, and he had chosen the exact thing to put his mark on it that I would have chosen if I had been married to Robert's mother.

Mr. Bloom did come home occasionally, but even then I didn't get to see him. He was sleeping, Robert would say, going on to explain how tired a salesman becomes after several weeks on the road. On two or three such afternoons, Robert's mother was also not to be seen, and he told me that she, too, was taking a nap and that we were to tiptoe carefully when we went past the closed door to their bedroom.

Christmas morning came and I was downstairs at 5 A.M., tearing into my carefully wrapped presents with impatient, greedy hands. The unexpected child of my parents' middle age, with all my brothers and sisters grown up and living away from home, I had spent my early hours of the past three Christmases all by myself, and I am certain that the pain of a child getting up on Christmas morning to find nothing under the tree cannot be much worse than the pain of one who finds everything there but has no one to show it to. It was not that my parents were really unfeeling. Indeed, they carefully kept my belief in Santa Claus alive beyond the customary age of disillusionment, perhaps because I *was* the last and much youngest child—even telling me that all my Christmas presents, except for some clothing from my mother, had come from Santa Claus. But it never occurred to them to get up early on Christmas morning in order to share my excitement, and I can still remember the sick emptiness of the hour and a half between my discovery of my presents and the first sound of someone else stirring in the house. That year, as usual, I finally heard the maid come upstairs from her basement room, and for the next ten minutes I held her captive while I gloated over each new addition to my wealth.

"Santa was certainly generous to you," she said, and it was so true that I didn't at all mind her saying it in the middle of a yawn.

"Look what Santa Claus left me!" I was able to say to my parents at last, when they came down for breakfast. I had been particularly struck that year by the great number of things he had given me compared to what my mother had given me, and I emphasized this difference by putting his gifts to me and hers in two piles, side by side. But a peck on the cheek and a cursory smile were all the tribute my parents paid to me, Christmas, and Santa Claus's generosity before they opened their own small presents from me, with an air of rather hasty embarrassment, and then turned to the newspaper and to breakfast.

Still, this year I knew someone who would take a second look at what I had received. It took some tight crowding, but I managed to tie all my presents onto my new sled with my new lariat, and I departed for Robert's house. I wasn't disappointed. Not only did Robert's eyes pop at some of the individual presents and at the sheer mass of what I had been given but his mother and, yes, his father, too, were as excited as Robert himself. Mr. Bloom, who got down on the floor to play with my new hook-and-ladder fire engine, turned out to be just the sort of man I had expected. He liked the fire engine so much that I wanted to give it to him, except that the idea of giving it up hurt too much. Out of this dilemma came a sudden inspiration to ask him if he would like to trade his sword for my fire engine. I was circling carefully about this idea, trying to approach it in the best way, when something happened to destroy the notion utterly.

It was not surprising that none of us had paid much attention to Robert's gifts during the first few minutes I was there. All three of the Blooms were too polite not to have gone all out to admire a sledful of gifts dumped into the middle of their living room by a guest as greedy for appreciation as I was. They would have done this even if my presents had come from the ten-cent store. But my gifts were both costly and impressive, and the Blooms, in their modest circumstances, had no need to be just polite; quite simply, they all gave in to the dream of having enough money to buy what I spread out before them, and wholly enjoyed themselves with my presents. I was too far lost in their appreciation to remember that Robert had also had a Christmas that day. But he soon reminded me of it.

"Look!" he said to me. He held in his cupped hands a bright, gold-colored wheel, suspended on a silver axle within a framework of two intersecting wire circles.

"What the heck *is* it?" I asked.

Robert's mother and father were both down on the floor with us, and while Robert threaded a length of green string through a hole in the axle and then wound it carefully along the axle's length, I could feel their eyes looking from me to the wheel and back, excitedly waiting for my reaction. Then Robert gave the wound-up string a sudden vigorous pull, putting the muscles of his back and arm and the tension of his clenched teeth and closed eyes into it, and brought the top spinning to life. The golden wheel hummed softly within its unmoving world of wire circles. Robert placed the top carefully on the smooth surface of a box lid, and there it rested, poised on its projecting tip like a dancer on one leg.

"Watch," he said, and he picked up the wonderful toy and rested its cupped tip on the point of a pencil his father held up. Once the top was spinning there, Robert pushed it, a fraction of an inch at a time, until it was no longer a continuation of the pencil's length but was hanging horizontally out over space, held from falling only by the quiet humming and the touch of the pencil point on the cup.

"My *gosh!*" I said. "Where'd you get that?"

"Mom gave it to me."

"It's called a gyroscope," she said.

For the next five or ten minutes, we shared the excitement of watching the gyroscope ignore gravity in every position we could devise. I was ready to trade Robert all the solid excitement of my presents for the magic that I could feel spring to life when I pulled the green string. I held the gyroscope in my hand and laughed to feel that quiet, determined will fighting mine as I tipped the wheel away from the path it had chosen in the air. And then, suddenly, the magic would be gone and I would be left holding the toy dead in my hands.

"And what did your father give you?" I asked, staring down at the wheel.

"That Chinese beheading sword."

I gave him back the top, but I couldn't look at him. I could feel the cold, sharp edge of that sword in me.

"Where is it?" I asked at last.

"He hung it over my bed."

"Let's see it."

We stepped around the scattered toys and went into his bedroom. There it was, hanging over his bed, just as I had dreamed it might hang over mine.

"I'm not to touch it until I'm older, but she's all mine," Robert said.

I could easily have cried. My mother had given me ties, socks, gloves, shirts, pants, shoes, underwear—all the things a boy could easily do without. But Robert's mother had given him a gyroscope! And the sword had come from his father, while I didn't even think that my father had given me anything! I seemed to have only one real friend right then.

"What did Santa Claus bring you?" I asked.

"Santa Claus? *Santa Claus?*" he hooted. "There isn't any Santa Claus, you big dummy!"

I had heard there wasn't—but only speculatively, never with this final, crushing authority. I could think of only one way to defend myself against Robert's having everything and my not having even Santa Claus. I hit him twice, once on the chest and once in the face, and then I tied all my presents onto my sled with my lariat and

started out of the living room, refusing to answer any of the
questions his parents asked me. Robert followed me onto the porch,
and when I was half a block away he called out to me, "What did
you hit me for?"

"Shut up!" I yelled back, and I went home and put my presents
under the tree for my relatives to see when they came around later.

Most of the rifts of childhood are as troubled, as tearing, and
as quickly smoothed over as the wake of a small motorboat, and by
the time Christmas vacation came to an end I had accepted the
death of another illusion and Robert had forgotten my naïveté.
We went on as before, with the abrasive honesty of his life wearing
away at the hypocrisy of my own until I, too, occasionally knew
some emotional truths. With that encouragement of truth which
had been given him at home, he was quite free to say, for example,
that he liked or disliked this or that person, this or that book, or a
threatening gray or a clear blue sky. But I knew no such freedom.
Caught within the attitude that this world was God's green acre
and too sacred to be regarded critically by the likes of me, I wasn't
free to decide whether I liked a dog better than a cat, or a mountain
better than a rosebush. Any expression of vital choice on my part
was seen as a blasphemous elevation and denigration of two aspects
of the divine order, and, pressed down by the weight of my blasphemy, I lost the power to make any choice. But Robert restored
this power during the next year of our friendship. He restored it
with a series of shocks that showed me that what he said about something and what I felt about it, way down, were often related. How
exhilarating it was to have him come out with a truth that my
bones knew but my tongue could not say!

"What do you think of Miss Brown?" I might ask him, speaking
about the elementary-school art teacher.

"She's a nice lady," he answered, "but she doesn't know anything
about art."

My heart pounded with the truth of what he had said. I half
knew she didn't know anything about art, but she had been put in
our classroom by authority as an art teacher, so it was certain that
I must be wrong about her. "What do you mean, she doesn't know
anything about art?" I asked—on his side, of course, but still fearful.

"All she draws is mountains," he said disgustedly. "Never people,
or dogs, or flowers, or trees, or boats, or water, or houses, or clouds,
or *anything* but mountains. And it's always the same mountain. You

should have seen the teacher I had in New York. She could draw a face on the board in two seconds and everyone knew who it was. Boy, was she an artist!"

If I was impressed at the time by the fearlessness of what Robert knew and said, it is only now that I can appreciate the full miracle of his freshness surviving the hothouse atmosphere of souls under cultivation for adulthood that existed in our third- and fourth-grade classrooms. Having known Robert, I now seriously believe that the right sort of parents can emotionally equip a child to survive the "civilizing" process of education. But my real appreciation of Robert came mostly in retrospect, and most of whatever I now know about truth I had to learn the hard way, for in the late winter of our fourth-grade year—about a year and a half after our friendship started—I cut myself off from the hope that Robert would go on indefinitely helping me to find truth.

It was one of those false spring days that sometimes appear toward the end of winter—a sad, nostalgic day, when the air teased our bodies with the promise of games and picnics, and the earth was still locked up and unavailable for our use, beneath two feet of grimy snow. Robert and I were walking home together. "Mom just put up some more dill pickles last night," he said, and suddenly the day came alive.

"First one who gets there gets the biggest," I said, and, with my longer legs, I was on the porch while Robert was still pounding up the sidewalk. We pushed the living-room door open, and when we weren't hit in the chest by a flying, dancing Buddy, we both understood the sign. Whenever Robert's father was out of town, his mother tried to keep Buddy in the house as a watchdog—I suppose on the theory that he might possibly trip up an intruder and break his neck as he frisked about him in indiscriminate welcome. But when Buddy was absent—off on some disreputable scavenging trip, no doubt—it usually meant that Mr. Bloom was home. Robert and I now peered out the back living-room window and saw the car in front of the garage, and he lifted his fingers to his lips. "Come on," he whispered. "Let's go into the kitchen."

We tiptoed past the closed door of his parents' bedroom and past the open door of his own bedroom. As usual, I looked in and saw the sword still hanging over his bed. The sharp pain of Robert's ownership of that sword had been replaced in me by a kind of dull wonder at his exasperating sense of honor. "No, I can't touch it until I'm twelve," he had insisted a dozen or more times that past year—times when nothing in the world but a three-foot-long Chinese beheading sword was appropriate to the game at hand. Now, in the kitchen, Robert whispered, "We better not have any pickles without asking Mom. Boy, was she ever mad the last time we ate them all! How about some apricot jam and bread?"

"Swell," I whispered back.

"Hey, would you rather have apricot or strawberry?" he whispered from the depths of the icebox.

"Let's have both," I said, regaining some of the excitement I had lost in my disappointment over the pickles.

He brought out the two jam jars, spooned large helpings of each kind into a bowl, and began whipping them together with a fork. I stared, hypnotized, at the clean colors as they ran together and faded to a pinkish tan. "Boy, are you ever lucky!" I said. "Eating any old thing you want when you want! Do you think my mother, or that old maid of ours, would let me eat *anything* between meals? No, sir! Our maid says you're spoiled because you're an only child and your mother doesn't know any better."

"Well, maybe," he said, shaking fist-size globs of jam onto the bread. "But Mom told me they're going to try and get me a baby brother or a baby sister pretty soon."

"A baby brother or sister? Which kind would you rather have?"

"Oh, I don't care. They're both O.K., I guess." He returned the jars to the icebox, and came back to the table and picked up his bread and jam. "How about taking these out on the front porch to eat?"

"O.K."

We crept past the closed bedroom door again and went out on the porch, being careful not to let the door slam behind us. When we were comfortably settled on the front steps, with our mouths full of bread and jam, I suddenly decided to ask him a question that had occurred to me many times. "Robert, is there something wrong with your mother and father?"

"What do you mean, 'something wrong'?" he asked.

"Well, you know. The way they're always resting when we come here. Are they sick?"

It seemed to me that they must certainly be sick, or something more than sick. For me, bed was a concept that changed entirely with the time of day. Bed at night was a completely respectable thing, both for myself and for my parents—so respectable, in fact, that I usually put up a spirited fight against going to it. But after the sun rose over the high, gray mountains east of town, bed instantly became something slack and irresponsible, even on weekend mornings, when there was no immediate reason for getting out of it. "What?" my father would say, standing over me at seven o'clock on a rainy Saturday morning. "Not up yet?" He never said it harshly but always with a friendly smile, kept just thin enough to give me the message that bed simply wasn't the place to be at that hour. So grave was this obscure crime that even when I was sick enough to stay in bed all day, I dreaded the long morning and afternoon hours there, and never wholly relaxed until it was 8 P.M. again and really time for bed. If there was one aspect of the irregularity of Robert's house that I did not enjoy, it was this matter of bed in the afternoon. There *was* something sick about it.

"Heck, no, they're not sick," Robert said. "Dad gets tired out on the road. I *told* you that. And Mom likes to be with him. They're just taking a nap. Or maybe they're trying to find me that baby brother."

I stopped in the middle of a bite and stared at him. If he had spoken the last words in Latin he could not have lost me more completely.

"They're trying to find a baby? In *there?*"

"Well, of course," he said, stuffing the last of his bread and jam into his mouth. And then the full extent of my darkness must have shown on my face. He swallowed with a little choking cough. "Oh, my gosh!" he said. "You don't know about *that,* either, do you?"

"Of course, I know about it," I said angrily. "I just didn't know what you meant."

But I couldn't cover up my ignorance or my need to know the truth, for he proceeded to tell me all about it. He told me in adequate detail and finished by saying that all babies were "found" in just this way.

"*All* babies?"

"Yep—me, you, everybody. That's the way everybody's parents get their children."

I jumped up, and, seeing the expression on my face, Robert stood up, too, and then I hit him twice—once on the chest to knock him down and once on the nose as he was falling. In its most impersonal sense, the idea he had given me was just barely tolerable, but in relation to my parents it was an unthinkable blasphemy. After all they had done for me, hitting him seemed the very least I could do. I stood over him, breathing hard and with my fists clenched. He looked up at me from the top step, where he had fallen, and slowly rubbed his nose.

"You big damn dumb!" he said at last. "I'll never tell you another thing as long as I live!"

"You just better not," I said. "You just better never say another word to me if you know what's good for you!"

And he never did. From that day forward, I was on my own.

WRITING TWELVE: Try to pull together, dredge up, or get flowing enough memories of someone to write a long story about him consisting of many little stories, like "Not Another Word." Take several weeks to work on this writing. You might write one or two of the little stories every day and then piece them together, throwing away those that don't fit. You may find yourself dealing with two persons who oppose each other in some way, as the boys did in Richard Thurman's story. Or you may find yourself dealing principally with one person. Whatever, be sure you've hooked into an opposition that keeps you discovering incidents that reveal the person or persons you're writing about. If you don't find such an opposition, you probably can't write a long story without padding it.

Persons are easier to write about than places, but if a place calls you, answer that call.

> *It is much easier to sit at a desk and read plans for a billion gallons of water a day, and look at maps and photographs; but you will write a better article if you heave yourself out of a comfortable chair and go down in tunnel 3 and get soaked.*
>
> STUART CHASE

There was a Boy . . .
>   *many a time*
> *At evening, when the earliest stars began*
> *To move along the edges of the hills,*
> *Rising or setting, would he stand alone*
> *Beneath the trees or by the glimmering*
>   *lake,*
> *And there with fingers interwoven, both*
>   *hands*
> *Pressed closely palm to palm, and to his*
>   *mouth*
> *Uplifted, he, as through an instrument,*
> *Blew mimic hootings to the silent*
>   *owls . . .*

WILLIAM WORDSWORTH

chapter 11
through facts to large meanings

DISTANCE AND MEANING

REMEMBERING CHILDHOOD is not childish, but wise and sweet and necessary. We go back because we loved those years of play. We go back because remembering moves us closer to the children around us today. We go back because in writing through these years we gain a second life.

The best writers take this journey. Mark Twain wrote *Huckleberry Finn,* a novel about a boy with a gifted tongue, who once said:

The widow she cried over me, and called me a poor lost lamb, and she called me a lot of other names, too, but she never meant no harm by it. She put me in them new clothes again, and I couldn't do nothing but sweat and sweat, and feel all cramped up. Well, then, the old thing commenced again. The widow rung a bell for supper, and you had to come to time. When you got to the table you couldn't go right to eating, but you had to wait for the widow to tuck down her head and grumble a little over the victuals, though there warn't really anything the matter with them. That is, nothing only everything was cooked by itself. In a barrel of odds and ends it is different; things get mixed up, and the juice kind of swaps around, and the things go better.

After supper she got out her book and learned me about Moses and the Bulrushers; and I was in a sweat to find out all about him; but by-and-by she let it out that Moses had been dead a considerable long time; so then I didn't care no more about him; because I don't take no stock in dead people.

Pretty soon I wanted to smoke, and asked the widow to let me. But she wouldn't. She said it was a mean practice and wasn't clean, and I must try to not do it any more. That is just the way with some people. They get down on a thing when they don't know nothing about it. Here she was a bothering about Moses, which was no kin to her, and no use to anybody, being gone, you see, yet finding a power of fault with me for doing a thing that had some good in it. And she took snuff too; of course that was all right, because she done it herself.

J. D. Salinger wrote about another boy with gifted tongue, who cherished his little sister Phoebe:

She was laying there asleep, with her face sort of on the side of the pillow. She had her mouth way open. It's funny. You take adults, they look lousy when they're asleep and they have their mouths way open, but kids don't. Kids look all right. They can even have spit all over the pillow and they still look all right.

These men wrote of childhood at the height of their mature powers. If you're under twenty, you need even more than they to write of childhood. Writers require some distance between themselves and the events they recall—not always, but usually. Then they are unfamiliar enough with the events to feel the need to relate them fully for their readers and themselves. If they write of yesterday's or last year's events, they usually remember them so well they leave them shrouded in their nearby intimate memory, which the reader doesn't share.

> *But don't expect to write well about the love affair that you are in the midst of, or have just mailed a letter to break off. One principal figure in that situation you can't see. At least one. Probably two. You are "involved." You don't surround it. You suffer or you triumph; you do not comprehend.*
>
> *Later, all those feelings will become your knowledge. They will be of your knowledge and your wisdom when they no longer possess you. Your subject must be something you possess and can move all the way around. The former feelings that come together in your subject may include the most glorious or devastating that you ever had. And you will re-experience them. But you must emotionally enclose and dominate them.*
>
> SIDNEY COX

In most truthful accounts of childhood by adults, a tension builds between the childlike way of doing and perceiving and the writer's present ways. Like most tension in communication, it often breaks open new insights for the writer and reader. The child can never know the adult completely or the adult the child, but in the act of writing the writer momentarily constructs a bridge. There's danger for you as a writer walking there. But also the chance you may get over to the other side where you've never been before.

In the following story a college student records selected details of her life as an older sister. She tells a startling truth about herself when she was younger: as a teenager she demonstrated the mature understanding of an adult. Never does she say this, but it nevertheless comes through the lines of her story.

THIRTEEN

A month after we placed my sister in the home, we went to see her for the first time. It was June fourth, her birthday. She was thirteen.

We brought a big chocolate cake with candles. She loved birthdays and had always helped to blow out the candles on everyone's cake.

Driving in our old car, we were crowded in spite of there being only three of us in back. The drive was long—we went through Battle Creek. There was a lot of traffic and the sun was in Dad's eyes. We were all tense. There had been tears in the strangely empty house for the last month. We had received one letter reporting that "Although Elaine was not eating for a few days, she soon made an adjustment and is now doing quite well." We couldn't imagine Elaine not eating.

When we got to the home, we went to the administration building. Dad parked the car and told us kids to stay put. He and Mom went inside. Left to ourselves, we stared at buildings and at the patients who shambled around, shifty-eyed and odd-looking, with discouraged manners. When one came toward the car, we shut the windows and locked the doors, sitting terrified in the hot, musty closeness. The man asked for cigarettes, but we just stared. He finally went away and we relaxed again. It was the first time we'd ever seen a real retarded person.

Mom and Dad were gone a long time. We sat in the heat growing crosser and more impatient every minute. Finally they walked into view. Between them, holding their hands, was a shrunken figure in a blue dress. The figure walked like the retarded people, stumbling and uncertain. We wondered why they hadn't gotten Elaine yet.

They brought her to the car and put her in the back seat between us kids. Instead of bubbling her usual baby talk, Elaine sat there as if dazed. Her eyes were cloudy like someone had spilled milk in them. We looked at Mom's cold, unspeaking back, then at Dad. There were tears on his cheeks. Suddenly Jenny and John were crying, too. Not sobbing or anything, but just crying, the tears pouring down their quiet faces. For once I did not cry. My voice was shaking as I asked, "Mom, what's the matter with her eyes?"

Mom's voice was blank. "It's the drugs."

No one said anything else. We lighted the candles and sang "Happy Birthday." Elaine didn't join in. I blew out the candles for her. She ate a piece of cake indifferently, pushing it in without care for the crumbs or the mess. Jenny and

John tried to talk to her but she just shook her head. At last Mom and Dad took her back.

Not a one of us mentioned her. It was as if we had never seen her. Dad took a different route, by Augusta, and we all laughed and exclaimed at the scenery. We drove for a long time in that area before we went home.

SARAH KNIGHT

Elaine's sister Sarah (both names are pseudonyms) perceived that experience much as an adult would, but most of the time as children we saw the world differently.

To tell large truths about childhood and how it differs from adulthood may seem an impossible task. But when you put down a telling fact that draws others to it, you may be able to go through them to a significant finding about childhood. If you don't come up with such a larger truth, a significance, you may still have an account that takes your readers back into your childhood and brings it alive so much that they find themselves also moving back into theirs. Here's another childhood memory.

CATCH THE BALL

It was warm, the sun flashed through the branches of the tall trees looking like flash bulbs going off in the sky. I didn't know where I was, but I was with my parents, so it didn't matter.

Dad had parked the car out on the street, and we had walked up a long driveway edged with greens and flowers. Past the big red brick house of English Tudor was a high wooden fence. My parents had opened the gate of the fence and there I stood, looking into the sky, counting the suns that sprinkled through the branches of the huge trees. The landscaped yard of flowerbeds and lawn chairs formed a circle around an old dirty cement bird-bath. It was full of blackish water left from the spring rain, and offered neither refuge nor pleasure to the small summer birds.

"Jack, Donna." I saw strange people coming toward my parents; they seemed to be smiling at me for no apparent reason.

"This must be little Bobby," said a tall ugly woman in a white dress that held a sap stain just below her knee.

Mother started introducing me to the smiles. "Bobby, this is Mrs. Morrison, Mrs. Agrestrom, and Mr. Agrestrom . . ."

I watched my dad take a bottle of beer from a cooler of melted ice. I was ushered to a lawn chair through little clumps of people all talking at the same time.

Someone gave me a bottle of Coca-Cola. It was wet and dripped on my pants. There were no other children in the whole yard. I looked for my father and saw him walking towards me with a big baldheaded man. The man wore yellow bermuda shorts and shower thongs; the sun reflected off his bald head, making it look wet and shiny. They motioned me into the middle of the yard where they stood by the useless bird-bath that distracted from the smell of grass and flowers.

"You remember Uncle Otis, don't you Bobby?"

I said yes even though I'd never seen him before.

We started tossing a red ball around. Dad kept telling me how good I was every time I managed to catch the ball. Uncle Otis said the cubs needed me, whatever that meant. The ball was tossed at me and it skidded along the ground and jumped through my legs. It came to rest next to the bird-bath. I ran after it. I heard Otis yell that he was going to get me. As I bent down to pick up the ball, I felt Uncle Otis's hands grab me around my waist. He picked me up and lifted me over his head.

I looked around from within the grasp of his strong hands, the people were laughing, even my father. Otis moved a hand down to my ankle, grabbed it, and held me upside down.

The branches of the big trees were on the bottom of the yard. If Otis dropped me, I would fall into the top of the trees, through the branches and out into the sky.

He lowered my head into the bird-bath. As I felt the water on my head, I heard the people laughing around me. I still stared into the inverted sky.

"Now you'll be bald like me," said Otis, laughing, as he put me down next to the bird-bath. I was dizzy. I looked into the bird-bath and saw the black waves Otis made with my head splash over the sides.

The laughter died. I looked at my father. He wasn't smiling any more. I ran. Out the gate and into the driveway. I felt the water drip from the top of my head down my neck and face. I thought the dirty water the birds wouldn't use would make me bald. As I ran into the street and towards the car, the water made my shirt wet and the back of my neck cold, and it ran down my cheeks with my tears.

In that story, for Uncle Otis the incident was carefree play; for the little boy, terror. When you write of your childhood, you needn't look for these deep revelations. If you try determinedly for truths, your story will probably help your readers get inside your childhood, and that act will put them inside theirs.

Here's a childhood story by a college freshman who in her class papers customarily recorded facts with brutal force even when she was speaking love and tenderness.

WE WERE GETTING ALONG

I was to stay with my Aunt Bertha, where good schooling and manners would be taught. What Mom needed was understanding and someone to talk to, since her brother recently died in an auto accident. She was always alone, with nothing to do while we kids were in school.

If only I had kept my whale of a mouth shut, she would never have had to leave Jim, Joey—my brothers—and me. Mom and Dad were divorced at the time. Since Dad was living away, I slept with Mom whenever I could because her bed was much bigger than mine. Sometimes she would say, "Go to your room!" but if I nagged at her enough, she would give in and let me sleep in her big bed.

Earlier that night, Jim and Joey got into a spat over what show we were to watch. Mom never said a word. We stayed up that night till the 11 o'clock news came on and we even made our own supper—peanut butter and banana sandwiches with Kool-Aid. "All you can eat. Mom's sleeping," Jim said, peeking into her room, then closing the door quietly. I washed the dishes, Jim dried, while Joey, the youngest, cleared the table, only breaking one dish— that was good for him.

Dad called to see how we were getting along, because he knew Mom wasn't feeling her old self. "We're fine, but Mom's still sleeping," I said. She slept about sixteen hours a day before we started complaining. We thought she had tired, iron-poor blood and needed Geritol, because on the Amateur Hour, they would come out with, "Are you tired?

Rundown? Get enough sleep? Try Geritol!" The next day we went to school, pooled our money ($2.97), and Jim went to the store and bought a bottle. Mom was sure surprised when we tromped into her bedroom. I handed her a spoon. "Here, Mom, I don't like it when you're not yelling at Jim and Joey for picking on me."

Joey said, "You always ask for it!"

Mom was so thrilled about receiving the Geritol she started to cry and told us she would use it later. That was the night before I told Dad on the phone that she was still sleeping, but she wanted us to wake her in half an hour.

"Well," Dad said, "OK, if you get frightened, just call 381-2001."

"Sure, Dad. Bye," I replied as if he were kidding. Me get frightened? After all, I was nine years old.

That night it started to rain. I crept into her room, knocked the book from the bedstand onto the floor. Mom didn't move, just made a groaning noise. I climbed into the huge bed, snuggled next to her, back to back, and covered my head with the sheet, which made me feel better.

It seemed four hours later (really, it was about twenty minutes) when a tree limb cracked down onto the roof of the house. Lady, our collie, started barking and ran around the house. It was droopy, black, and noisy from above the sheets. Then Mom started to groan as if she was in pain, someone pulling her hair out, strand at a time. All I could think about was Dad telling me to call if I got frightened. Me scared of a little old storm? Huh! After another hair, I asked Mom if anything was wrong.

"They're coming to get me! Run, get in the house! The plane will hit me!"

"Are you all right, Mom?"

She went on and on. I didn't want to frighten Mom, so I called 381-2001. Dad answered and I told him what had happened.

"Uncle Milt will talk to you till I get home. Call him. You hear me?"

I called Uncle Milt, told him what had happened. After Dad arrived, then he came over to help.

Mom never got up during the night. Just lay in her big bed. I felt like a fool calling everyone at 2:00 A.M. and getting them out of bed.

"Your mother's just having a bad dream," my Aunt
Bertha said when she arrived. She was Mom's sister, the
old hag. Always wanted you to do something for her.
"Make the beds! Clean the floors! Kids were made to be
seen and not heard." Jim and I knew Mom wasn't just
having a bad dream. Joey, being only seven, slept through
the whole affair.

About 7:00 A.M., Pastor Jones came to pray with Mom
and talk to the elders. He patted me on top of the head.
I got mad, walked away, and tried to talk to Mom, but
everyone kept me away as if she were poison.

A while later, an ambulance came. Two men got out, and
started walking toward the house. Lady bit one man on the
back of the leg. There was a "Beware of Dog" sign on our
front tree, so the man just bitched. I was glad Lady bit
him.

The two men walked into the house as if they owned our
place and grabbed Mom. She made a fuss. Then they
slowly walked her through the living room and away.
Everyone was staring at her as if she were some kind of
animal. I knew she was still my mother.

GRACE WENDELL

Such a piece of writing tells so much truth that it may hurt the persons mentioned in it, although what it says is worthy of the attention
of many readers. (The names in this story, including the author's—as
in many other stories in this book—are changed to protect persons.)

BEGINNINGS AND ENDINGS

Most good published pieces of writing have been created in several
drafts—each version tighter and sharper than the last. What you see in
print is almost never the first effort. Professional writers don't expect
to dash off a piece of writing that is beyond improvement. Each version
they think of as preliminary to another better version until finally they
have had enough of drafting and say, "Done."

About eighty percent of the time, professional writers and editors
find that the beginning of a first draft is no beginning at all. It's a mess,
a series of false beginnings in which the starter's pistol goes off once,
then twice, and the runners burst from their blocks only to stop and
come back again. Writers must expect these bad starts because when
they first meet their readers they have been thinking through all that

they want to tell them, not just the beginning of it. So they tell them
too about the end of the story or the chain of ideas, as well as the
beginning—or too little, on the false assumption that the readers have
just gone with them on this journey of reflection. In fact, it can't be a
journey of memory for the readers. It must be a trip into an unknown
woods in the partial dark where the stumps and branches leap at their
feet and the hanging spider webs clutch their faces.

> *I write my first version in longhand
> (pencil). Then I do a complete revision,
> also in longhand . . . Then I type a third
> draft on yellow paper, a very special cer-
> tain kind of yellow paper. No, I don't get
> out of bed to do this. I balance the ma-
> chine on my knees. Sure, it works fine;
> I can manage a hundred words a minute.
> Well, when the yellow draft is finished,
> I put the manuscript away for a while, a
> week, a month, sometimes longer. When
> I take it out again, I read it as coldly as
> possible, then read it aloud to a friend
> or two, and decide what changes I want
> to make and whether or not I want to
> publish it. I've thrown away rather a few
> short stories, an entire novel, and half
> of another. But if all goes well, I type
> the final version on white paper and
> that's that.*
>
> **TRUMAN CAPOTE**

Here's the opening of the first draft of a childhood story that took
too long to get going.

I had gotten Alice for a present on my fourth birthday. We
had finished my cake and Mommy told me to go into the
living room. I had just settled down in the big chair when
Daddy came out with a box. I opened it and threw away the
tissue paper and there she was—all dressed up in a pretty
pink chiffon bonnet and pinafore. She had booties and real
socks, too. Mommy gave me a nightie and a blanket she had
made for her. That was in the box, too.

That's not a bad opening, but nothing in it surprises, and nothing hints at the tough attitude the narrator is going to take later; so readers might quit reading after that first paragraph, thinking they were going to read a gooey little girl's story. The tale ends with such strength that such a beginning as this doesn't fit. It's commonplace. When a child gets a doll as a gift, she takes it out of its box.

In the final draft of the story, which follows, the reader is quickly taken on a walk with a baby carriage and soon finds the little girl treating her doll as if it is her baby—which is the central attitude exploited in the story. Upon the advice of an editor, the author dropped the original paragraph given above and started at a later point, in this way:

ALICE DEAR

She was the prettiest doll I had ever seen so I gave her the prettiest name I knew then, which was Alice. But *Alice* wasn't enough, so later I attached the last name, *Dear*.

One day Mommy took baby sister out for a walk in the carriage and I asked if I could take Alice Dear along. Mommy showed me how to wrap her up like baby sister and how to carry her so she would be comfortable, and we went for a walk. Whenever someone looked at baby sister, they had to peek under Alice Dear's covers, too. Everyone thought she was the prettiest doll they had ever seen, just like they thought baby sister was the cutest baby.

I had three dolls—Alice Dear, Patty, and Judy. Alice Dear was the oldest and my favorite. Patty was a nice doll, but she was big as a real baby—much too hard for me to handle. She had a hard plaster head, rubber arms and legs and a cloth body. You couldn't spank Patty very hard, because every time you did, she'd always cry at you—WAH WAH! I couldn't bear to hear any child of mine cry like that. Judy was a more grown-up doll. She would walk, but her body was hard and you always had to treat her nice because Mommy said she cost a lot of money. Alice Dear was more timid than Patty or Judy. They could take care of themselves pretty well, but Alice Dear needed me. She could be any age you wanted her to be, but Patty was always a baby and Judy was always seven years old.

Alice had an all-rubber body and I could give her a bath, which I did every day. She had rooted hair and I could comb it and set it. When I spanked her, she always knew it was for her own good and that it hurt me more than it hurt her. She could take it like a lady. She didn't cry back at me like that ole sissy Patty did.

Alice Dear was cuddly. She was just right in my arms. I could take her to bed with me, and if she landed on the floor at night, she didn't mind because she knew I loved her. Patty would get mad at me, I know, because Mommy told me once that if she ever landed on the floor, her head would break. I couldn't even consider taking Judy to bed with me. Her hard body always poked me and sometimes she'd get stubborn and stick up her leg.

The years soon took their toll on Alice Dear. She began to wear out from all the baths and her rubber skin got all black. Though Alice never grew up like normal children, she got bald from all the times I washed and set her hair.

One hot July day of my ninth year, Alice Dear got a spanking for being naughty. Her soft body couldn't take it any more, and she split right up the back. All her foam rubber stuffing fell out.

I looked at her in surprise. Alice Dear didn't cry, she just gave up. All those shots in her behind from the times we played hospital together, she the patient, I the nurse, stood out like bruises. Suddenly I cried for all the times Alice never did.

I ran in the house and told my mother what happened and she comforted me. Then she took a paper bag and a broom and cleaned up Alice from the garage floor. She saved Alice's head. Alice Dear had a pretty face—rosy cheeks and blue eyes and a dimple that was nice to kiss. I set her head on the window sill in my bedroom for a couple of weeks and then asked Mother about doll factories that take parts from broken dolls and make them into new dolls. The next day, Daddy took Alice's head away.

It was right around that time that I lost interest in dolls.

JULIE TEITELBAUM

Consider the openings to all the papers you've written. They should open the story—swing open, and let the reader in. In the story "Catch the Ball," printed earlier in this chapter, the writer spends several lines setting the scene, but he does so with originality that prevents boredom. Instead of writing the tired phrase, "It was a warm, bright day," he says:

> It was warm, the sun flashed through the branches of the tall
> trees looking like flash bulbs going off in the sky.

The metaphor probably earns the respect of the reader. It suggests that this writer can produce a telling fact even in an opening description, so chances are good the story will develop some hard and valuable truths.

In the first two sentences of the story "We Were Getting Along," the writer sets up a contrast between "good schooling and manners" and "understanding" and forecasts the probing she will do into the acceptance of the mother by the daughter and the relatively cold concern of relatives and institutional officials.

In writing an opening beware of the windy generalization:

> Everybody likes motorcycles and I am no exception.

Not true. Many persons detest motorcycles and consider them the most likely transportation to Hell. Don't turn off the reader by pretentious or coy behavior. In the beginning you establish your voice. If you begin squeaking like a monkey or thundering like an elephant, you have ruined your chances with the reader, who will be astounded later to find you writing in natural human voice. Beware of phony introductions, voice changes, and unnecessary apologies.

An opening often gains by being new, surprising; but if your writing is crammed with surprises all the way through, you may do well to begin quietly and conventionally. You don't have to amaze or stun or mystify your reader at the beginning. But you have to avoid alienating him with emptiness, phoniness, or unsuccessful attempts at humor. You may simply begin factually:

> East High School is located two miles from the center
> of the business district in Clarksville.

but don't use that fact unless it makes a point relevant to your story. Later in this story, the distance from the school to the business district should come up.

Think hard how your reader will take your first words. Consider this opening:

> **What's going on? This question might have gone through
> the minds of the grocery store owners when the students of
> Mr. McMahon's psychology class went to the different stores
> for an assignment that was done over vacation.**

"What's going on?" is a question that might be asked by anyone in any situation. Here the reader is required to wait too long before the question gains any significance.

Revision: "What's going on?" said the grocery store owner when he saw twenty-five students from Mr. McMahon's psychology class walking up and down the aisles writing in their notebooks. They were carrying out an assignment during Thanksgiving vacation.

When you have found or created a good beginning to your story, consider its ending. At both ends of a piece of writing, a writer is driven to explaining, almost as if he wanted to give advice to the reader on how to read what he has written, and nothing is worse than advice. If the Explainery comes at the beginning, it's lost on the reader who doesn't know the story yet. If it comes at the end, it tastes like soggy bread. The reader has read the story and is insulted by being told what he has read.

The first draft of "Alice Dear" ended like this:

> It was right around that time that I lost interest in dolls, so
> I put Patty and Judy away to rest. They're still very stiff and
> unfriendly, but maybe my daughters will like them more
> than I did, so I save them and take very good care of them.
> They still look like new after all these years.

This last paragraph took up points unrelated to the preceding sentence, which was "The next day, Daddy took Alice's head away." That sentence by itself might make a pretty good ending, for it jolts the reader and continues the humor established earlier. But as an ending it may leave the reader wondering whether the narrator ever saw Alice again. The whole paragraph suffers because it takes up Patty and Judy again, when by now the story is all Alice's. When an editor saw this paragraph, he suggested that the writer had already written a good ending with the sentence "It was right around that time that I lost interest in dolls" but hadn't had the courage to stop when she had scored.

It's pleasing to create a smashing ending to a piece of writing, but ridiculous to try for one and miss. As you'll see when you read on in this book, one of the fundamentals of good writing is alternation—of kitchen and elevated style, of fast and slow action, of idea and example. Practiced writers who sense that their writing must have early hit the reader hard often play down the ending, understate it, so that it really is an ending, not just a stopping of something that has remained at one level all the while. The author of "We Were Getting Along" did this in her next-to-last sentence.

> Everyone was staring at her as if she were some kind of animal. I knew she was still my mother.

This ending carries a great deal more feeling in its simple expression than would supercharged sentences like these:

> My God! Didn't they have any sensitivity? Their behavior was absolutely cruel and vicious and they didn't realize the horror of it.

After you've let your first draft of a childhood story cool a while, look it over for a spot near the end that's exciting or surprising. Consider stopping a little before you believe your reader will expect you to. If possible, find a good detail near the end or one of the main feelings or ideas in your story; chop everything else off that follows it, or move the good passage to the end position.

Don't drool an ending. Wipe your mouth, say the last word, leave your reader.

WRITING THIRTEEN: Choose an incident or several incidents in your childhood and reconstruct them with telling facts. If possible, go through those facts to some larger meaning, a view of childhood or the relationship between children and adults, which goes beyond your experience to speak to your readers' experience. But don't give a lecture. Let the story make the point.

Think about the voice in which you write. Are you purposely mixing the manner of adult and child as Richard Thurman did in "Not Another Word"? Or are you trying pretty much to capture the sound of a child talking? Does your ear allow you to include as part of the story the dialogue of children who appear there?

Repeat: *to double, re-double, renew, parallel, echo, match, mirror, reproduce, regenerate, reincarnate, multiply, revive, reaffirm, reassert, accentuate, emphasize, build, hammer, slap, thump, beat, bang, punch, jab, convince, charm, lull, caress.*

chapter 12
repeating

WEAK AND
STRONG REPETITION

IF SOMEONE you love keeps saying he loves you, the repetition is beautiful. But if someone you dislike keeps saying he loves you, the repetition is unbearable. And there are places and moments where you don't want to be told you are loved. Even the heartbeat, with its repetitious but slightly irregular liveliness, can become monotonous—for example, if recorded day after day in a laboratory.

Repetition can comfort or bore, clarify or confuse, astound or outrage. Consider these repetitions:

> **I think Ethel was rebelling when she refused to follow my suggestion. She was rebelling against her ability to recover, her ability to heal, her ability to retain her youth. She had lost her youth, yet she was still fighting. Fighting for a lost cause.**

They clog the passage rather than emphasize what needs to be emphasized.

Professional writers read their work aloud to themselves and to others. They hear repetition their eyes didn't see. The beginner and the professional need to find ways of getting inside their writing and hearing it objectively. One way is to listen for repetitions, which are easily detected. Those that writers are surprised to find are usually weak: they didn't intend them. They may become valuable to the writers as flags indicating other failures or surrenders. If they didn't notice them before, they probably missed other weaknesses. Read the following passage aloud and you'll find weak repetition. It will help you spot other weaknesses.

> One of the specific aspects of the speech was the question and answer period. I feel that the panel during the question and answering period was very biased in their questions to Governor Barnett of the state of Mississippi. In so much as the questions directed toward Governor Barnett were mostly concerned with segregation in general.

The passage needs massive cutting. Here's a possible revision:

> In the question and answer period, the panel was biased toward Governor Barnett of Mississippi. Most of the questions concerned segregation.

In another part of his column, this writer ran into a snag with the word *fact*.

> Governor Barnett has said that the North is just as segregated as the South. This is of course an overstatement of fact, but it still does contain a certain amount of fact. There are no signs forbidding Negroes from using a drinking fountain or from buying a bottle of Coke from a vending machine, but I have experienced prejudice in the North and even helped the cause of segregation in Lansing, Michigan.

The second sentence might be revised in this way:

> This is an overstatement but still contains a certain amount of fact.

Note that in both excerpts from this column, the writer employed weak repetition when she was generalizing, not when she was giving particular evidence. Her last sentence in the second excerpt ("There are no signs . . .") is well written. In it she has found her voice and speaks with her natural powers.

Often weak repetition blooms when a writer tries to impress his reader, as in this passage:

> When one sits before an open hearth and can see the flames shooting from the burning wood, hear the crackling of the fire as it engulfs its source of fuel, and feel the

> warmth given off, one enters another "world," a "world"
> which is quiet and peaceful . . . You may ask why we
> spend so much time by the fire, and that should be a diffi-
> cult question to answer. But I believe it is the "mystery" of
> the fire that intrigues us. This "mystery" of the fire has a
> way of captivating your thoughts and putting you in a
> trance-like atmosphere.

Here again words appear close to each other in ineffectual repetition.
To show how unprofessional she is, the writer also puts quotation marks
around *world* and *mystery*—which she uses in the commonest way—and
insults her reader. Instead of saying the crackling fire "engulfs its
wood," she says "its source of fuel." She so feared repetition that she
went to a ridiculous length to find a synonym. Wood is fuel, but here
the general subject of fuel isn't being discussed. If the writer can't stand
to hear the word *wood* repeated, she should remove its first use, not
its second. Then the passage would read:

> When one sits before an open hearth and watches the
> shooting flames, hears the crackling as the fire engulfs the
> wood, and feels the warmth given off . . .

Avoidance of repetition sometimes leads writers to silly substitutions
for a key word in a passage. If the principal subject of your writing
is *cats,* use the word *cats* frequently. Don't say *cats,* then *felines,
furry friends,* and *four-legged bundles of fur.* Sports writers often sin
with this "elegant variation." For example, a good sportswriter in a
student newspaper began his article with *The Rich track team.* Then
he calls them by their name *The Olympians.* Next he says, "Then
the squad began to show." Up to that point his variation in naming
is inoffensive, but next he says:

> Still improving, the Central cindermen then overran T. F.
> South and Lockport West, finishing the season in grand
> style. The Olympians captured nine firsts . . .

By that point the paper's regular readers are probably fatigued by
the writer's attempt to avoid repetition, and an outsider is probably
lost, wondering whether *the Central cindermen* still refers to *the Rich
track team* or to one of their opponents.

The writer who has found a voice that belongs to her repeats words
with power, not with weakness. If she wants to hit a word hard, she
repeats it. Dr. Seuss does:

Then Horton the elephant smiled. "Now that's that . . ."
    And he sat
        and he sat
            and he sat
                and he sat . . .
    And he sat all that day
    And he kept the egg warm . . .
    And he sat all that night
    Through a *terrible* storm.

Thomas Paine, the pamphleteer who helped persuade colonists to join George Washington's army, wrote:

> I call not upon a few, but upon all: not on this state or that state, but on every state: up and help us; lay your shoulders to the wheel; better have too much force than too little when so great an object is at stake.

These repetitions helped create the United States.

In Shakespeare's *Macbeth,* Macduff speaks to Malcolm, reminding him of the sad state to which Scotland has fallen under the rule of the murdering King Macbeth:

                        Each new morn
New widows howl, new orphans cry, new sorrows
Strike heaven on the face, that it resounds
As if it felt with Scotland and yelled out
Like syllable of dolor.

Here the word *new* murders husbands, fathers, happiness, and creates widows, orphans, sorrows. It's not at all like the *new* which appears on so many packages of detergent, toothpaste, and shampoo in the supermarket. The manufacturer thinks the word will sell his product and he changes the product ever so slightly once a year, or changes it not at all, and stamps *new* on the package. Too many *new's* on packages have killed the force of them all.

Professional writers usually avoid starting a sentence with the same word that ends the preceding sentence:

> I found out his name was John. John was an engineer.

> The last topic on the program was rehabilitation. Rehabilitation is an urgent matter in Michigan because prisons are overcrowded.

In their second or third draft, professional writers look for repetitions of this sort—they know they will be there—and expunge them. But frequently they achieve their best repetition unconsciously. An idea, or a fact, often epitomized in a key word, dominates their minds. They repeat it when they write.

A good way to utilize repetition without being dull is to shift the form of the repeated word, or play with it in some way. Here a writer makes the word *uncivilized* speak to the word *civilized*:

> **I don't like picnics. That's against the great American tradition, I guess. I don't like to combine the civilized way of eating with uncivilized surroundings.**

When you write out a first draft hurriedly, you may find one key word appearing again and again. Before you eliminate the repetitions of it, think twice. Some of the repetitions may give strength to your writing and let the reader know what objects or ideas dominate your thought. Here's a memory of childhood that needs cutting. It contains too much good writing to be allowed to remain in this state marred by weak repetitions. But some of its repetitions are essential; for example, of the word *outside,* which is central to the writer's point. (Some of the major repetitions are indicated here in italics.)

> **Summer seems more fun during childhood. I remember those *screen-door days.* The back *door* to my house was covered with two sections of *screen* that bulged from being pushed by an endless chain of small hands. I doubt that the *door* was ever shut without a *bang*; in fact it seemed to be there for the sole purpose of shutting with a *bang.* To butt out that *door* without hearing the familiar b-r-r-zing *BANG!* would have been as unnatural to me as giving my sister some of my candy—well almost. I was always in a great hurry to get *outside.* Summer is an *outside* time. I had an outside mind. I could only think in *outside.* Sometimes in my haste to join my mind *outside,* I would fly at the *door* only to discover, too late, that a security-conscious grandmother or some such menace of childhood had locked it. I would come to a tire-tearing halt, like a cartoon car stopping on a dime. I had to peel my face off the *screen* like a waffle, and looking very much like one only with much smaller squares. I would *cuss* at whoever locked the *door.* If I did not know who the culprit was I would *cuss* at**

everyone just to be on the safe side. However my anger was silent, or mutterings at best. My mother's children left much to be desired where brains are concerned, but she did not rear any of us to be *stupid*, at least not so *stupid* as to be caught *swearing*. My father was a great strong *swearer*. He could invoke deities and conjure up demons that made my bottom sore before the *belt* was even off his waist. I was always puzzled by the fact that I could say *"god-darn"* this and *"god-darn"* that depending on whatever I wanted *God* to mend, and yet *"goddamn"* always removed the belt from my father's waist. The sin was in the "damn" not in the "God." I always wondered what God thought about it and how big a belt he had.

MICHAEL MANUEL

In this reflection on childhood, the notion of *outside* is crucial to the story because it is the urge to get outside quickly that led the boy to swear and to confront his father and think upon the effects and causes of profanity. But too much emphasis on *outside* and the screen door makes the ending discussion of profanity seem like an afterthought rather than the major subject the writing builds toward.

Here's a revision of the story with a number of the repetitions cut out:

> The back *door* to my house was covered with two sections of *screen* that bulged from being pushed by an endless chain of small hands. That *door* seemed to be there for the sole purpose of being slammed. To butt out it without hearing the familiar b-r-r-zing BANG! would have been as unnatural to me as giving my sister some of my candy.
>
> I could only think in *outside*. Sometimes in my haste to join my mind *outside,* I would fly at the *door* only to discover too late that a security-conscious grandmother had locked it. I would come to a halt like a cartoon car stopping on a dime and would peel my face off the *screen* like a waffle. Then I would cuss—at everyone, just to be on the safe side—but silently, mutteringly. Mother did not rear us to be so stupid as to be caught *swearing*.
>
> Father was a great strong *swearer*. He could invoke deities and conjure up demons that made my bottom sore before the *belt* was off his waist. I was always puzzled because I could say *"god-darn"* this and *"god-darn"* that,

> depending on whatever I wanted *God* to mend, and yet
> "*god-damn*" always removed the belt from Father's waist.
> The sin was in the "*damn*" not in the "*God*." I always
> wondered what *God* thought about it and how big a *belt*
> he wore.

Repetitions remain but they are necessary, therefore not tedious but powerful. To gain their full effect, some words shouldn't be repeated at all. The writer should save them strategically for one best moment. In the above story if the word *bang* is to sound loud, it should be heard only once.

Rhyme is a form of repetition, of sound, not word. It can be used in prose if the writer remembers that its effect there is customarily humorous. Lilian Moore wrote a book she called *A Pickle for a Nickel* in which she had Mr. Bumble say truly, "Boys like noise."

REVISING FIVE: Examine your story about childhood. Omit the weak repetitions and consider adding strong repetitions. Use penciled brackets so that you may restore words or phrases should you later change your mind.

WRITING FOURTEEN: Dash off two 10- to 15-minute free writings in which you play frequently with repetition. Repeat words in as many different patterns as you can. Repeat a word three times in a row, then repeat it as the key word in three phrases: "He was a bumbling carpenter, a bumbling father, a bumbling fisherman." Then separate the repeated words even more from each other. Try repeating all kinds of words—verbs, adverbs, prepositions, adjectives, nouns, etc. Use a word once with one meaning and then with another meaning. If you feel stalled, study advertisements in magazines and commercials on television to find still other ways to repeat. Study poems; almost all good ones repeat words skillfully. In all your practice in repeating, do not make up nonsense phrases or sentences that are lists of words unrepresentative of thoughts or feelings in you. Try always to say something you mean but play while you do that. Play around—seriously.

PARALLEL CONSTRUCTION

One of the fundamental beats in all good writing is parallel construction, which is based on repetition. No competent writer's ear is deaf to it. Take this statement:

> **George liked Jean and often walked beside her on the way
> to school. Jean was also sometimes accompanied to school by**

Ronald, who also liked her, but who often could be seen walking behind her.

Here's a shorter version:

> George liked Jean and often walked beside her on the way to school. Jean was also accompanied by Ronald, who walked behind her.

But it's still awkward. Seeing that the sentences compare George's and Ronald's walking with Jean, the professional writer would cast each part of the comparison in parallel form:

> George liked Jean and walked beside her to school. Ronald liked Jean and walked behind her to school.

Tightened and paralleled in this fashion, the sentences now emphasize that Ronald was bashful. They could be paralleled in another way:

> The boys liked Jean. George walked beside her to school and Ronald behind her.

At the same time that most parallel patterning throws into simple and dramatic comparison two or more ideas or persons or things, it shortens a statement so severely that it requires work from the reader. This is an ideal combination of qualities: challenge and delight.

Writers who wonder how their words will strike their readers need only ask how the words strike themselves as they pattern them. If they find themselves unchallenged or bored, they should know they aren't writing well. Their words should speak to them as well as to their audience—and to each other. Parallel patterning helps give them voice. Here's a beginning writer making words speak to each other.

> **I like to bounce when I get into bed, and pick up my pillow and throw it down, then pick up my head and drop it into the pillow, like someone picking up a little kitten and dropping it in some out of the way place so that it won't get *under* foot. Good thing I've got the upper bunk . . . I couldn't be any more *out* from *under* foot.**

Train your ear so you hear a word when you write it, and then ask whether it needs an answer from another word soon. Here's a beginning writer who was listening as she wrote:

> Why not be natural, free, untimed, unlimited?

Here's a professional advertising writer listening as he wrote:

> You ought to watch Longchamps meat experts buying beef for your dinner. They stride through the refrigerators, sniffing and poking each rib on the rack. They know what's what. So butchers give them their best. Well marbled steaks, tender as butter. Naturally aged meat, with a rich, beefy taste. Longchamps experts are tough. That's why Longchamps steaks are tender . . .

All writers who want to hammer an idea employ repetition and parallel construction. A high school girl gets out her hammer in the following article from the Lakeview High School *Crystal* of Battle Creek, Michigan (May 6, 1966):

NASTY NAZI SYMBOL OR HARMLESS FAD?

> Most teenage fads are inoffensive and short-lived. A current fad in Battle Creek is far from inoffensive and should be stopped at once.
>
> Teenagers are adorning themselves with symbols of German militarism such as German army helmets. Some are wearing an Iron Cross on a chain around their neck. Elsewhere, the Nazi swastika is in style.
>
> These symbols recall the death of 291,000 Americans and the slaughter of six million Jews.
>
> They recall an upheaval during and after the war, started by a man who used the swastika as the symbol of an evil philosophy.
>
> Human memories are short, but not so short that they blot out this devastating period of history.
>
> These military symbols are probably just an expression of rebellion. Some kinds of rebellion are healthy. This kind is sick.
>
> JANICE NEMRAVA

IMITATING ONE: Practice parallel patterning so you can see how easy and hard it is. Read the following examples and imitate their structure while you're writing thoughts of your own:

1. Every day, the sun; and, after sunset, Night and her stars. Ever the winds blow; ever the grass grows. Every day, men and women, conversing—beholding and beholden.

    RALPH WALDO EMERSON

2. We have rates by the hour, day, week, month, or by the job.

DICK'S KALAMAZOO JANITOR SERVICE,
YELLOW-PAGES ADVERTISEMENT.

3. Other people cannot see what I see whenever I look into your father's face, for behind your father's face as it is today are all those other faces which were his. Let him laugh and I see a cellar your father does not remember and a house he does not remember and I hear in his present laughter his laughter as a child.

JAMES BALDWIN

4. Cut flowers at proper stage of development. Dahlias when fully open; gladioli when first floret is open; peonies when petals are unfolding; roses before buds open. In general, cut while in bud.

The Pocket Household Encyclopedia

5. Remember that young uncooked spinach makes a good salad; that cooked buttered spinach and grapefruit salad are an ideal reducer's luncheon; and that cooked spinach greens are superb with Hollandaise Sauce . . .

IRMA S. ROMBAUER AND MARION ROMBAUER BECKER

Pursue, keep up with, circle round and round your life, as a dog does his master's chaise. Do what you love. Know your own bone; gnaw at it, bury it, unearth it, and gnaw it still.

HENRY THOREAU

chapter 13 keeping a journal

"WHAT a square idea," you may have said to yourself when you read the title of this chapter. A journal! You kept a diary in high school and took it out the other day and looked away in embarrassment—

> This was the greatest day of my life. I met Tim. He was standing outside the dime store, this tall, handsome boy—a dream that's what he was—and I thought—"He ought to be on TV—and then Jeannie introduced me and I thought I'd die. I couldn't believe it. Before I knew what was happening I found myself being walked home by him. He's just absolutely—I can't say what he means to me already.

Or if you're a man, your diary went for two days and stopped. The entries looked like this:

> Played ball this morning. Had lunch at 12:30. Didn't do much the rest of the day.

The writer of journals like that can't say or won't say. The reader gets no telling facts and so can't go through them to essentials or significance. No oppositions, no tension, nothing to grab or be grabbed by. A few years later even the writers of these diaries will be unable to get any valuable meaning from them.

In contrast, here's an entry from a journal kept by a person who constantly tried to put down truths.

> **I have drained six cartons of lemonade and twelve glasses of tap water since this afternoon, and two quarts of milk. I have a fever but am on my feet, slushing off to class— reading, writing, and I get paid today.**

Like the entry about Tim, this one is intensely personal, but it records telling facts which take the reader through the door into some essences. Reading this entry twenty years later, the writer might sense the tremendous swallowing vigor of his youth. There's a tension between his fever and his elation. Not a developed or highly significant piece of writing, but it scores, it characterizes.

All good journals observe one fundamental: they don't speak privately. They can be read with profit by other persons than the writer. They may be personal and even intimate, but if the writer wants an entry to be seen by others, it will be such that they can understand, enjoy, be moved by. The trap has sprung on the writers of the first two entries quoted in this chapter. They heard of secret diaries and thought they should write secretly in their books. So they went Engfishing, writing in a pseudodramatic manner but supplying the reader none of the oppositions that create drama.

Society presses on the writer to say nothing in his journal. A weird country we live in, where, as George Riemer points out in *How They Murdered the Second R* (1969), over six billion greeting cards were sold in one year to people who couldn't bring themselves to write anything of their own to friends and relatives. The Engfish teachers have done their job. But you know how to tell truths that count for you, and to make one truth breed another.

Persons who only dream of becoming writers spend their time dreaming of becoming writers. Those who really intend to become writers keep a journal and work the mine. You may say you don't intend any such thing, but you are one already if you have taken yourself through the program thus far in this book. That is, you write a lot, and some of what you write moves other persons. If you keep a journal, you can make your letters and school writing better, for it not only provides practice ground, but also gives you entries you can combine into longer work. Henry Thoreau did that and called the book *Walden*. Samuel Butler did that and called the book *The Way of All Flesh*.

Asked to write a full portrait of someone, a class of writing students found they couldn't open up to tell enough. Most of the papers

disappointed the students and the professor. One young married man
read the class this entry from his journal:

1

My wife's Aunt Sadie died yesterday, and the wheels of
grieving were set in motion. Six months ago she wasn't
even sick (we didn't know it, anyway). She and K.C. (her
husband, whom we call Case) lived in Sellers, which is a
little dot on a township map. When Sadie complained of
being tired, her doctor (small town and country variety)
told her to take iron pills to fortify her blood because she
was at about that age for her change in life. So she took
iron till she rusted when it rained and then went to another
doctor after a year or so. He found out she had a form of
leukemia.

Mary's ma and Sadie were sisters and super close. They
were both cut out of the same hunk of gold. Whenever I
saw Sadie and Case, Sadie would hug me with one arm
and start shoveling food at me with the other, and Case
would open me up a beer and start getting out a new (or
an old) gun to show me. Real folks. Sadie always talked
loud and real fast so I couldn't keep up or disagree, just
like Mary's ma . . . and Mary. But I never wanted to shut
Sadie up. She was always where it was at. Before I could
agree with her, she'd hand me a bowl to lick or the last slice
of ham, or Case would slip me another beer. I remember
holding bowls of food in my lap all the way back to Kalamazoo when we'd come from Sellers.

Now I have to go to her funeral. I don't like funerals
because of the people that lots of times go to them. That's
why if I want to pay respects to someone, I go to the home
and sit by them when I'm alone. Some people actually
rejoice at the sight of a person crying at the death of
another. They think the greater the display of emotion,
the higher the reading on the love meter. The reaction of
one person to the death of another is a personal thing.
Some people cry for the dead person's suffering. Some cry
for their own guilt feelings about their treatment of the
deceased. Some cry selfishly at their personal loss and future
inconvenience. And maybe some people just cry.

There is so much energy wasted at crying. Sadie at least
fed people, and she couldn't have always felt as good as she

acted. Probably the worse she felt, the better she cooked. But her worst probably doubled most people's best.

Isn't it barbaric to put dead people on display? Tomorrow we are going down there a full twenty-four hours before the funeral so that Mary's two youngest sisters can get used to things—what they mean is get used to seeing a corpse. I say a person should be allowed to remember another person in the way they want to. About all I can remember about my grandmother is how she looked in her casket and how her hand felt so cold and wax-like when I kissed "Nonnie" good-bye. The corpse shouldn't even have to be present for a funeral gathering. Having a group of people standing around watching a person being buried is like having friends in to witness a birth. There should be glad things doing at a funeral gathering. Sadie couldn't have stood to see all those people without feeding them. They should all talk about her and sing and toast to her good things.

And now I don't think my favorite dessert that Sadie used to fix me will taste good any more because everyone's going to spoil it and I hope she understands that I'm just a minority of one, but I loved her quite a bit for an aunt that's just adopted.

DAVE CONNOR

The students liked that writing. One said, "Write more. I want to know still more about Aunt Sadie." The writer promised, but didn't force himself to continue the story right away. When more strong feelings hit him the next day, he wrote another entry.

2

I'm in Sellers. Everyone has seen Sadie at the funeral home. I wonder why they call it a home. I stayed there for about an hour and every time a new bunch of relatives would get there, the crying and sobbing would start again. The parlor has overflowed into two extra rooms with flowers. This evening, Mary said that people just kept coming in and there have been several hundred through there since yesterday. Tonight Mary said that there was little sadness displayed and that all of Sadie's friends were talking and visiting and I think sharing some of the love that all these people had for Sadie. She was such a worker. She

helped everyone and never sat still long enough for anyone to do anything for her. I think she wanted them to do
something for somebody else and start a chain letter of
doing good things. And it is sad now that she can't do things
any more. When Becky, my fifth-grade aged sister-in-law,
was crying so hard this afternoon, I talked to her because
she's never been in a funeral situation before—all of her
grandparents are still living. I asked her if she ever saw
Sadie cry, and she kind of whispered "No," and I said,
"Sadie didn't let people stay sad when she was around, did
she?" And I got another "No." "I think it might make Sadie
sad if she saw that she was making you so unhappy," I
got a soft head on my shoulder and a hug from one skinny
arm half-way around the middle. I told her that Sadie had
been in a lot of pain when she was sick and felt very badly
even after the doctors had done everything they could,
and shouldn't we be thankful that she wasn't feeling badly?
"Now she can rest and be peaceful and we should be happy
for her."

Maybe I sounded like a preacher and maybe it wasn't me
talking, but she needed someone to hang onto who wasn't
already tear-soaked. Mine were the only dry eyes in the
house at the time. My wife is one of five girls and my sister-
in-law's husband and I are big brothers quite a lot. I'm a
big brother anyway, except I only have one sister, and she's
the youngest in my family, so I don't know much about
little girls.

Sadie would be happy if she could see the kitchen at her
daughter's house. It's piled full of food that people have
been bringing over all day long. There's like ten pies, six
cakes, five potato salads, four beans, eight Jello things,
and about three dozen home-baked dinner rolls. Small
town folks help so much. They come into Nancy's house
after each group leaves and wash up all the dishes and
clean up the house. Nancy's got her dad to tend to now
and so many things to do. She's a pretty strong person. It's
hard for an only child to shoulder the bulk of a load like
she's got now because Sadie took care of Case and the
bookwork for his garage and she did all of Grandpa and
Grandma Lewis's cleaning and washing and then some.
But I think Nancy inherited her mother's will to do good
things, come hell, high water, or locusts.

I don't think tomorrow's going to be as sad as I thought
at first.

Waiting a few more days, the writer felt moved to complete the record
of his changing feelings about funerals. He wrote this entry:

3

We buried her today. Lots more family came and I saw the
rural roots of their upbringings emerge in their sincerity,
frankness, and strength. Few of the people were verbal
wizards or well-versed, and few were under forty. They
were tanned from years of exposure or from their retire-
ment quarters in Florida. As I shook hands with them
during the day, I could sense their feelings. The men were
big and grasped my hand firmly, and extended their
friendliness and welcome in their simple and straightforward greetings. My hand felt small in the grasp of these
working hands that were still calloused and showed the
marks of their toil. Streaks of gray were common in even
the sons of the older men, but the gray was apparent only
on the outside. The men were dressed neatly and each man
filled his jacket through the shoulders so that you didn't
notice the missing button-down collars and herringbone
suits.

The women were stout and unpretentious. Their hands
too had steered many a tractor and pitched more than a
few bales of hay. Their dresses were fitting to the occasion
and to the women wearing them—not a lot of style, but a
lot of class.

After the funeral and the graveside service there was a
gathering at the American Legion Hall, where we ate some
more and where I watched people a lot. The atmosphere
was pleasant and I think it helped people to relax from the
tension and emotional strain and start getting back to the
matter of picking up from where they were so sadly interrupted.

The minister who gave the service was a carpenter and a
minister—a becoming combination. He spoke to a full
house about the privilege that it was for all of us to help—
each in his own way—to share the burden that had come to
the family. We can all be strengthened by the love that
Sadie had spread to so many in her life and that abounds

even at her death. He talked a lot about walking the path of life and how great it was for all of us to take a step together in that atmosphere so filled with love.

The sun was bright and you could tell that winter was just about over and something was getting ready to happen to all the farmland we passed on the way to the cemetery. The line of cars stretched a long ways down that tarvy road, and parked cars were wound all through the grounds while the minister read the last simple words.

During the service there were a lot of private tears running down already red and swollen cheeks. Mine had remained dry until almost the end of the service when I put my arm around skinny little Becky, who sat next to me. This time when her head pressed on my shoulder, it was me who was trying not to cry. I felt the grief of the family then and didn't care much about why I was upset. Lots of people had wept openly in the past two days when I had not.

I love a lot of those people like I was a blood relation, and feel only now I was really part of them. During the service I had flashed ahead to my aunt's funeral, or my folks' deaths, and I began to understand a little better and to feel the feelings that everyone had. I cried too because I'm not an omniscient narrator . . . . I'm just a little slow to feel.

When the writer and his professor looked at the three entries together, they saw they made a record of a whole journey from the writer's scorn for funeral rituals to his acceptance of them, and how and why he moved from that place to this place.

> *Look sharply after your thoughts. They come unlooked for, like a new bird seen on your trees, and, if you turn to your usual task, disappear; and you shall never find that perception again; never, I say—but perhaps years, ages, and I know not what events and worlds may lie between you and its return!*
>
> RALPH WALDO EMERSON

Students in school seldom have the opportunity to consider an experience or idea over a period of time and from different and developing viewpoints. That's one of the reasons they seldom write moving, deep stories or discussions. Keeping a journal forces writers to put something in the sock every day or so. Often when they review what's there, they see things that, taken out and sorted, come together with new meaning.

All sorts of odds and evens and ends can go into the journal sock. Here are some lines from Henry Thoreau's journals, which ran to fourteen volumes when printed.

1

April 22, 1851. Had mouse-ear in blossom for a week. Observed the crowfoot on the Cliffs in abundance, and the saxifrage. The wind last Wednesday, April 16th, blew down a hundred pines on Fair Haven Hill.

Having treated my friend ill, I wished to apologize; but, not meeting him, I made an apology to myself.

It is not the invitation which I hear, but which I feel, that I obey.

You may say those lines don't amount to much. The hundred pines down on Fair Haven Hill make a fact, but what does it tell? The last two sentences are generalizations and don't bring a person or act alive. True, when the mouse-ear came into bloom may not be significant, but then again for Thoreau it may some day bloom again in conjunction with another thought of his. Think of your journal as a place where you may write anything, even a fact that doesn't tell. It's a chance book, where every phrase put down might later speak to you or to another phrase recorded days or months later.

The last two sentences in Thoreau's entry #1 are generalizations, and therefore run the risk of being empty or boring. They don't reveal the persons they must have been based on. Yet they contain oppositions, so they are more than half-hearted remarks. In your journal, record simple facts, opinions, preferences—anything that counts for you at the moment. Here are entries from college students' journals:

A

Lines I liked: When Queen Mab drums in the soldier's ear and he, awakening suddenly, "swears a prayer or two and then sleeps again." (63:87) Seems to me probably just what a soldier does.

I also like Benvolio's line on 47: 131, "Being one too
many by my weary self." Sometimes I feel the same way.
I don't even like my own company.

B

My son turned over today and I never imagined the happiness that an apparently trivial move like this could bring.
I guess I'm growing up faster than he is.

Here's Thoreau characterizing one of his neighbors in his journal.

2

October 4, 1851 . . . I was admiring his corn-stalks disposed about the barn to dry, over or astride the braces and
the timbers, of such a fresh, clean, and handsome green, re-
taining their strength and nutritive properties so, unlike the
gross and careless husbandry of speculating, money-making
farmers, who suffer their stalks to remain out till they are
dry and dingy and black as chips.

Minott is, perhaps, the most poetical farmer—who most
realizes to me the poetry of the farmer's life—that I know.
He does nothing with haste and drudgery, but as if he loved
it. He makes the most of his labor, and takes infinite satisfaction in every part of it. He is not looking forward to the sale
of his crops or any pecuniary profit, but he is paid by the
constant satisfaction which his labor yields him. He has not
too much land to trouble him,—too much work to do,—no
hired man nor boy,—but simply to amuse himself and live. He
cares not so much to raise a large crop as to do his work well.
He knows every pin and nail in his barn. If another linter is
to be floored, he lets no hired man rob him of that amusement, but he goes slowly to the woods and, at his leisure,
selects a pitch pine tree, cuts it, and hauls it or gets it hauled
to the mill; and so he knows the history of his barn floor.

Farming is an amusement which has lasted him longer
than gunning or fishing. He is never in a hurry to get his
garden planted and yet [it] is always planted soon enough,
and none in the town is kept so beautifully clean.

He always prophesies a failure of the crops, and yet is
satisfied with what he gets. His barn floor is fastened down
with oak pins, and he prefers them to iron spikes, which he
says will rust and give way. He handles and amuses himself
with every ear of his corn crop as much as a child with its

playthings, and so his small crop goes a great way. He might well cry if it were carried to market. The seed of weeds is no longer in his soil.

He loves to walk in a swamp in windy weather and hear the wind groan through the pines. He keeps a cat in his barn to catch the mice. He indulges in no luxury of food or dress or furniture, yet he is not penurious but merely simple. If his sister dies before him, he may have to go to the almshouse in his old age; yet he is not poor, for he does not want riches. He gets out of each manipulation in the farmers' operations a fund of entertainment which the speculating drudge hardly knows. With never-failing rheumatism and trembling hands, he seems yet to enjoy perennial health.

Thoreau found telling facts and significant oppositions between the way Minott and other men lived. He brings the reader up sharp with the last sentence, saying that a man with rheumatism and trembling hands enjoys perennial health. After the whole account of Minott's solid way of life, the pressure on the last two words is so strong that they speak of more than simply physical well being.

You may never match the depth and vigor of Thoreau's journals. You don't have to. No one is requiring a *Walden* from you. But you will write a valuable journal if you practice the fundamentals presented in this book. Note how these entries from beginning writers' journals come alive:

C

I worked again and about seven Ed came into the store. Until three months ago, he was drinking four to six quarts of beer every night. Then one night he choked on his phlegm (he has bronchial asthma), fell over backward into the bathtub, breaking his pelvis, and almost choking to death—when he got to the hospital, the doctors diagnosed also a weak heart, bad liver, and almost shot kidneys. His doctors warned him to stay away from alcohol or die in five years. He bought only Coke for about a week after he got out of the hospital.

Then one night that I happened to be working, he walked in—twenty pounds thinner and looking like death warmed over, and ordered one bottle of Pabst. I involuntarily hesitated but I'm not there to be a moral judge, so I sold it to him. He bought four last night, and I figure that gives him about four years and nine months.

A constant charge made by professors is that students do not relate what they read in class to their own lives. True of Engfishers, but not of students who have found their own voices and are willing to put down their truths. A line sticks in their minds and helps them see better at a later time, in another place. Here are two journal entries in which that happens.

D

In class once we talked about how much we forget of each day and it's still true. A few days ago I was walking through Bronson Park and noticed a cigarette butt squashed into the pavement still wet and soggy from the melting snow. The brown paper that covered its filter was faded. I thought how many other times I'd seen ugly cigarette butts smeared on sidewalks and forgotten them, but this one I remembered. Oh joy! Then I reached the street and gazed at the brown parking meter that clashed with the green lamp post and the purple car. Usually I would ignore such a color combination and walk on oblivious, not to be avoiding seeing it, but forgetting it as fast as it was seen. Kierkegaard said in one section of *Either/Or* that there is an art to forgetting just as there is to remembering. And I wondered how much of one day's comprehensions do we train ourselves to forget.

E

"Every man is the builder of a temple, called his body, to the god he worships, after a style purely his own, nor can he get off by hammering marble instead. We are all sculptors and painters, and our material is our own flesh and blood and bones."

While sitting in church three weeks ago I saw an example of what Thoreau is telling us in the above statement.

Mrs. Churchpillar came into our church and sat down beside me. I was *indeed* privileged, for everyone praised Mrs. Churchpillar as a large contributor to the new church. We happened, *in fact,* to be sitting in one of the *very* pews donated by the Churchpillars. But, *somehow* I found it difficult to praise Mrs. Churchpillar because of the sight of her own temple, the one Thoreau talks about. *Her own temple was a mess!*

The artificial paint on her face was so thick that if I were to chip it with hammer and wedge I could not reach flesh.

Her dress was so tight that if she had left it on for any length of time her circulation would have been paralyzed from diamond choker to spike-heeled alligator shoes. Her breath was still clouded, and her head, too, from the whiskey-sours of Saturday night. But, *such as it is,* her body is her own temple to God.

Like most first versions of writing, this entry could be cut to its advantage. The words italicized above might go. "Her own temple was a mess!" is a giveaway line that prevents the subsequent description from surprising the reader.

WRITING FIFTEEN: Keep a journal for at least two weeks.

REVISING SIX: Revise and sharpen two to five entries you think carry truths and oppositions and present them for criticism.

Don't feel that everything in your journal should be excellent, or that right now you should be able to tell what's good and bad. A journal is a place for confusion and certainty, for the half-formed and the completed. Thoreau said:

Of all strange and unaccountable things this journalizing is the strangest. It will allow nothing to be predicated of it; its good is not good, nor its bad bad. If I make a huge effort to expose my innermost and richest wares to light, my counter seems cluttered with the meanest homemade stuffs; but after months or years I may discover the wealth of India, and whatever rarity is brought overland from Cathay, in that confused heap, and what perhaps seemed a festoon of dried apple or pumpkin will prove a string of Brazilian diamonds, or pearls from Coromandel. [January 29, 1841]

You too.

chapter 14
sound
and
voice

ALL PERSONS employ sound skillfully
without being taught. In a speech given to American teachers in 1966,
Edmond Wright, a British schoolteacher, pointed out that under
extreme emotional stress all persons speak in strong rhythm and often
with alliteration.

You *d*umb, *d*amned fool, you *d*isgust me!

He told students to write down what persons at home said under
stress: they found considerable alliteration. One student complained
that he didn't hear any, so Mr. Wright suggested he go home and
pour a glass of milk over his brother's head and then listen to his
father. He did. He heard considerable alliteration.

Knocking around in every person's head are the sounds of his
native language: spoken or muted echoes of what he has read, the
lullabies his mother sang him, the rich cursing of men hunting or
playing games, the formal rhythms of a trained voice reading in
church or synagogue, the skip rope song, the hurried swallowed
phrases of other children singing the "Star Spangled Banner" or
chanting the "Gettysburg Address," the taunts they sang in the street:

Simpy Sam is a stupid old man!

Without trying, most persons can write rapidly such sound effects
as these by a high school girl:

> I like to go fishing. But I don't like to touch worms or slippery, slimy fish. They wiggle. I went with Anne three years ago. That was fun until she broke her promise and made me take the fish off. Then it swallowed the hook. It was terrible. It wriggled and writhed in the bottom of the boat. Then it just lay there. Dead.

This is not an exceptional piece of writing. The seventh sentence suffers from It-ache. In the sixth, *it* refers to the fish; then suddenly *it* refers to the whole struggle of the fish with the hook. But in sound, the passage is strong. *Slippery* and *slimy* and *wriggled* and *writhed* alliterate with force and their sounds echo the sense of what they say. The last two sentences allow the record to run down appropriately, and *Dead* stands by itself, final—in its. position, its shortness, and its two hard *d's.*

In the phrase "bottom of the boat," the writer has repeated the *b* sound skillfully. You may say that she didn't mean to hit that sound hard and that it adds nothing to the passage because the *b* sound does not suggest *boat* or *bottom* as the *sl* sound in *slippery* and *slimy* suggests the squirming fish. True, but one of the marks of a strong writer is that through his sentences appears from time to time an occasional repetition of sound that gives his words a strength like the "bone" in spaghetti cooked not too soft by an expert Italian cook. Note this pattern of sound repetition in these next passages. The authors were probably not trying for any effects, but they achieved them nevertheless.

> Men are *h*orribly *t*edious *wh*en *th*ey are good *h*usbands and a*b*ominably concei*t*ed *wh*en *th*ey are no*t.*
>
> OSCAR WILDE

> It's like *wh*en you break up *w*ith a girl and you've explained all your reasons to her *wh*y. And *sh*e *s*ays, "I *s*till don't *s*ee *wh*y it *w*on't *w*ork." And you've *s*een *it* ou*t* and you've hi*t* *th*e *b*lank har*d* col*d* *w*all of *s*olid no*th*ing.
>
> HIGH SCHOOL STUDENT WRITING FREELY

Another way to create faithful and exciting sound in your writing is to try to put down what you hear. The sound of a bullfrog? In *Walden,* Thoreau calls it a *trump* and put it down *tr-r-r-oonk*! In his *Journals* he describes the pigeon woodpecker's "whimsical ah-week ah-week." In *The Field Book of Ponds and Streams,* Anne Haven Morgan writes the American toad's call as "wheep."

When she heard the sound of traffic on a nearby street, a mother working in a beginning writers' course remembered her children's youth through sound:

HOME

At noon, traffic on Stadium transmits an even, steady sound, the passing of many cars blending together in a deep, harmonious hum. At two o'clock in the morning, a single car creates a gradual crescendo as it approaches, a diminuendo as it moves into the distance.

One car at night carries a lonesome, nostalgic sound. I am reminded of times I've lain awake waiting for teen-agers to return. In the deep quiet of the country night I can hear the first faint sound of a car coming down the highway a quarter of a mile away, slowing down to turn the corner onto the gravel of our country road, the gradual increasing of sound as the car approaches; then a momentary lowering as it slows for the bump of the little bridge; an increasing again for the rise of the little hill where our house stood. I can remember lying tense and breathing lightly, waiting for the moment when the noise of the car would continue on past the house into the distance. Or—it would pause, diminishing abruptly as the driver pressed the brake and the car coasted with its own momentum into our driveway. I heard the final beat of the motor, the quick staccato of young feet, first on the porch steps, then on the stairs. Soon the hall light, always left on for the last one in, was snapped off.

My child was back under my roof again.

GERTRUDE ANDRESEN

Here the writer not only remembers sounds but evokes some of them by her choice of words and building of sentence rhythms. The statement

> then a momentary lowering of sound as it slows for the bump of the little bridge

employs the word *bump* perfectly—a short word with a little burst and closure in it, coming in the middle of the statement so that it sounds exactly like what the writer is describing. Maybe *bump* was the only word that came to the writer's mind, luckily right in sound for her purposes. Maybe she also thought of saying *slight rise in the road, ripple,* or *protuberance,* and discarded them because they didn't contribute anything in sound. Often writers don't know how they achieved good sound effects. Sometimes they don't hear them until a reader points them out. Yet writers have a right to take credit for them.

You may train your ear by reading aloud good writing. Then when you read aloud your own writing you're more likely to hear skillful sounds. In reading a second or third draft you can change a word here or there.

To write fully, you must use all your senses. Remember how places and objects smell, the taste of the back of your hand, the touch of concrete, the sound of a laugh—an American's laugh, a Southerner's laugh, a Northerner's. Such variety.

The representation of sounds in words can become conventional and even trite—"bang!" "screen," eek!" Here's a beginning writer recording sounds in fresh words:

> **I like the quiet crackling of root beer foam; the swish, then flap of the net as the basketball passes through . . . squeaky popcorn; slept-on mattress . . . moccasins treading soft sand, crisp as toasted linen; steel door weightlessly slammed shut; secret roar of sea shell; whirr of a movie reel; the ps-s-s-t of freshly opened coffee . . . whirr and buzz of the WALK signal; a Band-Aid coming off . . . creaky wicker chairs . . .**
>
> SISTER MARY LOIS GLONEK

IMITATING TWO: Put down in words a page of sounds you like and dislike. Study the passage above by Sister Mary Lois. Note her accuracy and restraint. She avoided the obvious and conventional representations of loud sounds. You may follow her direction or others. Like all symbolizing of experience through words, the representation of sounds is complex and subtle. Sometimes it's almost a precise rendering of actual sound; sometimes a satirical conventionalization, as in the *Batman* series—"Zowie! Blat! Pow! Bam!"

The most significant sound in life is that of other voices. The best writers seem born with an ear's memory for the way a person speaks, and if they write down the conversations of a dozen persons in one story, all speak recognizably differently. Maybe this is a natural gift, not to be learned. But you may try, at least, to see whether you have it.

The following two statements by William Carlos Williams differ completely from each other in sound. They move differently—that is one of the effects a writer can achieve by controlling sound.

THE DANCE

In Breughel's great picture, The Kermess,
the dancers go round, they go round and
around, the squeal and the blare and the
tweedle of bagpipes, a bugle and fiddles
tipping their bellies (round as the thick-
sided glasses whose wash they impound)
their hips and their bellies off balance
to turn them. Kicking and rolling about
the Fair Grounds, swinging their butts, those
shanks must be sound to bear up under such
rollicking measures, prance as they dance
in Breughel's great picture, The Kermess.

POEM

As the cat
climbed over
the top of

the jamcloset
first the right
forefoot

carefully
then the hind
stepped down

into the pit of
the empty
flowerpot

Dr. Williams' mastery of sound should come as no surprise to readers who know he was a poet. A practicing M.D., he wrote poems in his office in between seeing patients or on the way to visit them in their homes.

In "The Dance," Dr. Williams writes only two sentences, listing again and again a few nouns joined by prepositions, or a verb form ending in -ing. Once he says they go round and round, his parts of sentences repeat and repeat and thus go round and round themselves:

the squeal and the blare and the tweedle
a bugle and fiddles
their hips and their bellies

One way he gets the parts of sentences to swing is to join them with *and,* a word he uses six times.

Read aloud, the poem almost flies off the page, because Dr. Williams has employed so many sound effects—alliteration and assonance, the repetition of *ound* in *round, around, impound, Grounds, sound.*

`Dr. Williams' second sentence is not actually a sentence but a jamming together of the parts of several sentences which don't keep straight their subjects and verbs. For example, the shanks are not "swinging their butts"; the dancers are. Dr. Williams knows what a sentence is, but here he deliberately violates grammar in order to increase the feeling that the speaker is himself breathlessly swinging around and around rather than reciting a carefully composed statement at a speaker's podium.

In the second poem about the cat, Dr. Williams has arranged his words to slow down the reader as he speaks the lines. Instead of the constant repetition of words ending in *-ing,* he uses many words ending in sounds that stop rather than prolong sound: the word *top* not a word like *new,* the word *jamcloset* not a word like *see.* Also many of his words begin with hard sounds: *cat climbed, flowerpot.* In "The Dance," he wanted beer-drinking peasants to swing in circles; in "Poem" he wanted a cat to step precisely and carefully. The poet must be able to control sound as a pitcher controls a curve.

You may hate poetry or fear it because you have been tossed too many knuckleballs, those slow and slower mushy pitches that take forever to reach home plate. Because of that possibility this textbook has not asked you to write poetry, although to learn to write some poetry is to learn to master language, and thus to write any sort of statement, whether a business letter or a novel, with power. If you have urges to write poetry, give in to them.

But know what contemporary poetry is before you try it. Not a bunch of vague private thoughts about reforming the world or feeling sorry for yourself because you're lonely. Like all good writing, good poetry puts you somewhere in reality—perhaps in the mind of a real person. It's alive. You can see what William Carlos Williams wrote about, a Flemish painting he liked and an American cat.

Write about your experience. You don't have to try poetry; but if you do, remember that it's first of all a concentrated form of expression. Pack the word. Pack the meaning. Play with words. Make one phrase say three thoughts or feelings. Remember, sound should speak the feeling you wish to communicate. Use rhyme if you wish, but keep it

alive, fresh, surprising. If it comes out blue, true; moon, June, swoon
—give up. Poetry must have guts and bone, whether it's delicate or slam-
bang. It must have all the attributes of good writing discussed in this
book, only brought to their ultimate concentrated power. That way,
underneath, it carries truth.

> *Poetry is a response to the daily neces-*
> *sity of getting the world right.*
>
> WALLACE STEVENS

VOICE

In free writing a person frequently finds that his pen or typewriter
seems to have taken over the job of writing and he's sitting there
watching the words go down on paper. A writer should do whatever he
can to help bring about this state. In his book *Making It,* writer and
editor Norman Podhoretz says:

> The poem, the story, the essay, and even something so ap-
> parently inconsequential as a book review (I mean one
> which is approached with seriousness), is already *there,*
> much in the way that Socrates said mathematical knowledge
> was already there, before a word is ever put to paper; and
> the act of writing is the act of finding the magical key that
> will unlock the floodgates and let the flow begin.
>
> .   .   .
>
> . . . The key, I believe is literally a key in that it is musical
> . . . it is the tone of voice, the only tone of voice, in which
> this particular piece of writing will permit itself to be writ-
> ten.

Mr. Podhoretz goes on to describe a writer who has found a voice
right for what he wants to say.

> In this beatific condition, he will sit with a pen or at a type-
> writer and watch, in delight and amazement, sentences
> mysteriously shaping themselves into rhythms he *knows* to be
> right . . . He will find that he has not only been permitted to
> uncover things he did not know he knew, but that he has
> also been allowed for the first time to say many things he
> knew he knew and had never been able to get onto a page
> because they had never *fitted* anywhere and only what fits is
> allowed.

There's nothing so good as *feeling* to control actions. Lots of talk flying around these days about developing intellectual control, but to learn to tap feelings so they control actions and words is far more useful. If you can find the feeling that belongs to a piece of writing you want to create—your feeling toward the subject and the persons you're writing to—then the composing may be accomplished almost without your help, and it will be true in tone, and compelling. Note how feeling holds together the following passage.

> A sun-bleached beach in Monterey, California, that's where he wrote the letter. He said the moon was full, and beautiful, and it hit the ocean just right, that he was glad it was a weekend and he didn't have detail, that he was wearing the sweater I got him for Christmas and was drenched in Pub, which I also bought him, that he thinks he's landed the radio job, that he wishes he could be home in Michigan and be going to college again.
>
> He asked me if I liked the valentine he sent and the flowers and do I miss him and think of him and how did I do on my chemistry exam?
>
> He said it was getting too cold to write outside by the ocean, so he better leave. He was going to San Francisco for the weekend and would I stay home over the weekend because he was going to call Saturday night? I did. He didn't.

Finding the right voice will help you write better than you ever thought yourself capable of writing. The author of the following story let her emotion take control of her words. Her judgment of the durability of Volkswagens may be incorrect but her defensive feelings about being in an accident ring true. School often implies that to be emotional is to lose all judgment. The matter is more complicated than that. To be emotional is also to be human.

"A" IN DRIVING

> I hit a car. Can't believe how stupid I am. My lack of concentration has been bothering me. VW's are so cheap. To hit one going 5 mph and damage the bumper—with a Pinto yet. VW's are so cheap.
>
> Oh no, I know the guy in the V-dub! Everyone's running out of the car screaming and staring at the stupid bumper. You'd think I'd murdered someone. Guess I have to get out of my car. "I'm really sorry, was looking in the rear view

mirror, didn't know everyone stopped. Just find out how much it costs and tell me, OK? Sorry ..."

More bumper stares and everyone gets back in (VW's are so ugly. The bumpers are made out of tin). My face was hot when I got back in my car. I could just hear them now, "Stupid ——, ——, ——, ——, girl, dumb woman driver, etc. etc."

They don't have to get personal. And it's not fair to generalize. Besides, more accidents are caused by men, and why did they have to stop like that? That stupid light always backs up traffic. Why don't they fix the road?

They should deport VW's, they're so cheap and ugly. How am I going to pay for that car? A red light?—it was only orange I think.

I have to concentrate. It's hard when there's so much on my mind, and now that car—how am I going to pay for it? No, I have to concentrate on my driving. Red light—stop. Very good. Got an A in driving in Driver's Ed, only got a C in lecture though. Green—start up slowly—don't stall, shift into second, third, great! But do I need a tune-up? How can I pay for it and that stupid VW? Turn left—forgot the blinker. In the driveway, home. Major sigh. Turn off the car, lock the door. Better not drive any more, at least today. Just can't seem to concentrate.

In that paper, a truthtelling voice speaks, and its rhythms rush and build like the human mind traveling at high speed. Rhythm, rhythm, the best writing depends so much upon it. But as in dancing, you can't get rhythm by giving yourself directions. You must feel the music and let your body take its instructions. Classrooms aren't usually rhythmic places. In kindergarten students swing more than they do in college. But you can let your pen find the rhythms of your life if you'll only let go. Note how the rhythm of the following passage contrasts with the weightiness of the statements. It's alive.

How do you turn down a marriage proposal gracefully? How do you say, "Thanks, but I'm only twenty and I have a million and one things to do and places to go before I even begin to think of committing myself to one person, and please don't be offended. Honest, it's not that I don't love you; it's just that it's too big a responsibility to think about right now and I'd be saying this to anybody who'd ask such a question at this time in my life. I love you, but I won't let you own me."

Before you write your next paper, sit still a moment and listen to yourself speaking inside. If you hear a voice that takes on a clear tone—happy, calm, humble, arrogant, loving, irritated, enraged, soothing, or ironic, listen as you write and get it on paper.

> *I've never liked the conventional con-*
> *ception of "style." What's confusing is*
> *that style usually means some form of*
> *fancy writing—when people say, oh yes,*
> *so and so's such a "wonderful stylist."*
> *But if one means by style the voice, the*
> *irreducible and always recognizable and*
> *alive thing, then of course style is really*
> *everything.*
>
> MARY MCCARTHY

Finding a true voice gives a piece of writing unity. Everything seems to belong together and the whole speaks in one rhythm that can't easily be denied or forgotten. And it keeps the sentences pouring out and thus gets by the danger of stopping somewhere along the line wordless, and then stopping again, and perhaps becoming absolutely stopped, so the writing can never be finished. In the following letter by a mother, there's no doubt that the writer is going to finish her statement.

Dear Mrs. Grint:

My son Robert is in your music class. As you know, he left his music book on the school bus last Friday. Robert has searched the bus, asked the drivers, the principal, the janitor, his teacher, even the school cook—without success.

You told him you could not understand how a nine-year-old boy could be so careless, irresponsible, and ungrateful and strongly suggested that he lacked proper home training.

Robert is careless and irresponsible, and most of the time I wouldn't change him if I knew how. He's careless and irresponsible, Mrs. Grint, about your values and mine, not his. Robert's world consists of baseball, frogs, snakes, bubble gum, and more baseball. He takes his mitt to school every day and doesn't lose it. He spends hours down at the pond collecting frogs and snakes.

Ungrateful! Why should he be grateful to you for driving out every natural musical desire he has ever had? Sending that damn book home to be covered is a case in point. You've made it a sin for a child to have an uncovered book

in your class. You shout at your students, humiliate them
before their friends if they sing a wrong note, or sing too
loud or not loud enough. If their attention wanders, you
assign them an extra report on Bach or Mozart.

It is true, as the school administration points out, that
your students learn music—music theory, music history, and
music antagonism. I'm sorry for your students, Mrs. Grint.
They've been cheated. They've had to pay too high a price
for learning to sing on pitch. I'm sorry for you too. You've
paid too much for the covers on those music books.

A writer's tone should be natural to him or her in the circumstances,
and above all it should be justified. Nothing is more ridiculous than a
person who takes on the wrong tone—unless as a joke. The prissy
schoolmarm who pretends to be offended by a bit of gossip that you
can see her licking her lips over becomes a buffoon. When I was in the
army, I knew a corporal who was always affecting a pompous delivery
and then misusing big words. Once he shouted at several soldiers talking
noisily outside the captain's office, "All right now, cut out the levitivity!"
Another time, explaining the rules of the Geneva Convention for behavior of war prisoners, he said, "Give the enemy officer only your
name, rank, and serial number; and then step forward one pace and lay
your prudentials on the ground."

In the following letter, taken from a campus newspaper, the writer
tries to speak in a condescending voice to persons he thinks his intellectual inferiors, yet he doesn't command his own elevated language
firmly enough to deserve the superior position he has given himself.
He berates a columnist for not getting down to criticism, but he himself doesn't make a clear statement of what was bad about the columnist's writing. He's showing off his vocabulary rather than using it
powerfully, so the tone is arrogant, but ill-founded.

To the Editor:
I do not imagine that it is the usual thing for graduate
students to seek to disturb the lethargy which has obviously
enveloped the undergraduate staff of The Daily Orange, but
having in mind the high cost of newsprint, I feel obliged to
speak out against its unforgiveable waste as noticeable in
some sections of your paper.

I speak here directly of one column, authorized by a chap
named "Bernie," and which purports to be a critical review
of television offerings. More specifically, I am concerned
with the column as it appeared on Tuesday, Dec. 11.

Such writing as appeared in this item is, I fear, only too typical of collegiate journalism on the whole, and of the undergraduate "critical" mind in particular.

The subject of these review columns is not criticized, but, rather, serves as a springboard for the author's inane solecisms, painfully born in a vacuum, and nurtured by insipidity.

The use of Irish orphans as the basis for a crude observation on the televised appearance of Elvis Presley is only a gross example of stupidity compounded with poor taste.

The criticism directed at Kate Smith made claim to intelligence only in that it was written in fairly correct grammar, (though it should be said that the hyphen is still considered a part of English grammar).

In that last sentence the letter writer makes fun of a columnist for not being perfect in grammar and himself errs in punctuation by putting a comma before a beginning parenthesis mark. The intelligent critic allows other human beings a few slips in form, lest he leave no place for himself to stand. To continue the letter to the editor:

In pertinence to material, descriptiveness of such relevance, and the other accepted canons of artistic criticisms the column was woefully lacking and the author, apparently, equally ignorant of the existence of such.

But the world has had its great writers and, I suppose, we must have our Bernies. However, as the editor of a college newspaper, you, sir, should feel exceedingly culpable for allowing such execrable prose to reach your pages.

It degrades not only your capabilities and those of the rest of the staff, but also offends the intelligence of all connected with a university that sponsors writing of this calibre.

There is enough wrong with the "Ed Sullivan Show" that it provides ample material for stimulating criticism. Resorting to pseudo-witticisms for a few strained laughs is a luxury which no publication can, economically as well as aesthetically, afford.

Whew! A graduate student Engfisher. He really had nothing to say except that he was superior to this stupid "chap" Bernie. When that's the message, the tone can't be anything but affected or arrogant. When you have something to say you know will be of value to others, then you'll respect words and choose them honestly. And they may take on a tone you want them to have.

Here's an essay that won a hundred dollars in a contest sponsored by a national sorority for women educators. It's all marble or plastic, like most of the winners of contests asking for statements on "Why I Am Proud to Be an American" or "Why I Believe in the United States." The writers presume the judges want Engfish and give it to them. Then the judges are left with the job of deciding which is the best paper among several hundred or dozen hopeless, dull statements.

WHY I WANT TO BE A TEACHER

I want to be a teacher because, by teaching one can help students toward the world of tomorrow—of the 100-year life, of supersonic speeds, of visits to the moon, and yet maintain and enrichen the American Teaching traditions.

"Help!" you may be saying. "Already I can't stand it." But it gets worse:

A teacher can help to guide the future businessman, the scientists and the leaders of our country toward the future

Where else would they be guided to? Perhaps the businessmen to jail for violating antitrust laws or the scientists to Hell for inventing diabolic engines of death?

in an era when education has become a vital part of the American life . . .

Was there some era in which education was a deadly rather than vital part of American life? If it taught this girl how to write, perhaps that era is the present one. The essay goes on in that platitudinous way and becomes more fatuous in the later paragraphs.

I want to teach because I like people and I like to work with people. One learns by teaching; each day holds a new experience, problem or personality. One meets people of different backgrounds and with new ideas.

Where does a person meet only people of the same background and with old ideas?

Through her years of teaching, each teacher experiences many different personalities. She has the opportunity to help develop these personalities and become more enriched from the experience. With the guidance of a good teacher, students learn more than math, history, or whatever the subject, They can learn a lesson in living.

> Getting students to think original thoughts, feel honest emotions, listen, respond and arrive at their own conclusions is a rewarding experience in itself . . .

Trouble is, this girl hasn't the first notion of what it is to think original thoughts or feel honest emotions when she's writing. Her voice is borrowed, and badly. She's an All-American Engfisher.

As a writer, at times you may not feel close to your subject: it doesn't produce love or hate in you. You may not feel close to your audience; you're not entirely sure who makes it up. The subject or the occasion may seem so mechanical or formal that any appropriate voice you choose doesn't belong to you. At these times you need more than ever to search hard for a voice. Remember the directions written by the teacher taking trippers to Chicago in Chapter 3. She found a light voice in which to speak ordinarily heavy instructions. Here's a part of a pamphlet titled "How to Take Care of Cats," published by the American Humane Association. How would you describe the writer's voice?

> There are few greater compliments than the friendship of a cat. You can't *buy* friendship from a cat. You can't *force* friendship. You get affection and respect from a cat only when you earn it—and a cat's standards for human conduct are high.
>
> The cardinal need, in making a friend of a cat, is to understand cats.
>
> For example, you should understand that punishment has almost no effect upon a cat—except that the cat may get indignant and leave home. A folded newspaper, banged loudly on a table *before* a cat jumps on the table, may make the cat decided not to jump. But a smack on the tail, *after* the jump, will merely convince the cat that *you* are an objectionable person. The cat won't connect the blow with the fact that it is on a table.
>
> Don't expect to get "obedience" from a cat. Cats simply don't recognize authority. The word "obedience" isn't in their vocabulary. If you ask a cat to do something that it wishes to do, it will consent very graciously—and that is the best that can be had.
>
> If this characteristic irritates you, try a tankful of fish instead of a cat.

So many of the strong voices in this chapter speak in anger that you may think a person writing with dignity and control can't sustain a voice that will give unity to his words. Here's part of a speech delivered by one of the most eloquent men of the nineteenth century, Frederick Douglass. A slave until the age of twenty-one, he was largely self taught and therefore didn't always use Engfish as did some of his better educated contemporaries. He's here dedicating the Freedmen's monument in memory of Lincoln in Washington, D.C., April 14, 1876.

We fully comprehend the relation of Abraham Lincoln both to ourselves and to the white people of the United States. Truth is proper and beautiful at all times and in all places and it is never in any case more proper and beautiful than when one is speaking of a great public man whose example is likely to be commended for honor and imitation long after his departure to the solemn shades, the silent continents of eternity. It must be admitted—truth compels me to admit—even here in the presence of the monument we have erected to his memory, that Abraham Lincoln was not, in the fullest sense of the word, either our man or our model. In his interests, in his associations, in his habits of thought and in his prejudices, he was a white man.

He was preeminently the white man's President, entirely devoted to the welfare of white men. He was ready and willing at any time during the first years of his administration to deny, postpone, and sacrifice the rights of humanity in the colored people in order to promote the welfare of the white people of this country. In all his education and feeling he was an American of the Americans. He came into the Presidential chair upon one principle alone, namely, opposition to the extension of slavery. His arguments in furtherance of this policy had their motive and mainspring in his patriotic devotion to the interests of his own race. To protect, defend, and perpetuate slavery in the states where it existed Abraham Lincoln was not less ready than any other President to draw the sword of the nation. He was ready to execute all the supposed constitutional guarantees of the United States Constitution in favor of the slave system anywhere inside the slave states. He was willing to pursue, recapture, and send back the fugitive slave to his master, and to suppress a slave rising for liberty, though the guilty master were already in arms against the Government. The race to which we belong were not the special objects of his consideration. Knowing this, I concede to you, my white fellow citizens, a preeminence in this worship at once full and supreme. First, midst, and last, you and yours were the objects of his deepest affection and his most earnest solicitude. You are the children of Abraham Lincoln. We are at best only his step-children, children by adoption, children by force of circumstances and necessity. To you it especially belongs to sound his praises . . . But while in the abundance of your wealth, and in the fullness of your just and patriotic devotion, you do all this, we entreat you to despise not the humble offering we this day unveil to view, for while Abraham Lincoln saved for you a country, he delivered us from a bondage, one hour of which, according to Jefferson, was worse than ages of the oppression your fathers rose in rebellion to oppose.

The voice in which Douglass speaks (he wrote his speeches for delivery) is dignified. Many sentences are of about equal length and start in much the same way. The language and the effect are elevated, befitting words spoken at a highly formal occasion. But Frederick Douglass was not showing off his vocabulary as was the graduate student writing about Bernie. Douglass never for a moment forgot his truth. He spoke hard words about Lincoln, and many whites have been shocked by them. His statements gain in surprise because they are delivered in grand tones. Like everyone else who has ever spoken a word, Frederick Douglass and you have at your command a number of different voices. Use them.

> *Concentration upon honesty is the only way to exclude the sounds of the bad style that assault us all.*
> DONALD HALL

WRITING SIXTEEN: Do two 15- to 20-minute free writings on any subjects that strike you at the moment. Whether large or small matters, you must know them and care about them if you are to find a voice that speaks rightly your feelings. If this task intimidates you, look back over the chapter and see how different subjects brought on different, but real, voices for writers like you. Don't expect too much. If you write one paper of the two in an authentic voice, you have done well.

Objectivity does not mean detachment, it means respect; that is, the ability not to distort and to falsify things, persons, and oneself.

ERICH FROMM

chapter 15 writing responses

FROM ELEMENTARY SCHOOL through college, students are asked to write book reports, which are assigned mostly to find out whether the students read the books. The teacher's hope is for a profound analysis of a book, telling only enough of the plot to show the author's skill or weakness, and revealing insights that the book provided. Instead, most such book reports are dumb. They summarize the plot and tack on a vague or pompous comment about the "theme" of the book. They bore the teacher and student. You would never give such a report to friends to enlighten or delight them. Note that both of my last verbs have the word *light* in them. Book reports are usually heavy, and dim.

In college you'll be asked to move from writing book reports to critical papers. You'll read a couple of stories and compare them. Or you'll review a work of literature, history, politics, or sociology and discuss its meaning, organization, symbolism, or rhetoric. Most such student papers never find their way into a reader's heart. There's no point in writing such junk. Rather it's a crime to take all that time to produce something no one, including the writer, wants to read. Such papers damage your truthtelling habits. They're bad behavior all around.

If you can understand why people commit such crimes, you may be able to avoid them. Teachers have a "body of knowledge" they're expected to communicate to students—in this instance, the terms and forms used in a special field of study. So they ask you to read a work they know well and to dissect it, using terms they learned when they became teachers. Conditions are right for producing Engfish and un-communicative writing. People are asking *you who don't know* to tell them *what they know.*

But it's not hard to avoid this trap. Read a story or poem (you could read again Richard Thurman's "Not Another Word," page 97), and respond truthfully to it. You don't need to employ certain terms or approach the work in a specially learned way. It was written for human beings to read and enjoy, so they could see how other people are living—both like and differently from the way they themselves live. Then respond with feelings or thoughts that come to you as you read or after you're finished.

As you read you may be thinking, "But I'm not having any great ideas. Sometimes I'm bored or don't understand the author's point." That may be the way school has sometimes made you feel, but you're a thinking being. That's the difference between you and animals. Most of the time your mind is running like a motor, reacting, responding to stimuli before you. It hums both consciously and unconsciously, making connections, marking differences, coming to conclusions rapidly and sometimes brilliantly, unless you slow it down and distract it by attempting to show off. Frequently you then become frightened "out of your mind."

As you're reading a page or finishing a chapter of a story, record what your mind has been thinking. Try for truth rather than bluff. You'll get down on paper valuable human responses, the best of which will be worth sharing with others. Here's such a response written quickly for a high-school class. It isn't a professional piece of writing and doesn't sound like one. It could be improved if the writer made clearer to her readers which of her statements about cats come from the articles she read and which from her own observations. But it says something that counts for the writer and is apt to count for her readers. Although not professional or scholarly in form, it's a step in this person's development as a writer. Many papers written in school that are more professional *in form* say nothing valuable to anyone. They're first steps in the development of dishonest or empty writers whose works will never profit themselves or others.

1

Patricia Moyes, "What Is Your Cat Trying to Tell You?" *Woman's Day,* February 20, 1979.

I never realized all of the messages cats can tell us by their body, until I read the magazine article "What Is Your Cat Trying to Tell You?"

> I enjoyed the article because I have a cat and wanted to understand how my cat was trying to communicate with me.
>
> I noticed how my cat will lick me on my arm or hand when it wants attention. But I learned from this article that there are several types of licks. The worried lick is when the cat is scared or worried about being brushed or sprayed with flea spray. The affectionate lick is most frequently used by my cat, along with the purr, to show contentment and trust in its master.
>
> The ears and tail work together to show signs of anger. I have noticed my cat in a fight with another cat will put her ears back and wag her tail, ready to go into action. Sometimes my cat will fluff her tail and fur. It depends on how angry she is.
>
> When my cat is happy about something, possibly the arrival of her meal, she will carry her tail high and straight. When she is disappointed about something her tail droops.
>
> The paws of cats are used to express love. My cat will place her paw on my hand when she wants me to rub her.
>
> The whiskers droop and the cat smiles to show contentment. I never noticed my cat smiling but according to this article cats do smile. They do not show their teeth, but they move the corners of their mouth slightly upward.
>
> A cat's eyes are quite like human eyes. When cats are being rubbed their eyes are in a half-closed position while purring. My cat also tries to outstare me with her bright eyes. It can look at me a long time without blinking her eyes or turning away.
>
> Since I read this article I have become more aware of my cat's expressions, and now I realize how my cat is communicating with me.

Many critics worry too much about making themselves look good. If you're honest in writing responses, you can talk about places that lost you in a person's writing or speaking. Sometimes you'll reveal to readers weaknesses in what you were reading or hearing; other times you'll reveal your own weaknesses as a perceiver; but that's all right. Most of your readers like to know that you're human, like them. The difficulties you have as a responder are apt to be crucial for all responders, and your discussion will therefore be useful.

Here are some truthful responses from students who had just read Harriet Beecher Stowe's *Uncle Tom's Cabin*—a book that helped turn many Americans against slavery before the Civil War. I'll give an excerpt from the book so you'll have a sense of what these writers were responding to.

". . . Eliza came in here, after dinner, in a great worry, crying and taking on, and said you were talking with a trader, and that she heard him make an offer for her boy—the ridiculous little goose!"

"She did, hey?" said Mr. Shelby, returning to his paper, which he seemed for a few minutes quite intent upon, not perceiving that he was holding it bottom upwards.

"It will have to come out," said he, mentally; "as well now as ever."

"I told Eliza," said Mrs. Shelby, as she continued brushing her hair, "that she was a little fool for her pains, and that you never had anything to do with that sort of person. Of course, I knew you never meant to sell any of our people,—least of all, to such a fellow."

"Well, Emily," said her husband, "so I have always felt and said: but the fact is that my business lies so that I cannot get on without. I shall have to sell some of my hands."

"To that creature? Impossible! Mr. Shelby, you cannot be serious."

"I'm sorry to say that I am," said Mr. Shelby. "I've agreed to sell Tom."

"What! our Tom?—that good, faithful creature!—been your faithful servant from a boy! O, Mr. Shelby—and you have promised him his freedom, too,—you and I have spoken to him a hundred times of it. Well, I can believe anything now,—I can believe *now* that you could sell little Harry, poor Eliza's only child!" said Mrs. Shelby, in a tone between grief and indignation.

"Well, since you must know all, it is so. I have agreed to sell Tom and Harry both; and I don't know why I am to be rated, as if I were a monster, for doing what every one does every day."

"But why, of all others, choose these?" said Mrs. Shelby. "Why sell them, of all on the place, if you must sell at all?"

"Because they will bring the highest sum of any,—that's why. I could choose another, if you say so. The fellow made me a high bid on Eliza, if that would suit you any better," said Mr. Shelby.

"The wretch!" said Mrs. Shelby, vehemently.

"Well, I didn't listen to it, a moment,—out of regard to your feelings, I wouldn't,—so give me some credit."

"My dear," said Mrs. Shelby, recollecting herself, "forgive me. I have been hasty. I was surprised, and entirely unprepared for this;—but surely you will allow me to intercede for these poor creatures. Tom is a noble-hearted, faithful fellow, if he is black. I do believe, Mr. Shelby, that if he were put to it, he would lay down his life for you."

"I know it,—I dare say;—but what's the use of all this?—I can't help myself."

"Why not make a pecuniary sacrifice? I'm willing to bear my part of the inconvenience. O, Mr. Shelby, I have tried—tried most faithfully, as a Christian woman should—to do my duty to these poor, simple, dependent creatures. I have cared for them, instructed them, watched over them, and known all their little cares and joys, for years; and how can I ever hold up my head again among them, if, for the sake of a little paltry gain, we sell such a faithful, excellent, confiding creature as poor Tom, and tear from him in a moment all we have taught him to love and value? I have taught them the duties of the family, of parent and child, and husband and wife; and how can I bear to have this open acknowledgment that we care for no tie, no duty, no relation, however sacred, compared with money? I have talked with Eliza about her boy—her duty to him as a Christian mother, to watch over him, pray for him, and bring him up in a Christian way; and now what can I say, if you tear him away, and sell him, soul and body, to a profane, unprincipled man, just to save a little money? I have told her that one soul is worth more than all the money in the world; and how will she believe me when she sees us turn around and sell her child?—sell him, perhaps, to certain ruin of body and soul!"

"I'm sorry you feel so about it, Emily,—indeed I am," said Mr. Shelby; "and I respect your feelings, too, though I don't pretend to share them to their full extent; but I tell you now, solemnly, it's of no use—I can't help myself. I didn't mean to tell you this, Emily; but in plain words, there is no choice between selling these two and selling everything. Either they must go, or *all* must. Haley has come into possession of a mortgage, which, if I don't clear off with him directly, will take everything before it. I've raked, and scraped, and borrowed, and all but begged,—and the price of these two was needed to make up the balance, and I had to give them up. Haley fancied the child; he agreed to settle the matter that way, and no other. I was in his power, and *had* to do it. If you feel so to have them sold, would it be any better to have *all* sold? . . ."

There was one listener to this conversation whom Mr. and Mrs. Shelby little suspected.

Communicating with their apartment was a large closet, opening by a door into the outer passage. When Mrs. Shelby had dismissed Eliza for the night, her feverish and excited mind had suggested the idea of this closet; and she had hidden herself there, and, with her ear pressed close against the crack of the door, had lost not a word of the conversation.

When the voices died into silence, she rose and crept stealthily away. Pale, shivering, with rigid features and com-pressed lips, she looked an entirely altered being from the soft and timid creature she had been hitherto. She moved cautiously along the entry, paused one moment at her mis-tress' door, and raised her hands in mute appeal to Heaven, and then turned and glided into her own room. It was a quiet, neat apartment, on the same floor with her mistress. There was the pleasant sunny window, where she had often sat singing at her sewing; there was a little case of books, and various little fancy articles, ranged by them, the gifts of Christmas holidays; there was her simple wardrobe in the closet and in the drawers:—here was, in short, her home; and, on the whole, a happy one it had been to her. But there, on the bed, lay her slumbering boy, his long curls falling negligently around his unconscious face, his rosy mouth half open, his little fat hands thrown out over the bed-clothes, and a smile spread like a sunbeam over his whole face.

"Poor boy! poor fellow!" said Eliza; "they have sold you! but your mother will save you yet!"

No tear dropped over that pillow; in such straits as these, the heart has no tears to give,—it drops only blood, bleeding itself away in silence. She took a piece of paper and a pencil, and wrote, hastily,

"O, Missis! dear Missis! don't think me ungrateful,—don't think hard of me, any way,—I heard all you and master

said to-night. I am going to try to save my boy—you will
not blame me! God bless and reward you for all your
kindness!"

Then, after a stop to see Uncle Tom, Eliza and her boy
made their escape from the plantation, over the frozen river.

Having read the whole book from which that excerpt was taken,
these seminar students responded to it. They weren't told what to
respond to or how, but simply to write down reactions that came to
them, trying not to show off or pretend.

2

I think I can see some of H. B. Stowe's biases coming through
in her book—as sort of a "sign of the times" attitude toward
Blacks no matter where one was living at the time—North,
South, East, West. I seem to catch an air of superiority (not
inequality) or maybe it would be better to say the book
is written with more of a "maternalistic" attitude toward
Black people. They are thought of as a people that must be
helped. I don't mean to put H. B. Stowe down. She had good
intentions but when you feel you must help someone it's
hard for the helper not to feel a bit superior.

Maybe that's why in recent years Black groups have gotten away from wanting to be incorporated into white society (integration desires of the past). To do this, you would
have to say the white man "helped" the Black to incorporate
and because of the "help" Blacks are somewhat put down
again because they "needed help." I'm probably not getting
across the idea that I wanted to. Back to Stowe and her
biases—she's always grouping the Blacks and giving them all
the same characteristics: "They all have *this* kind of nature
or *that* kind of nature" and they're all like children. She
writes of individual Blacks but I don't know if she really
sees them as individuals. It was also interesting to me that
she should make George—one of the heroes, an intelligent
person able to read and write and to invent some kind of
machine—a *mulatto!* and she also made his wife Eliza a mulatto. Why didn't she make someone in the book so intelligent etc. all *Black?* Why did she feel she had to make
George half "white." Or at least his wife Black? That really
bothers me!

The passage above was written as an entry in a reading journal.
While these students were reading *Uncle Tom's Cabin,* they stopped

whenever they were moved and wrote down responses. Their writing could be improved by editing. But what is said in it was valuable to the class. Some readers—all white—thought Stowe understood black people fully because she was writing a book that in effect asked for their liberation from slavery. But several agreed with the writer of entry 2, for example:

3

I have been quite surprised by several of the passages I've read so far in *Uncle Tom's Cabin*. For example: "Tom, who had, to the full, the gentle, domestic heart, which woe for them! has been a peculiar characteristic of this unhappy race . . ." (p. 96).

"This nerves the African, naturally patient, timid and unenterprising . . ." (p. 98).

"The boy commenced one of those wild, grotesque songs common among the Negroes . . ." (p. 3).

Perhaps the most blatant stereotype of all is: ". . . it must be remembered that all the instinctive affections of that race are peculiarly strong. . . . They are not naturally daring and enterprising but home-loving and affectionate" (p. 97).

As I just stated, it seems that Harriet Beecher Stowe was stating some pretty blatant stereotypes—she seems to be speaking in a condescending, although benevolent, tone. What she's said about the Black race here, taken alone, would be positive points, but in the context that they're used they make Black people sound like obedient pets! I don't think she meant to downgrade them at all, but was unwittingly voicing many of the common misconceptions of her day about the Black race. I think everyone has been in a situation where you've been misinformed or are simply naive about the circumstances, and when you try to say something good, you only show your ignorance or misconceptions.

I also found it interesting that George (Eliza's husband) who was so smart and dignified was supposed to be half white (p. 111). This, too, I believe, shows something about Mrs. Stowe. Why does George—so far portrayed as the brightest Negro—have to be half white? Why couldn't he have been all Black? I know that the fact he is so light-skinned helps him pass himself off as a person of Spanish descent, but I wonder why she doesn't let us continue thinking he's just lighter-skinned.

Maybe I'm reading too much into these passages. As far as George is concerned, perhaps this was only said to point

out the large number of cases where white men sired mulatto children. It's impossible, I guess, to know why the author portrayed certain instances in a specific way. I hope,
as I continue reading, that I find some deeper insight on the
part of Mrs. Stowe toward the Blacks because if I was Black
and read these passages, I would feel extremely offended.
As it is, I hope that when I'm finished with this book, I can
understand better than I can now why this book had such
a tremendous impact on the U.S. in the 1850s.

> *What I wish to do is to plead for passion-*
> *ate criticism for the sake of the passion-*
> *ate itself. Just as passion reveals the*
> *artist, so does it reveal the critic . . . To*
> *write passionately, the critic must invent,*
> *or, to use a more accurate word, he must*
> *create his criticism so that it reveals a*
> *work of art, through the critic's feelings.*
> BARNETT NEWMAN, PAINTER

    The writers of entries 2 and 3 made the same points: They thought
Stowe considered blacks inferior or child-like as human beings, al-
though she was advocating their freedom, and they thought she made
George half-white because he was a hero.

    When responses are written truthfully, they help make the practice
of *criticism* (saying what's good and bad about a book) valuable. In a
way, reading criticism is dangerous, because the critic may prevent
you from thinking and learning to perceive better on your own. You
may simply echo the opinions of the critics you read. If in school you
get the chance to read honest responses of other class members to a
work you've looked at, you're fortunate, for then criticism will do
its two principal services for you: (1) show you that your perception
of a work is sound, and thus increase your confidence in your powers,
or (2) face you with responses that teach you. You learn from others.
They learn from you. A misperception—yours or someone else's—may
finally be more instructive than a brilliant insight. If you realize why
you misperceived, you may be able to avoid such misperceptions in
the future.

    Entries 2 and 3 are natural responses to reading. Another natural
response is to remember similar or contrasting experiences in your
own life to those in the work before you. For example:

4

When I was a freshman in high school my parents sat down with me and my older brother and told us that they were getting a divorce. They had always fought a lot and Dad was an alcoholic, but I was absolutely stunned. They went further to say that we had to decide who we wanted to live with.

When they said that, I couldn't stand anymore. I was hysterical. I ran out of the house and just kept running. It was still summer weather and I didn't have any shoes on and my feet as well as my legs were all cut to heck because I had run through the woods and a stream. When I was through the woods and on the road, my ma found me. She had the car. She got out of the car, chased me, grabbed me, and threw me in the car.

I cried all that night. I didn't want my family to be split up. I have five brothers, four of which were younger and were not old enough to decide with whom they wanted to stay, and I couldn't decide myself. I loved them both very much. I couldn't hurt them. Eliza ran because she didn't want to be torn from her family. I ran because I would rather be with neither than one, for the sake of their feelings. Eliza had no choice and at the time neither did I.

I must admit that I was not very rational then. For a time we all lived with my mother but she had sort of a nervous breakdown and now we all live with my father. We still see my ma a lot. She's remarried and doing well. I never did decide.

That account touches the nerve of the family ties that Stowe was writing about. And that's one of the principal functions of literature and other forms of art—to remind us that we all experience deep suffering and joy, so that we know we're not alone. The writer of entry 4 could have developed more fully the likenesses and differences between her run and Eliza's but she was writing a quick journal entry and what she said made a point for the other students. Her writing could be improved by editing, yet it has virtues. Note how when she tells the climax of her run, and her mother is pursuing her, her sentences become short and the key ones become staccato ("She got out of the car, chased me, grabbed me, and threw me into the car"). She recaptures the physical and emotional truth of the act. Her unconscious is supplying rhythms appropriate for the feeling of the experience.

After you've recorded thoughts and feelings true for you, you're committed in a way that you're not when you simply answer a teacher's questions. If others in the class as well as the teacher are recording their true responses, and sometimes the true responses of professional critics with whom they agree, then you're all genuinely prepared to learn from each other. You've put yourselves on the Moebius Strip, made yourself a part of the work you've witnessed and the work a part of you.

Write in your journal several responses to something you've perceived. Don't try to think up something grand that you believe a professional critic might say. Just respond. Record your reactions the way the writers of the first four responses in this chapter did.

WRITING CRITICISM

Some people make careers out of writing criticism. They're given the job of reviewing and evaluating books, movies, TV shows, sports events, or any other human activities. They may work for General Motors, tour the company's plants all over the world, and make estimates on their efficiency. Theirs is a clear function: to write evaluations so persons who haven't themselves seen what the critics are evaluating can have a notion of its worth. A movie—is it worth seeing? A book—worth reading? A site for a plant—is it feasible? A long report on a new scientific work—is it worth attention?

The obligation of these critics is larger than just responding to certain things in the work that interested them. They must give an overall view of what was there, or what happened. If they're criticizing a movie or play, they talk about the story, its meaning, the actors, the direction, the production, because they're *reviewing* it. They care about the art form they're discussing. They want to set high standards for it. They hope that their judgments will help the actors—and all other workers—to become better at their jobs. They care passionately about what they do because they believe that good plays and movies help people understand their lives better as well as provide them with entertainment. And so they feel a threefold responsibility—to their readers, to the people who created the work, and to high standards for theater.

Because professional critics don't know their readers individually (except perhaps in an instance like the one I mentioned of a critic reviewing plant sites for General Motors), they must be careful to *give enough of what they're judging so that readers will be able to judge their judgments of it.* That's the fundamental principle in writing criticism of any kind. Here's a small entry in a student's journal about

a movie she saw at home on TV. She's not attempting to write a professional critique, but she remembers this principle:

> **There was Frank Sinatra kissing this frigid Creative Writ-
> ing teacher who really liked him but was too serious about
> being a writer to live. It was afternoon and they were in a
> summerhouse. The lights dimmed. He plucked one hairpin
> from her hair and tossed it away.**
> **All at the same time—**
> > **Her hair dropped around her shoulders,**
> > **her eyes had twice as much mascara,**
> > **and the hairpin clattered to the studio floor.**
> **I laughed and said, "What a move!"**
> **The fifteen-year-old boy across the room didn't hear my
> laugh, but answered, "Yeah, he's really got it!"**
> **I looked at him—searching for his sarcasm.**
> **He wasn't looking at me. He hadn't moved his eyes from
> the TV.**

The writer is making the point that she thought the movie scene
was corny, but a fifteen-year-old boy found it absorbing. She gives
enough of the film incident to allow her reader to judge her judgment
of the boy, and to show that her reaction was different from his. But
she expects her readers to form conclusions; she doesn't lapse into
Explainery.

Below I'll reproduce a professional critique about the leader of a
musical group. You'll see that the critic knows a great deal about
this musician and others in his field. That's the difference between a
responder and a critic. A responder can give readers insight into a
performance or work by being rigorously truthful to her own responses
and drawing upon her experience as a human being, but that's not
the same as being a critic who writes from a great fund of knowledge
about a field and the performers in it. To know a great deal about
what you're writing on is to have an advantage over amateurs, no
matter how truthful they may be.

The mistake that many teachers—including me—have made is to
expect students to write like professional critics on subjects they know
little or nothing about. Students should be encouraged to become
habitual, truthful responders to what they encounter in school, but
comprehensive critics only when they're writing about matters they
have known intimately and long. Having said that, I'll present two
professional critiques and then suggest how you might emulate them
as a beginning critic in a field of your own.

Here's a critique of Roger McGuinn's album *Thunderbyrd*, Columbia Records, in *Focus*, April 15–30, 1977, Columbus, Ohio:

I buy Roger McGuinn's albums because I can't help it anymore. I'm a Byrds junkie, and what began easily enough with *Mr. Tambourine Man* is now a habit 20 albums long. *Thunderbyrd* is McGuinn's fifth solo album since disbanding the group. The lilt and drone, that sweet whine that was the Byrds, is now mostly just a memory, and I've been buying his albums to see where that sound has gone, to be there as it winds down and finally out. It's been winding down for some time. It has yet to wind up into anything as specific or as good as it once was. But there are signs that McGuinn is stirring.

We pay attention to his albums because of his past. He remains an important figure on the landscape of rock, not so much because of what he has done for us lately, but because of the promise contained in his past. Oh, there have been some good songs on his solo albums, but basically we are waiting on him. And making demands—the legend will always be there, for him and for us. In concert McGuinn still covers the old Byrd hits in a one-legged sort of way, running through "Turn! Turn! Turn!," "Eight Miles High," and the others with his Rickenbacker and the help of some anonymous sidemen. It occasionally borders on travesty, it is always painful—watching an aging Byrd struggling with the myth.

Like his concerts, his albums have been uneven mixtures of that old sound no longer quite remembered and some new sound not yet found. *Thunderbyrd,* though stronger and more cohesive than the past few albums, marks that same unresolved search for form. The conflict is in its title. Think of the Byrds and you think of almost anything *but* thunder. They had, at their best, a controlled, cyclic, beautifully self-contained thunder, but they did not deal in the straight stuff. Yet McGuinn is trying to push them together —a Byrd rising from Dylan's Rolling Thunder Revue and getting tough. He is not anywhere in particular just yet.

In fact, if you look at the solo albums, *Thunderbyrd* included, they chart a course that goes something like this: they are increasingly rock-and-roll; the sound is harder; there are fewer and fewer overt Byrdsongs—no more of that high church density, that jingle-jangle wall of sound created by McGuinn's 12-string Rickenbacker. More and more the Rickenbacker is merely a background rhythm slipping in and out (McGuinn has been farming out lead guitar work for some time now). His voice, however, has the same haunting, hard edge to it; it remains one of the most distinct and powerful voices in rock. And he has been testing its possibilities more each time out, in the process neglecting the vocal harmonies that were a Byrds trademark. That neglect hurts him. Too often his voice is out there all alone without the pure harmonic counterpoint of the early Byrds or the rawer harmonies of the later Byrds.

But that is due at least in part to the fact that nobody seems to stay around from album to album. On each of them McGuinn has fronted a different group of musicians. Another crowd, another miscellany: some McGuinn-Levy originals, some borrowed material, and a Dylan tune for good luck. *Thunderbyrd's* original material is occasionally powerful, but McGuinn and Levy do not give us any "Chestnut Mare"'s here. The Dylan song, "Golden Loom," written in 1975 and never recorded by him, is one of the few McGuinn interpretations of Dylan that seems to gain nothing in the process. McGuinn and company sound like mere stand-ins for Dylan and the Band. It's on some of the borrowed material, however, that McGuinn gets close to the kind of coalescence he has in mind with the album's title. The Frampton/Gallagher song, "All Night Long," and "American Girl" are scorchers. They have a raw, almost sinister drive, yet in both of them is an innocence, a transcendent Byrds sound. They shimmer and sear all at once.

It's songs like these that make *Thunderbyrd* more than some ad man's title. They are partial delivery on McGuinn's promise and the statement of a new sound created from the old. Should you buy this album? That's probably a question you don't ask yourself if you've hooked into the Byrd myth somewhere down the line. If you haven't, if you're free of the obsession, you might want to spring for the *(Untitled)* album of several years ago (a Columbia two-fer) and catch McGuinn and the late Byrds at their peak. If you want to witness a struggle, an artist seriously at work on both the legend and the future, then buy *Thunderbyrd*. It's flawed, certainly, but what albums these days aren't?

GEORGE FELTON

That musical review was written by an English teacher at the Columbus College of Art & Design. It took him more hours than a student should be expected to spend on a daily assignment. He had to jot down ideas and reactions, rearrange them into a unified piece of writing, and edit and proofread a final draft. But professional models of writing are good for you to study to suggest the outer limits of skill and thoughtfulness to which you might aspire. Here are some comments George Felton sent to me about his experience writing the review of *Thunderbyrd:*

> I have had an obsession with Roger McGuinn and the Byrds since I was old enough to drive around town in Dad's car and listen to the radio cranked all the way up. I can't think of anything I've ever wanted to write about more. What I like about the piece is that I've managed to blend my feelings with what's actually on the record. I wrote out of my life about a public thing. I believe that is the best kind of criticism. When it is right, it is honest and real. The reader knows where the writer is coming from. And the writing, instead of feigning omniscience, concerns itself with the space between the writer and his subject. . . .

I could give a dozen rules or suggestions for writing critiques—what topics, for example, are usually touched on by a drama or music critic, but you'd probably forget them quickly. Better to think of a pursuit you're grabbed by—whether skiing, painting, or working with wood or cement—and then try to find professional critiques in that field, and study what they take up. Think about what your readers, the other students and the teacher, would need and like to know about the work you're critiquing.

Since George Felton's review of *Thunderbyrd* may be a longer article than you have time to write, it may be an unrealistic model for you. Here's a shorter musical critique, published in *The New York Times* for February 24, 1979.

> Nina Simone made her first appearance in a New York nightclub in 10 years on Thursday evening at the Village Gate, and she made it in what has become Nina Simone fashion.
>
> She kept the audience waiting for an hour before she went on. During that hour, she sat in her dressing room complaining about the financial arrangements for her appearance, objecting to the size of the audience. When she finally appeared, she did 45 minutes of an uneven, relatively perfunctory performance, punctuated by interpolations in her songs of "I must get my money!" and "I will get my

money!" Although she was scheduled to do two shows, she did only one.

Miss Simone told the audience at one point that "we had planned to do a very cold show." And to some extent it was a "cold" show—one in which she virtually threw away one of the basic songs in her repertory, "I Loves You, Porgy," racing through it, skimming the surface; breaking off another song to engage in exchanges with her audience.

Miss Simone is still, as she always has been, an angry woman. But whereas, on other occasions, her anger has been channelled into her performance, giving a high, emotional edge to the moods that she can build, this time her anger was focused on personal annoyances and, instead of stimulating her performance, it tended to stifle it.

But even in a "cold" show, Miss Simone could not help responding to the warmth and adulation of the audience at the Village Gate. Her artistry kept bubbling up in her. A song would gain in emotional tension as she got into it. The fires would start to light up, but she never let them burn long enough to burst into the flames of which she is capable.

All through her performance, Miss Simone had the steadying assistance of Al Shackman, a guitarist who has been with her for 20 years. Bob Dorough, with Bill Takas on bass, opened the program, on time, playing a lively, swinging piano while he sang with an intense, rhythmically phrased involvement.

Miss Simone is scheduled to be at the Village Gate tonight and next week, Thursday through Saturday, doing shows at 9:30 and 11:30.

JOHN S. WILSON

John S. Wilson is the regular jazz critic for *The New York Times;* he writes several critiques a week. He puts more time in on critical writing than George Felton does. Both men have been listening critically to music for years; memories of hundreds of performers have been stored and compared in their minds, partly consciously, partly unconsciously. In that respect these men may have an advantage over you: They may have lived longer and can draw on a greater bank of firsthand knowledge. Also, they have probably read more musical criticism than you have. But don't despair: Instead, lead with your strength—write about something you love as much as they love music, and draw upon your knowledge.

Critics can never reproduce in words the whole work or performance they're writing about, but they can provide facts that partially put their readers in the work. You might be thinking that if readers saw the play or movie being reviewed they would resent any recapitulation of it. Not so; they need to be reminded of what details the critic is evaluating. Not all spectators remember all parts of a performance and sometimes they miss entirely a specific act or line that the critic wants to discuss.

Note that in his review of Nina Simone, Mr. Wilson supports his charge that she was unprofessional in her performance: (1) "She kept the audience waiting for an hour"; (2) "She did 45 minutes of an uneven, relatively perfunctory performance [that's a judgment unsupported by facts] punctuated by interpolations in her songs of 'I must get my money' and 'I will get my money' "; and (3) "Although she was scheduled to do two shows, she did only one." Once a critic has clearly supported his opinions with evidence—as a lawyer in a courtroom supports charges with evidence—readers are apt to believe his subsequent assertions. Mr. Wilson never characterizes Ms. Simone's performance as unprofessional or irresponsible; he doesn't have to. The facts he cites do the job.

Another fundamental of critiquing is to be fair, to mention the good as well as the bad aspects of a production. Without wasting space, Mr. Wilson lets his readers know he has observed Ms. Simone a number of times and so is qualified to judge this performance. He's angry at her for treating the audience so shamefully, but he doesn't rant and call her names. Instead, he remains cool enough to say, first, that she has always been an angry woman; second, that in the past she has "channelled" her anger "into her performance, giving a high emotional edge to the moods she can build"; and third, that this time she let personal annoyances "stifle" her performance. He doesn't allow his own anger about Ms. Simone to make him forget the performance of Al Shackman, her accompanist on guitar, and the piano and bass players, for whom he has good words. It's a remarkable critique in which a critic's disapproval of a performer's actions takes on authority because it's controlled and substantiated, rather than petulant and opinionated.

In many ways, writing a good critique is like writing a good story or report. Critics put readers there in the action and provide the ground out of which opinions, feelings, or conclusions grow. And they give readers enough fact and detail that they can begin to judge the critics' judgments. Enough, but not too much. In my critique of Mr.

Wilson's critique, I've quoted only short phrases from him, not whole sentences and paragraphs. A common weakness of school book reports is long, boring quotations or summaries of plot. It's a childish habit that writers need to grow out of. Remember your seven-year-old sister answering your question, "How did you like the movie?" She went on and on, like this:

> Well, you know, this man had a little boy who owned a rabbit and this rabbit was in a cage in the backyard and one day the postman came and opened the cage and forgot to close it and the bunny ran out. The next-door neighbor saw the bunny run away. The neighbor's name was Jones, and he had a little boy, too, only this boy had freckles, and when the bunny got out of the woods. . . .

You couldn't get your sister out of those woods, and she kept getting mad at you for interrupting and trying to find out why she thought it was a good movie. You knew it wasn't that there was a bunny and a man named Jones; it had to be something about the way the bunny acted, maybe humorously, endearingly. And something special about Jones, too; but your sister hadn't articulated in her mind what made the film powerful for her; so she remained hung up on the plot. When you write a critique, remember the oldest writing principle—just enough; not too much, not too little.

I began this chapter talking about the response of a human being not trained as a professional critic in a field she has become knowledgeable about over many years. But I think that you can see that the professional critic is still writing a response. It arises out of more experience but is basically a response: truthful, personal, human—although made through a screen of comparisons and history, which renders it more objective.

WRITING SEVENTEEN: Think of a performance, event, process, or activity you love and know a lot about. Maybe it's basketball, dancing, housebuilding, roller skating, motorcycle racing—whatever. Then choose a particular instance of it, one game or one building, for example. Something you think deserves or needs critiquing. Go look at it and write a critique. You might attend a game, play, or musical concert that you know will be reviewed by a professional critic in a newspaper or magazine. Write your critique before you see the professional's version.

Then bring both reviews to class. If several students in your class are interested in reviewing the same event or work, you might post all of them next to one another on a bulletin board in the hall or classroom where other people can compare the differing perceptions of the same event. In that way you can learn from one another and from the professional critic.

If you'd like to approach the quality of a professional's critiques, you can't give excuses. Don't say you didn't have time. The drama critics for a newspaper have to see a play and then rush to a typewriter to write the critique, revise it, and give it to editors and printers that night so it will appear in the next day's paper. To do this, they take quick notes and don't write a full plot summary. And ahead of time they gather any material that may be helpful in the hurried writing later—biographical notes about the actors, publicity releases, the printed program. Who is the author? Was it the performance or the script that made the evening memorable? Maybe both, or neither. The critics do whatever they can ahead of time to help prepare themselves for working under pressure.

Remember, the critique is still your personal response. If you try to use it as an opportunity to show off, it will fail. Tell your truths, and others that you learn from other people. You work under that obligation to your readers and to the persons who created what you're reviewing.

chapter 16
creating
form

PATTERNS

A RECENT TEXTBOOK on writing says:

> Since learning to outline is one of the most important
> steps—perhaps the most important—in writing well, we
> want you to make at least four outlines.

The man who wrote that must never have talked to a real writer.
Eight out of ten writers say they never use outlines and the other two
say they use them only in late stages of writing, in the second or
third draft when they have all the materials captured and need only
to rearrange them strategically.

In the first place, outlines freeze most writers. Professionals are
looking for ways of breaking up the ice and poking around in new
waters. They want writing and ideas to flow.

> *I have often at the beginning of a book
> found myself very uncertain what I
> would do, and appalled at the difficulty
> of knowing what to put where, and how
> to develop my incidents. I never have
> that feeling now because I have always
> found that there is some one point or
> other in which I can see my way. I im-
> mediately set to work at that point and*

> *before I have done and settled it, I invariably find that there is another point which I can also see and settle, etc., etc. . . .*
>
> SAMUEL BUTLER

In the second place—Wait a minute. The second place. By their form, outlines always imply there will be a second place. Maybe there won't be. Or shouldn't be. I.a., I.b., II.a., II.b. "Express all your points in the outline in the same style, all complete sentences or all phrases." The Outliners are full of stuff like that. They get writers so interested in the form of the outline that they quit thinking of the writing they're outlining.

Yet readers need some form or they become confused, get lost, give up. Making anything—a table, a fishing fly, a piece of writing—involves a struggle between form and content. Only the dull assembly-line maker can avoid that struggle by drawing up a perfect plan, or outline, before beginning creation. Punched out, every one the same, no surprises anywhere. A good planner allows for departures from plan, sidetrips down alleys full of discovery. The best trip you ever took in your life—could you have written an outline for it beforehand?

Yet the reader and writer need form, some direction, some over-riding mood, or they will sense only chaos. When the folks at home send George on a trip, they expect more than a bagful of chaos spilled on the kitchen table when he returns.

Many professionals say that the more experienced they become, the more certain they are of where they're going before they start. But they still keep their eyes and ears open as they go, hoping for fortunate accidents.

Beginning, you may find a direction, even a conclusion, flowering in your mind. Then all you do is find experiences to embody it and bring it alive. But if there is not an example or experience clinging to the idea or direction when you first get it, the chances are you will never bring it alive. Better start with something already alive and kicking. A butterfly caught and squirming in the net, wings flapping wildly. Not a lot of preserved specimens lined up in the glass case neatly and systematically labeled.

But the glass case is good. Something to enclose the things flapping around in your mind and experience. Place something else with the butterfly. Does it go with him? Or does it contrast in some significant way? Is it a leaf in shape—half of the butterfly? And then a bird. Look at her. How do her wings differ from the butterfly's and the leaf's? Let these pieces of experience knock around against each other in the case and in your mind.

> *It doesn't matter which leg of your table*
> *you make first, so long as the table has*
> *four legs and will stand up solidly when*
> *you have finished it.*
>
> EZRA POUND

If what you are thinking about doesn't fit into a case, you may simply jot down the elements in a list, informal, like the one you take to the supermarket.

Any piece of writing needs a point. What that means is hard to say but easier to sense. Everyone knows the meaning of the word when listening to a person talk on endlessly through boredom into sleep, and someone says, "He talked on and on but to no point." What *point* is and why it is needed can be seen by reading most term papers written in high school and freshman college classes. They have subjects but no points. For example, Harry Smithers writes "about Switzerland or the things he has seen in Switzerland don't make a paper simply because they concern one country. What about Switzerland? Do any of the facts he has collected do anything to each other? Contradict? Surprise Harry in some way when compared with facts he knows about other countries? If he thinks he will write about Switzerland because the library has a number of books on it, or because no one else has written about it recently in school, or because he once heard that watches are made in Switzerland, his paper is doomed. When he starts in on a good piece of writing he'll have an itch or he'll never scratch hard, with purpose and enjoyment.

Switzerland might be Harry's subject, but never his point. To cover Switzerland would be to write an endless number of volumes, describing its government, postal system, watchmaking industry, role in European and world wars, people's dress, food, social customs—all with that dreadful emptiness of a travel brochure or a bad children's encyclopedia. Take this statement by a writer in a political magazine:

> The Swiss make watches, speak many languages, act as
> peace arbitrators, never commit themselves to the cause
> of right in any war, and act as holding companies for all
> sorts of high-level financial wheeling and dealing, aiding

persons all over the world in avoiding taxes and financial responsibility.

Maybe this statement is not true. But it is full of assertions, of points that could be pursued with genuine curiosity. It was not made by the Chamber of Commerce trying to attract tourists, but by a woman puzzled and inquiring, who said what she truly believed. If you came upon this statement as the opening paragraph of an article, you would probably suspect that the writer was going to take you on a journey.

An editor of a university press once said that most Master's and Doctor's theses submitted to him for possible publication were unpublishable. No one would want to read them, he said. Some contained ideas and material that could be brought together with point if the author could bring himself to see why anyone might want to know what he had found in his research. When he came upon such a thesis, the editor said he returned it to the writer with the query: "So what?" If the writer could rewrite his thesis so that it answered that question, he had made what could be justly called a book.

To construct a good piece of writing you need to go somewhere in it. If you haven't taken a journey, no amount of outlining or structuring can make the writing live. Whatever the type of writing—article, essay, story, case-history, poem—it must contain surprises and questions. Else it will remain dead for you and the reader. They must be genuine surprises and questions. Many beginning writers are affected by the worst, most gimmicky writing. They spin a long description of a man they have known, disguising who he is and where they have known him, and then in the last sentence they say: "There he was, smoking his pipe in the big rocking chair in the living room—my father." Surprise is valuable, but it must make a point or give truth to experience. This trick ending about Father does neither. If the writer told of a man exhibiting behavior shockingly unlike his father's, then as indication of the shock the writer himself felt, he might properly hold back the identity of his father until the end. The first-rate writer produces surprise after surprise for his reader, in his expression, in the events he records, in the thoughts he comes to through comparisons. But he does not play practical jokes on his readers.

What shape will you give a piece of writing? Or better yet, what movement? It needs a pattern. Formlessness is too hard on human perception. You'll lose your readers if they have no hint of what journey you're taking them on. They need surprise and wondering, but can't stand one question after another with no intimation of answer or direction. As a writer you need form, a limit which will force you to invention. Henry Ford didn't say one day, "I think I'll invent something great" and then build one of the first American motor cars. He was thinking about a form—a wheeled, self-propelled vehicle; and a purpose—faster travel on roads than was provided by horse-drawn carriages.

What's the right form of your piece of writing? There's no manual in which you may look up the answer. Like all good questions, this one cannot be answered simply. If you remember that a good piece of writing is composed partly through plan and partly through accident which the writer keeps himself ever ready to exploit, you may guess that a good form involves both discipline and freedom for writers and readers. It gives readers a sight of the path at times, at other times the realization they have to work hard to open it up. Occasionally it will lead them astray on exciting side trips. Give readers a small sense of direction for the journey, but don't keep nudging them in the elbow— This way! No! Over there! Now back again!

Professional writers are often mystified by the way they put together writing. They know it has a form but they seldom know its origin. They're afraid of outlining because they want things to happen to them as they write. Nevertheless their final draft usually possesses sure form, a movement that gives power to the events they've written about. Some emphasize freedom to discover. Some emphasize the need for plan. James Thurber said of Elliott Nugent, with whom he wrote the play *The Male Animal*:

> He could plot the thing from back to front—what was going to happen here, what sort of situation would end the first-act curtain, and so forth. I can't work that way. Nugent would say, "Well, Thurber, we've got our problem, we've got all these people in the living room. Now what are we going to do with them?" I'd say that I didn't know and couldn't tell him until I'd sat down at the typewriter and found out. I don't believe the writer should know too much where he's going. If he does, he runs into old man blueprint —old man propaganda.

Because Thurber wrote this passage doesn't mean that he never paid attention to the shape of his writing. He rewrote his stories dozens of times until he got them moving right.

Probably the reason professionals are so unsure in discussing form in general is that good form always comes out of the materials of a particular piece of writing. As they gain experience, writers come unconsciously to a sense of form for their materials. Always they hold in mind a few simple, fundamental forms that will limit them wisely and give their readers a sense of certainty among all the surprises they encounter.

> *A plot is a thousand times more unsettling than an argument, which may be answered. It is not a pattern imposed; it is inward emotion acted out. It is arbitrary, indeed, but not artificial. It is possibly so odd that it might be called a vision, but it is organic to its material: it is a working vision, then.*
>
> EUDORA WELTY

Here are a few such fundamental forms or patterns of movement. They may be useful if you don't let them bind you. Allow one to dominate your complete piece of writing and at the same time introduce several of the others to shape small pieces of the same work if you wish.

(a) *Simple Comparison.* X is different from B. You may show how X's arms differ from B's, then the legs of both, the shoes, etc. Or you may describe X completely and then B completely. As you make your observations and as you write, keep thinking: So what?

(b) *Before and After.* It was *this* way once. Now it is *that* way. You may emphasize the difference. You may ask why the difference. You may tell how the difference came about.

(c) *The Journey.* I (he, or it) started here and went through this experience or that country and came out there. Chronologically. First this happened, then that.

You may present the whole matter as story, or occasionally interrupt to explain significance. Show. Give the story. Tell. Explain why or discuss the significance of an act. But don't interrupt a story to tell or comment unless you do so frequently and regularly.

The Journey pattern is useful in writing about ideas (as well as events) which are apt to confuse the reader unless controlled. If it's your idea, you may show where it came from, how you took it on, and what you did with it over the years or days. If it means a good deal to you, the tale of your journey with it should be exciting, for the truth is that the journey was full of surprises—traps, bogs, a mountain with a view.

(d) *David and Goliath.* David has only a slingshot and courage against a gigantic warrior armed with spear and shield and wearing a coat as heavy as five thousand shekels of brass. Any little or deprived or disadvantaged person against great forces. Who will win?

(e) *Will It Work?* An idea, a plan, an invention new and untried, or old but now standing against the established order—a variation of the David and Goliath story. The odds are against it because it's not now the accepted thing. Will it win through?

In deciding upon a form, a writer constantly juggles

1. the needs of her materials (they may cry out for a certain treatment),
2. the weight of her purpose,
3. the limitations and potentialities of her medium (is it a letter, an article in a picture magazine, a paper to be read aloud or silently in class?),
4. the knowledge and needs of her audience.

The professional knows she's writing to other human beings, who can be bored, who are often insulted by gimmicks, who have normal human needs for rising excitement, for hoping that every trip they take will pay off.

THE HOOK

A good device to remember is the fishhook. It rises slowly and then hooks back, so it will dig in and stick. It is barbed. Its curve points back to its beginning, to remind itself and the reader where it came from.

Many professionals employ the Hook in their writing: They begin with a word, action, or symbol and at the end of their article or story come back to it. All that has intervened between the first and second mention makes its second appearance more exciting or significant than its first. For example, on page 52, Mindy Stiles says early in her story "Golden Leaves" that the girl she saw was "fat and ugly." Then in her last line she employs the Hook, coming back to how the girl looks—now, "laughing and very beautiful."

In the story on page 51, by Jann H. Cain, the first sentence and the last sentence both talk of leaves. This is a Hook of subject rather than phrasing, but it makes a point. Because the elephant-shouldered boy in football uniform had noticed Jann was picking leaves out of the piles along the curb he gave her a tiny pale yellow leaf.

Using Hooks in your writing often comes naturally: something has burned itself into your mind and you write about it. Without planning, you begin and end with that something.

Hooks can be made in different styles. On page 58 the writer of "Through the Gates" hooks his story by beginning with the narrator speaking of walking past the experienced workers to his first day on the job ("everybody was watching") and feeling uncomfortable because no one smiled. At the end of the story the narrator walks out past the newly arriving morning workers, and he doesn't smile at them. All the events between those two moments explain the lack of smiles at the beginning and ending.

The Hook is a natural way of forcing the reader's attention on what you want to emphasize. The repetition of a word or act at the end of a developed piece of writing will probably please rather than bore your reader; for what you say is yours in some way and must be unfamiliar to him. The hook allows him to experience something that is familiar now to him.

The Hook is only one of the strategies available to you as a writer. Often you will use it without planning to. Sometimes you can improve a paper by consciously introducing the Hook into your second or third draft to drive your major point home. But it's only a possible strategy, not an inflexible rule. It can become a cheap trick that doesn't arise out of the materials or needs of the writing. At times a story or article must provide a setting or present a preliminary action before it gets into the major act or idea. Then a Hook would snag the lines of development, and shouldn't be used.

So there are no sure-fire formulas for shaping a piece of writing. But the strong writer keeps the pressure of form upon himself. He keeps asking:

Where is this going?

Does it arrive somewhere?

Does it add up?

Is something happening between things here?

Have I made clear, directly or indirectly, why I wanted to write this?

What did I want to say? Did I get it said?

WRITING EIGHTEEN: Choose one of your free writings you like and shape it more powerfully. You may have to expand or contract it radically. Does it already follow one of the patterns discussed in this chapter? Can you improve it with a Hook?

THE ALTERNATING CURRENT

Bad preachers don't use the Alternating Current. They drone on in an unrelieved elevated vocabulary. Bad editorial writers do the same. They have no sense of the lightness that can be achieved in writing that discusses a solemn subject in sober setting.

We hold these truths to be self-evident . . .

This statement from the Declaration of Independence would be spoken by few persons in their kitchens, but

all men are created equal

might well be there. Speaking of King George III, the writers of the Declaration said:

He has plundered our seas, ravaged our coasts

in language again not of the kitchen, but the rest of the sentence might have been said there:

burnt our towns, and destroyed the lives of our people.

Note the alternation of language in Robert Lipsyte's baseball article:

METS BEAT GIANTS 8-6, ON SWOBODA'S HOMER IN 9TH

Ron Swoboda, who won it in the ninth inning with a three-run pinch-hit home run, said: "It was a story-book game. Holy Cow!" And it was just that.

Most of the crowd of 41,038 at Shea Stadium sat stunned yesterday long after the Mets had beaten the Giants, 8-6. Swoboda's drive cleared the leftfield fence and the 22-year-old outfielder jogged around the bases in a mood he later described as "elation . . . the epitome . . . my greatest thrill!"

More than 24,000 in the crowd had bought their tickets just before gametime because the great Juan Marichal was starting for the Giants. For almost six innings they got what they paid for—perfection from Marichal and something less than perfection from the Mets.

The 27-year-old Dominican righthander, out of action recently because of a sore finger, had registered his 17th victory Tuesday night, by the official scorer's decision, after retiring the last four Mets. Yesterday, kicking high on a dusty mound, he retired the first 17 Mets.

3 OUTS ON 6 PITCHES

In the second inning, with six pitches, he put out the side so quickly that he had to wave his sleepy outfielders back to the dugout. In the third, facing Dennis Ribant, the busy little Met starter, he was worked for his first full count before Ribant lined out to Willie Mays, a well-hit ball that Mays had to hustle to catch and gave a few plaintive voices reason to holler, "Let's go Mets."

In the sixth, Ribant bounced one over Marichal's head for a single, and the crowd prepared to console itself with a brilliant one-hitter instead of a perfect game.

The Giants, meanwhile, were doing what was expected of a team that started the sunny afternoon game leading the National League and fresh from having beaten the Mets three times in a row. They scored a run in the fourth on Willie McCovey's 21st homer of the year, a run in the fifth on Marichal's double and Jim Davenport's single and a run in the sixth on Jim Hart's 24th homer.

GIANTS GAIN 5-0 LEAD

In the seventh, San Francisco made the score 5-0. Tito Fuentes drove one of Ribant's pitches into the leftfield corner. Larry Elliot dropped it in foul territory and examined it, apparently thinking the ball was foul, while Fuentes went to third, credited with a double. Ossie Virgil, who had replaced Davenport at third base, then singled and McCovey walked.

With the bases loaded, Darrell Sutherland replaced Ribant, and Mays singled home two runs.

In the last of the seventh, the Mets began to move at last. They needed three singles and a throwing error by Marichal to get one run. The people who had come to see at least a shutout went home.

Tom Haller hit a homer for the Giants in the eighth, making the score 6-1, but it was a wasted gesture. In the bottom of the eighth, the Mets charged.

Jerry Grote reached second on a two-base throwing error by Virgil, and John Stephenson, a 25-year-old catcher pinch-hitting for Dallas Green, the third Met pitcher, blasted his first homer of the season. Singles by Chuck Hiller, Al Luplow and Larry Elliot made the score 6-4.

In disbelief, the crowd froze.

HAMILTON IS VICTOR

Jack Hamilton, the winning pitcher, put out the Giants in the ninth. Then Marichal strolled back to the mound. He demanded that it be dampened because he was kicking dust into his own face. A little man with a green sprinkling can scurried out and dampened the mound.

Satisfied, baseball's best righthander pitched two balls and a strike to Ken Boyer. Boyer hit the fourth pitch over the fence for his 11th homer of the season, and Marichal was pulled out for some showering of his own.

"Let's go Mets." There was no plaintiveness now, no whine. There was hope.

Ed Bressoud, who had been playing an erratic shortstop for the injured Roy McMillan, singled to left. Ron Hunt, pinchhitting for Grote, bunted, forcing Bressoud at second. Stephenson, hero of the eighth inning, hit a wrong-field single to right. There was one out, two men on base, and the score was 6-5.

The roar was swelling now as Bill Henry, a left-hander, replaced Lindy McDaniel, a right-hander. The next scheduled batter, Chuck Hiller, was called back for a right-handed hitting replacement and Manager Wes Westrum said to Swoboda, "Get a bat."

Swoboda later admitted he was excited because "that's it, when everybody's relying on you." He kept telling himself to "stay loose" and he forgot that the last time Marichal had started against the Mets, on May 20, Swoboda had won the game with a tenth-inning homer against the same Bill Henry.

The first pitch was high; it would have been a ball if Swoboda, overanxious, hadn't swung and missed. The second was a ball, low and inside. The third, waist-high and fast, was thrown with the stuff that dreams are made on.

Kitchen	*Elevated*
they got what they paid for	perfection from Marichal
hustle to catch	plaintive voices
The people who had come to see at least a shutout went home	a wasted gesture
Marichal was pulled out	In disbelief
he was kicking dust into his own face	an erratic shortstop
There was one out, two men on base and the score was 6–5	The roar was swelling now

Elevated language is usually more precise than kitchen language and comes to us trailing associations different from those carried by kitchen language. In many ways it's superior as a vehicle of expression, but no one wants to hear it steadily throughout a lecture or a column. The ordinary speech of the common man is our anchor, and no good writer forgets it.

The Alternating Current is not difficult to turn on in your writing. The secret lies in the genuineness of its juice, the speech you already have in your unconscious memory. If you remember your native dialect—the language you learned at Mother's knee—and alternate that with the language of writing you've picked up through reading and listening to teachers in classrooms, you'll find the current naturally coursing through your prose. Finding it is again a matter of honesty. What is your voice? Do you hear how you speak when you're not thinking of your language? Listen to the country, the kitchen, the ball game, the streetcorner talk in your life. Introduce it sparingly into your writing. At the same time you'll find yourself varying the length of your sentences, and that's another form of Alternating. You often talk in shorter sentences than those written in books.

The Alternating Current flows in this quick piece of writing: rich, full descriptions and then short iron, punchy sentences.

> I used to hunt with Gramp. He didn't hunt like my father. We would walk along the cramped, hollowed-out cowpath. The bushes and weeds would push out at us from both sides. I always walked behind. It led along the murk-filled brown-greenness of the channel that connects his two lakes. I would wait for something to break. He taught me never to kill anything unless I was going to eat it. He helped my brother shoot a pigeon once. He would have eaten it if it had not smelled so much.

When the hunting was poor, we would go down by the lake and shoot beer bottles that some ass had left behind. There were always some there. Gramp would sit on a rotten stump and remember. He used to shoot pickerel as they pulled their heavy egg-filled bodies up the narrow channel. He said that they would spawn near the roots of the silver-gray pussy-willow trees. They're gone now; so are the pickerel. He would sit and laugh. And tell how the warden had chased him for two miles up to his slate-gray house. He had hid in the barn until he had left and then fried the warm fresh pickerel on the old black stove that was the heart of the house on a cold misty morning. We all learned something from him although he never taught us anything. I never knew it until he left. Tomorrow is never the same.

TOM CRONK

This is the way writers keep their writing alive. Tom Cronk may not have known that he was following an age-old tradition, but he was. Preachers use this method, poets, men and women who tell stories around pot-bellied stoves.

Whenever you write, consider using the juice provided by the Alternating Current.

*Do not hunt for subjects, let them
choose you, not you them. Only do that
which insists upon being done and runs
right up against you, hitting you in the
eye until you do it. This calls you and
you had better attend to it, and do it
as well as you can. But till called in this
way do nothing.*

SAMUEL BUTLER

chapter 17
your subject choosing you

By NOW A PERSON in the circle has prob-
ably said that once when she was writing, everything flowed together—
her choice of events and ideas, the form in which to put them, and the
sound of her words. This is what is meant by inspiration. Maybe it has
happened to you. Then writing becomes effortless. That may sound
overstated, but it's a fact in the life of working writers. Not all the
time, but often enough that you would be foolish not to try to set up
conditions which welcome this spirit, this Muse.

In fifteen minutes a college freshman wrote this:

> I know what it's like when it gets to the point where if I
> were dying I wish they'd drop me off a cliff and I don't care
> about anything, especially school, because there doesn't seem
> to be any reason, and no one seems to care anyways, and my
> mother calls and doesn't ask how I'm doing, or what I've

200

been up to; she just bitches about the house and her ex and then she starts to cry and has to get off the phone and later my dad calls and he complains about money and how's Mother and I say, "She's just fine," and he says "good" and has to go to New York this afternoon, so he must rush off now, but he'll get back to me later, and I know I really should do my homework, but I'm too bummed to get into it, so I sarcastically write the tragic story of my life in three parts on the window in soap, making sure to include my braces and the bicycle I never had, and then I finally sit down to write and I'm so depressed and all I can think about are the dippy girls who have nothing more to think about except what they're going to wear tomorrow, and I thank God for the Tab in front of me and the cigarette in my hand, and I realize I'm the real reason for my frustration, which frustrates me even more, and I have to write something for class, but I know no one wants to hear me bitch, so I go for a walk.

Only one false note there: some people do want to hear bitching like that, it's so funny and true.

If you didn't amaze yourself in free writing, go back and try more. It's a guaranteed activity: if you write fast—without thinking of spelling, grammar, punctuation, or form—and try to tell truths, sooner or later you'll write something that moves you and others. Then you'll become more confident and begin to respect your own experiences because you realize they're different from every other person's in the world—and so the ultimate source of your power as writer.

Once you know in your bones where your power is, you can follow Samuel Butler's advice given at the opening of this chapter, and run with it. Write with it. Butler says that if you aren't called by a subject, do nothing. School often insists you must follow the assignment whether or not you feel called. In the circle you'll have more options than school customarily offers. For example, you may be allowed to write three papers and turn in only one. But even if assigned a general topic, within that you can let a more specific topic choose you. This chapter will show you how to do that.

Here's a dialogue by a student:

Mother sat down on the couch. Her face was flushed red under her rough skin.

"Now Victoria—" she began, patting my knee and clearing her throat. "A woman is something . . . er . . . to be a woman

is one of the most beautiful things . . . um . . . uh . . . because
love is something beautiful and you'll fall in love someday
and . . . we . . . um . . . when you do . . . you'll know it and
you'll get married. But until then . . . ahem . . . you meet
some nice boys and well . . . um . . . you'll have crushes on
them but you'll think you're in love but when you grow up
all . . . I mean when you get older, you'll realize that it
wasn't love and you'll be glad that you didn't . . . um . . .
what I mean is . . . well, when you're with these boys, they'll
want to kiss you and . . . well . . . you know things like that
but . . . uh . . . well, honey . . . ah . . . a boy won't—respect
you if you do . . . uh . . . let them. Well, you know, boys
aren't like girls and they get carried away easier and they
can't . . . um . . . stop themselves . . . and they'll try to make
you do things you'll be sorry for later because you're a nice
girl, I mean . . . you'll want to save that . . . um . . . well,
marriage is the place to . . . um . . . Well, you'll understand
when you're old . . . I mean . . . the girl has to say no. Ah
. . . a girl can control the situation best by not leading the
boy . . . um . . . you know what I mean, don't you?"
    "Sure, Mom."

VICKI CARON

That brief, one-sided conversation makes no statement characterizing
Mother. She speaks at length and Daughter speaks shortly. Nevertheless,
the writing describes the gap between generations—one of the pressing
issues of the day. The paper is persuasive because it puts readers in
the situation, makes them feel the embarrassment of the mother and the
superiority of the daughter. An overwhelming sense of superiority that
is evidenced by the daughter's short ending comment. The words on
the page say, "Sure, Mom," but in the reader's mind they say, "I know
so much more than you, Mom, that there's no use my trying to explain
it to you. The discovery of your ignorance would shock and hurt you."

Once read to the class, Vicki's dialogue pointed the way for other
students. A man wrote of his relationship with his father:

    "Don, could you come in here a minute?"
    "No thanks, Dad."
    "I said get your ass in here!"
    "Yes, what do you want?" (with a sarcastic smile).
    "We received your marks from school."
    "And—?"
    "And it looks like we need to have a little talk."

And so we have our "little talk," except it's more like one of his long sermons on how stupid I am and what a failure I am for not equalling his accomplishments and grades he had while he was in school. Dad carried a 4.0 through college and even worked somewhere in the area of sixty hours a week while getting it. Now that's quite a feat, just ask him and he'll tell you (and tell you, and tell you). Granted, that is great, but it shouldn't mean that since he did it that way that I should have to, nor does it mean that if I don't have a 4.0 that I'm a failure. But in his eyes I am.

"Your grade point is only 2.93. You're not even in the 3's! You're beautiful, real beautiful. You've gone from a 3.8 to a 3.1 and now to, to this, this crap."

"Gee, Dad. I'm sorry, so sorry. What will the neighbors think?"

"Shut up and don't get smart. When I was in college I—"

"You got a 4.0 and you worked so hard to get it. Your parents were both gone and you had no one to help you. You did it all by yourself. Well flip you a fish! You're so wonderful, and I'm such a dumb ass. I've got everything going for me, even two very loving and understanding parents. Both of you with your Doctor Degrees, and yours in child psychology. Can't you see that I'm not you, and I may not have the same desires or the motivation you had? You were poor, you hardly had a thing; but now you've made it and not just for yourself but for us kids too. We're spoiled, Dad, and therefore don't have that drive you had. But you can't see that. This is why I don't have that same motivation in school that you had."

"But can't you see, Don, can't you—"

"No, and I won't see until you get off my back and accept that I may not want what you wanted and that it may be better for me to do things differently than the way you did them. We're drifting apart, Dad, because of all this, and I don't want to. Accept me for what and who I am and try to encourage me, not threaten or downgrade me. I'm almost getting to the point where I don't want to come home any more or see you and Mom, and that's being really poor."

"I'm sorry, son, I just want what's right for you."

"I know, Dad, so do I."

DON DRUMMONDPORT

Powerful writing is often dangerous. Truth about things that count in our lives has a way of spreading rapidly. For example, if you were a parent of a college student and suspected that she and her classmates were writing revealing portraits of parents, you would be curious to see them. Maybe you or the parents of your child's friends were being revealed to a class at one of life's worst moments. You might feel awkward, embarrassed, or outraged. That's why I have used the names Vicki Caron and Don Drummondport rather than the real names of the writers of these two papers. I want to protect them and their parents and at the same time makes it possible for truth to do its thing—give power to the writer's language and rhythms.

Think of your writing as possibly useful to you and others. In this class it's not an exercise to be done for Teacher's grade. Maybe you have more distance in your view of your parents than Vicki and Don: you see good sides of them as well as bad. Perhaps I shouldn't imply that Vicki and Don aren't aware of good sides of their parents; for their papers present only single encounters with them. If they were asked to write of events in which their mother and father appeared generous or loving, they might present similarly strong pictures. Here's a more rounded portrait of a mother. It might well induce Vicki and Don to think more comprehensively about Mom and Dad.

KEEPING BALANCE

At home this weekend Mom remarked that it sure felt good to her to have some satisfying projects of her own. She showed me a dress she was making for the sewing lessons she'd started, and described some of the kids she taught gym to in her new teacher aide job at the elementary school. She seemed less fidgety than I'd remembered her.

"You know," she said, "I've let you and Dad push me around for a good many years."

It's true. My mother lived by her rule that "Your father's word is law," and she let him be right, asked his permission for anything important, made way for his projects. And we all hated her when she had a spell of self-righteous hurt because she didn't get attention and concern enough to satisfy her.

"And you know," she says now, "Dad kind of resents it when I have projects of my own. He'll come in with something all cooked up for me to do, and if I'm busy sewing or something, I just say, 'You go ahead and do it if you want to, dear. I'm kinda busy here,' and he just doesn't know quite how to take it."

Seeing the results of my father's dominance and my mother's submission as I grew up taught me that Dad's way was a lot more satisfying. So I adopted it. I learned to think like him, demand like him, cultivate a drive for getting things done like him—and to use Mom like him.

On shopping trips she wanted me to see her in a hat or dress or pair of shoes and approve before she bought. If I didn't look pleased enough she said, "I guess maybe I'd better wait on this, don't you think so?" If I really liked the way something looked on her, she bought it. But if Pops didn't like it after she brought it home, she returned it to the store, apologizing to me for asking my advice and then not taking it.

"It really is your father, after all, that I have to dress for, and it will just be easier this way." She was agonizingly serious.

Pop would give his opinion on an issue and Mom would say, "Yes, dear." Later I'd give a conflicting opinion on the same issue and Mom would say, "Yes, dear."

I disrespected her for that. "She doesn't think!" I'd say to myself, and believe that I despaired over her.

This is my third year away from home, but only in the last few months have I come to see that she was simply loving two people in her life, and for that it didn't matter what our opinions were.

It's beginning to dawn on me that yes, I learned to think like a man, but I missed a lot of my mother's womanly lessons because I scorned their value in her. She knew all along that what she believed to be correct wasn't necessarily the most important thing to get across. People have to feel those things out for themselves anyway, and they can do it if they have love.

And it's wonderful to Mom and me that it's at the same time that each of us is understanding better the ways we've been and grown. She feels more comfortable about my obsession with change, and I'm beginning to grow a few roots that can soak up some of what she's poured into me.

CARMEN HINSDALE

Although this portrait shows both strengths and weaknesses in Mom, I have still changed the name of the author so this mother will not be identified in a public examination by her daughter. Mother might be able to accept this portrait of her, but if she were identified through her daughter's name, some of her friends or acquaintances might gossip about Carmen's picture of her.

Samuel Butler said, "Let your subject choose you." He did that himself, as many professional writers do, because he wanted to put himself into the flow of words and experience and ideas that sometimes comes to a writer free. You can do that and still be writing about a national or local issue. Think of the society you live in. Right now it is testing all its institutions. Thoughtful priests are leaving the church and getting married; thoughtful teachers are leaving established schools and setting up alternative schools. Thoughtful men and women are living together without being officially married. And—thoughtful priests are staying in the church and praising its traditional ways. Thoughtful women and men are speaking up for conventional marriage. Thoughtful teachers are warning against the dangers of undemanding education. These are controversial times. You can't have avoided experiences which touch some of the changes in church, law, race, school, marriage, children-parent relationships, government, the armed forces, war, bureaucracy, business, natural resources, narcotics, welfare, old age—the list is almost endless.

The experiences you write of don't have to be extreme: you needn't have witnessed or committed a crime. Perhaps you attended a wedding recently that took place in a pine woods and included rituals written by a bride and groom dressed in bluejeans. You were present at the breaking of an ancient tradition. A report of what you saw is evidence in a national controversy. You need only tell what took place. If you wish, you can include your own feelings, but that's not necessary. This isn't a conventional school assignment which requires you to make "a concluding judgment at the end of the paper expressed in not more than twenty-five words."

The smallest experience, fully brought alive on paper, may illuminate your readers' understanding of national issues. You had a car accident and the policeman insisted you go to the hospital. You said, "No, it's only a scratch on my forehead." He said, "It might be a concussion," and it was, and you are grateful to him. A story to put up against those which depict arrogant, bullying cops. Without thinking one thought or planning one move, you're always assuming a role that's being debated these days—going with or against the expectations society has for men and women. A simple way to write a paper on this topic is to tell of one moment (remember the Secret of Once) when you chose to play the role of man or woman. Or played it unconsciously, without choosing. Again, the easiest and most powerful way to write this paper is probably to tell the story of how you got into this act and what you did. No need to talk about the general subject—your readers are intelligent. They'll get your point if you dramatize it rather than deliver a lecture.

Here's a young father in college telling how he played man's role while his wife was playing woman's:

MAN

I felt like a kid dressed up to play in the snow in the gown, hat, and mask. My eyes and hands must have been all you could see.

I was guided into a small room. On the table was Sue at her final destination after all the waiting.

"Sit on the stool there next to her," said one of the masked faces. "Put your head next to hers."

My cheek next to Sue's, we both looked down toward her feet. The mirror overhead showed two hands in rubber gloves working inside an opening. The opening was hidden from our view by the totally expanded tummy under a green sheet.

I offered my hand to squeeze but she had handles to grip and they would do just fine.

"Watch the shoulder, watch that shoulder," one said to the other and then went on talking about something else. Both of them were chatting as they worked, as if they were changing spark plugs in a car.

Sue groaned for what must have been the one hundred and third time today.

"Pull the shoulder around!" he said.

There it was. A pair of eyes, a nose, and a mouth learning to cry. Sue groaned again and when I opened my eyes again I heard, "Got a fine-looking little girl. Had some trouble with those bronze shoulders, heh, heh, but she's fine."

They told me they would call me in the waiting room when Sue was ready. On my way out I watched the new life kicking in the incubator. Sue's face was relaxed a little now.

Walking down the hall, my hand ached a little from rubbing her back for what seemed every three minutes over the past eight hours. My hand ached hard. I felt silly just being a man.

DON HORNER

That account of a birth was written tersely in its first draft, which appears here. The people in the circle had nothing but praise for it, except for the dangling construction in the last paragraph. A listener suggested that it was not Don's hand that was walking down the hall, and he ought to rephrase that sentence.

That was a man playing an unusual role, assisting in the delivery room. In the following paper a woman complains that she played a classic female role.

FOOL

Running, I just barely caught the bus. I was the last one to board, and I waited until I was inside the warmth before searching my pockets for bus fare. Shifting my packages, I pawed my left coat pocket, then my right, then the front pocket of my jeans . . . damn, please let me have 15¢ bus fare. I couldn't have spent it all . . .

"Diana, hi, forget it, will ya? Fare's on me."

Startled, I looked up to see Scottie's smile, that chip-toothed grin that used to make me smile inside. Never outside, though—that was almost a commitment to Scottie, and he wanted no attachments.

I crouched next to him between the driver's seat and the change box. The doors of the bus locked me in, the gears slid the bus forward, and Scottie and I were once again separately together. Damn Metro Transit—but God, don't damn Scottie.

What in hell was my college graduate friend doing driving a city bus? Scottie, the backpacking winter camper, the bearded wonder, who left after graduation to discover himself in far away places. He wasn't supposed to come back—we said goodby long ago, and I knew life would go on.

He glanced at me, checked his rearview mirrors, looked at me again; waiting for me to say what was on my mind, he

silently psyched me out, knowing my mind as well as I. Didn't want to fill any air pockets with useless conversation— I'm still the same, Scottie, so read my mind.

"Where are you living now, Diana? Write it down for me." He handed me a pen and a bus schedule, and I held it in my hand, fighting my feelings, weighing my doubts. You can't go back, right? But I signed myself away, almost like selling myself, and now I wait for that special knock at the door.

Diana, how can you be so damned gullible when you know he's just adding your name to his string again? I'm such a fool.

DIANA GARSTI

In the following story of a woman dating a Vietnam War veteran, several man-woman roles are presented.

SOLDIER IS HOME

We used to talk about school and fishing and the war. Ron was smart, a bittersweet kind of smart that comes from seeing too many of life's problems too soon, and I was smart from books and vacations. He told me about poverty and hungry children, the army and helicopters, dead friends and psychotherapy wards. Then it didn't matter whether I'd seen Boot Hill and Hungry Horse Dam. Not to him. At times I felt he might as well talk to a washcloth. He didn't want a response, just something to talk to. So many feelings about so many things were revealed but never about each other. But always I was there because he mattered to me.

I hadn't seen Ron for three months. Then he called and asked me out. A date. I wondered if this meant a new kind of relationship. It didn't—he never came. I consoled myself: "But Ron's so different."

A week later I saw him at the bookstore.

"Hi Ron."

"Hi. Hey, I'm sorry about last Friday. Had some family problems."

"That's ok. I wasn't really mad, so don't worry about it."

"So understanding." He laughed. "If you'll risk another try, how about this Friday?"

"Promise to come?"

"Promise."

He didn't. This time his difference wasn't as consoling. So what if he was bittersweet? I still had some pride. Damn his sad existence and his heart-wrenching knowledge. They weren't my problems.

"Pardon me, Miss, but I have a problem." I finished buckling my seatbelt and glanced up. It was Ron. "I need a ride downtown. Which way you goin'?"

"The other way." I unbuckled and rebuckled my seatbelt. Something to keep my eyes off his.

"Mad?"

"Shouldn't I be?"

"Yeah, I suppose. Sure you're not going downtown? I have to be at an interview in five minutes."

"You're still the same."

"Well, I wasn't going to go but at the last minute I changed my mind. How 'bout a ride?"

"All right."

Neither of us spoke. The news came on the radio. Ron turned it off. "I'd still like to take you out."

"Why?"

"Because you're good looking."

"Is that a ploy?"

"No, it's the truth."

"What? That I'm good looking or that's why you want to take me out?"

"Both."

"Well, there's no way." And I meant it. I told him that twice was all I'd take, but it wasn't true. I told him he needed at least a little conventionality, knowing it was his unconventionality I liked. I was sarcastic and belittling and I knew I was and I didn't want to be so I didn't say anything for a while.

When he got out of the car the hard feelings were gone and we had a date for Saturday. I wondered if he was going to come, telling myself I didn't care, and I didn't.

He came this time: half an hour late and high because "A buddy stopped over and we smoked a little. Sorry."

"Yeah, me too." I was afraid to ride with him, but didn't say anything because what good would it have done? Just an empty bunch of words to him.

The movie wasn't any good. Ron said he liked it but since he was high during the first half, he couldn't be sure. So we left it at that and bought a pizza. That wasn't any good either.

"This pizza seems to be indicative of the whole night," Ron said. "Know what I mean?"

"I think so."

And he told me what he thought of dates and girls. Girls were stupid, especially college girls; and dates were a part of their game. College was a shelter from the hard things in life. It kept them soft. "They walk around saying 'I love you' to half the boys they meet and don't know what half of anything's about. If a college girl told me she loved me, I'd tell her she was full of crap."

I realized I wasn't one of those girls. I was a washcloth. "Oh Jesus," I said. "Why don't you realize that people don't have to go through hell to have feelings and emotions. Just because a girl has an easy or sheltered life doesn't mean she can't be in love. It happens all the time."

"Yeah, it happens but it's not real. First you have to know hate and bitterness and you have to be hungry and you have to bleed and hurt and cry."

"And then you're like you are and you can't find happiness or fulfillment in anything. Adversity *may* have made you wise, but it hasn't made you happy. And since you can't find happiness you begrudge all of us simple people trying."

And there was more but it said the same thing. I came home wondering what had ever made him so special to me. He wasn't smart, he just had different ideas, narrow ideas. I didn't want to see him again.

A month passed and I hardly thought of Ron any more. Then one day I read "Soldier's Home" by Ernest Hemingway. Krebs came home from war and death, and all the things that used to make a difference didn't any more. Girls were fun to look at but their patterns were too complicated to get involved with. It didn't matter that he had no girl— or job or religion. These things bore complicated consequences and for Krebs death had already uncomplicated everything.

CHRISTINE LELDON

In "Man," "Fool," and "Soldier Is Home," the writers have recorded experience so truly that it forced them to see themselves objectively, and their experience becomes irrefutable evidence in a controversial matter. The fact of what they say is incontestable, as true as a statistic like

"One out of every four marriages ended in divorce in 1976 in Eustrasia." And yet more significant, because it reveals motives, causes, tone, mood, and consequences.

How different these writings are from the usual college essays on women's and men's roles. You shouldn't scorn students who write pompous-sounding empty lectures or sermons of that kind. School has a way of unwittingly encouraging such writing. It wants to pass on truths that have been discovered by authorities. Since they often believe they are speaking the last word, they are apt to state their ideas generally, to promulgate the Truth. Therefore students feel pressed to do likewise. Asked for a paper on feminism, for example, a young man writes, "After many centuries of enduring male chauvinism, women in America have finally begun to liberate themselves." That's his statement of the general idea he's read in many articles. Or a young woman writes, "In the future, women will find themselves hired for jobs at the same pay as men, and in general will be accorded the same rights and privileges." And so on. Nothing there anyone wants to read at this stage in the movement. "But how could I write any other way about feminism?" says a student. "I've only read one article on the subject. I'm not an expert."

But every person in the country has encountered changing sexual roles. A father lives in relation to the movement—he increasingly accepts and brings about changes, or he resists them, or he shuttles back and forth between the two positions. A mother likewise. Every time the student—male or female—encounters the other sex, the experience touches this subject. Examine yourself. If you're a man, are you treating women like sex objects? If you're a woman, by your behavior are you asking to be treated like a sex object? We need to have a current history of young women and men spending time together inside and outside the custom of dating. How do young people act toward each other through sexual roles? Differently from the way older people act toward each other? First we should not generalize but begin writing the record, putting down the evidence. Dozens and hundreds and thousands of little accounts of the behavior—including the talk—of persons of the opposite sex working, studying, meeting, sharing, or retreating from each other. These stories are in your past experience and all around you.

> My pen is a lever which, in proportion
> as the near end stirs me further within,
> the further end reaches to a greater depth
> in the reader.
>
> HENRY THOREAU

WRITING NINETEEN: Write the story of an experience you've had which touches one of the national controversies of the time. You don't have to name the controversy or make general statements about it. Just a piece of your life, or the life of someone you know, down on paper, fully realized, and your readers will get your point.

If you and your teacher wish, you may later write another account on another national isue. And another. With this method alone you can find topics for a dozen papers, enough to fill up the work of a whole semester.

WRITING TWENTY: Sometime in your writing experience, try looking at one subject, person, place, relationship, act, or habit, at different times during the day, week, or month. Then you can utilize the power that comes to most professional writers who stay with a subject over a long period of time. Write down what your boss said this morning at work. Then something she said next Tuesday. And several days later. Maybe you'll find that she differs according to mood, according to the pressures that build up in her job, according to the weather. And you, too, in the way you come on with her. Late at night, right after a full dinner, in cold weather, under dark skies—whatever, your subject may change and the differing views of it you put down will enrich your writing.

At Caldwell College in New Jersey, where some foreign students study English while taking college courses, Isabel Marquez began the year by writing six or seven journal entries about the death of her mother, an event that had profoundly shaken her. When she was asked to write about one of her deepest experiences, she went back to those journal entries and made them the basis of this paper:

WHERE ARE YOU?

November the twenty-seventh. It would be her birthday. I can't believe yet that my mother died three months ago. This has been my deepest experience I have ever had in my life, maybe because I'm very young. I know it has impressed my mind even though sometimes people could think that everything is all right for me now.

We had many good times when I was younger. When I came back from school, she used to wait for me to eat together because I got home at two o'clock in the afternoon. I told her everything about my day at the school, and we shared our opinions about my work in some of the students' activities. Then, we used to laugh a lot because I told her the funniest things about what I had done during the day.

The idea of coming here to Caldwell College was hers. It came to her mind after I told her at lunch one day, "Mama, today a teacher from an American College came to visit the school and to show us the system to apply there." I had always told her, "I want to learn English. I want to travel." We are not poor, but we are not rich either. So, she told me, "Take it easy. I have to save enough money in order to send you there." And she did it. I couldn't believe that! One of our best dreams was almost done. I was going to the United States alone.

While all of that was happening, I was really fighting with her. My life had changed at the same time that I met new people out of my school, but I didn't tell her anything about them because she had always thought that we were very young and the society was very dangerous. Well, I have to accept that she was right, after all. We had terrible communications problems because she never could figure out which ones were my thoughts, my opinions about several topics, and I never tried to understand her point of view. She was still seeing me as her little baby who needed her for everything. Of course I needed her, but I also needed to meet people. I couldn't tolerate her and my whole family being so strict with me. This fact was given when she became sick. I remember one of the discussions we had. That was a day when I was talking by phone with a guy that my mother didn't approve of. She suddenly appeared in front of me asking, "Who is it? Oh! I know! It's Antonio! I don't want you to talk with him anymore!"

I didn't answer anything. So she took the telephone from my hand and hung it up. I was so upset. "Why did you do that?" You can imagine what followed when I asked her that question. First of all, she was angry while I started to cry. I was trying to explain to her many different things, all of them related to a principal one.

"If I die, don't worry about it. I don't want you to be worried about me. I would like to live by myself. My life is mine, not yours." She became more upset than I was while she started to threaten me.

"I will tell this to your father. You aren't an adult yet. You can't do whatever you want."

My brother Martin was coming back from his work, and he heard part of the discussion. He told my sisters (Elsa and Irene) who were in the kitchen, "Isabel is killing our mother.

If you allow that and mami dies, I'm not going to carry her coffin over my shoulders." He has a very strong temper.

So, you can suppose that my brothers and even my sisters were almost hating me because they thought I was the principal reason of my mother's worries. For them, I was just a stupid girl who wanted to be liberated or something like that. My oldest sister, Elsa, was the closest daughter of my mother, who looked at everything through Elsa's eyes. One day Elsa went to pick me up at school (something unusual), and we began to discuss aloud in the car.

"What do you think you are, stupid girl? Don't you see that my mother is sick and she's terribly afraid because she thinks she could have cancer? It doesn't matter to me what you decide to do with your life, but don't bother her because you will be in trouble with me. Do you understand?" We were angry with each other.

Finally, I had to tell her, "OK. I'm not going to see Antonio anymore. But you, leave me alone."

Since May of this year my mother felt bad. Nobody knew her illness, but she couldn't get up out of her bed because she had a pain, a terrible pain in her back and in her stomach too. Because of that, she always lay down or sat in a swinging chair in her room. My family took her to see many doctors in different hospitals. They made lots of tests and gave to her a mountain of medicines, but she was still feeling the pain. The doctors never said what the illness was because they were confused about it. I began to feel guilty because I thought that our fights were the reason for her illness. Can you imagine the feeling of a person who thinks she's killing her mother step by step? That was my feeling. I couldn't go every morning but for a few minutes to her room. Her face, her eyes were guessing every thought I could have in my mind. There were other times when her face was turned to. a sweet expression, as if she were saying, "What did I do to you?" But I couldn't keep my eyes from seeing her. She was like a small candle which was extinguishing gradually. I felt a mixture between guilt and sadness that was also killing my feelings and my mind. I didn't know what to do. I wanted to reach the things I was sure were my right, but, at the same time, I was wondering how I could arrange everything to take away my mother's worries without any fights.

To go to her room was so hard for me. First of all, because all the medicines (a lot of them) that she was taking were on a small night table near her bed. After some weeks, we had to bring a hospital bed for her. So her room was almost like one of a clinic. There was a strong smell in her room's atmosphere and a partial shadow that made the room even more mysterious than it could normally be.

We had to call my oldest brother Xavier, who was in the United States studying a post-graduate course in medicine, to see if he could do something for her. While he was coming we took her to a hospital because she was suffering extremely. When Xavier arrived, he talked with another doctor (Dr. Ayala), a friend of his, to make her a complete series of tests. We were scared, but especially, I was more so than them because that guilty feeling didn't let me live in peace.

Dr. Ayala told Xavier after a few days, "Your mother has a pancreas cancer, and she needs an urgent operation to see if we can save her. I'm really sorry, Xavier, because she's sweet, and I know you love her very much."

We knew about this conversation only later, because when my brother went to my mother's room, he didn't say anything about the illness. Instead he said, "You just have a silly calculus in your liver, and with the operation you are going to get well soon. Come on, mami, you have to say 'yes' now because the operation is so simple. It doesn't have any risk."

In that moment, I was in the room, and I became glad because I didn't know the other information, and I believed my brother completely. When I came back home that evening, my sister Elsa told me about her illness.

"Do you know what's wrong with mami?"

I was smiling when I answered, "Sure. With the operation she is going to live for a long time."

She was almost crying when she had to tell me, "No, that is not true. She has cancer, and probably the operation is not going to be useful." I was eating some bread, but my throat stopped swallowing. My eyes didn't see anything clearly. My mind was confused, mixed up. I couldn't believe that. Suddenly, my house was involved in a heavy silence. That was for me the symbol of her absence in our lives. All the stupid thoughts that were going around in my mind disappeared. At least, Elsa and I have been excellent sisters. We love each other a lot, and if one of us is going through suffering, the other consoles her. That was helpful for me at that time.

Since the day when my mother was at the hospital, we had to spend the night with her in order to accompany her because she was really scared about nights alone in a hospital. She thought (like I do) that it would be terrible if she could die without her family beside her.

The operation hadn't been useful at all because the cancer was extended into the aorta, behind the pancreas, and if the doctor extracted it, she would lose much blood dying on the operation table.

To see my mother in that situation was terrible for all of us. She had been a dynamic woman and now she couldn't move by herself. She needed help all the time. She didn't eat normally but with tubes of serum, vitamins, and even a bag of blood.

How can I describe those nights? I have to go to the hospital at seven o'clock at night, when the people who were with her during the day left the room to go back home. I kissed her forehead softly and held her hands between mine The sickness was doing her to fade her natural skin color which was becoming a really horrible yellow. Day by day, I was more impressed with the contrast between both of the colors. My skin looked so healthy beside hers and there were nights when I prayed to God.

"Why can't she have my same color? I want to lose mine just to give it to her." Then, I was sitting silently beside her bed looking at those respirators and tubes going inside her nose, throat, to reach the stomach. She called me.

"I love you," she said. Now I'm remembering that and I'm crying in that moment, I couldn't. If I do that in front of her, she would surely know what her sickness was. I had to hide my face and say:

"I do too."

The seventeen of July was my Graduation of High-school. My mother and I had been waiting that moment because she knew that maybe I would say a speech in the name of my classmates. It would be a great day for the two of us, but she was at the hospital and she couldn't go with me. My brother Axel recorded the speech. In these kind of acts, they use to give the medal that you have won to your mother when the act is over. I cried when that moment came because I had to receive the medal in her place, and we went almost running (by car) to the hospital. When she heard my speech, she also cried, adding,

"It's beautiful." I had written a paragraph at the end of it, mentioning some words of a book that in my family we have as a treasure. It's "The Little Prince" by Antoine de Saint-Exupery. It says as follows:

So the little Prince tamed the fox. And when the hour of his departure drew near—

"Ah," said the fox. "I shall cry. . . . Good bye. And now here is my secret, a very simple secret: It is only with the heart that one can see rightly; what is essential is invisible to the eye. . . . You become responsible, forever, for what you have tamed. You are responsible for your rose. . . ."

And then, the little Prince went away.

As always happens, it's now when I realize that I didn't take care of my rose, and that was my fault. I would like to see her alive now because I know she would be proud of me. I'm doing well at the United States. I'm alone, but however I have been responsible for myself. She is not here to see it but that is my lesson. I learned that I have to be as perfect as possible even though that it doesn't mean I'm going to change extremely my past ideas. With her death, she taught me the way I have to adjust them with society's point of view. She made me stronger with her wisdom. I could realize that when a month later I saw her death certificate. A whole set of memories crossed my mind. In it I saw her the day she told me at the hospital,

"Mi amor, I think it's impossible for me to go to your school the seventeenth."

"Mami, you have to see me that day. I'm encharged of the speech. And what about the new white dress you bought for me? Moreover, you have to be there to receive the medal. Mami. I need you to be there!" I was desperate.

"You know I can't. But I want you to write a great speech. Don't talk about the same thing everybody always does. Write about your future as humanistics students, about specific problems that the youth has and how you can solve some of them if you make the purpose of working together. Don't be afraid. You are young and the world is opening its doors to you. Study hard and you are going to be a success."

> Everything happened as she said, as she had always been
> saying. The death took away her body, but never her spirit.
> But there is no more warm, no more from her. Where is
> she? In the darkness? Where?
>
> I have to continue living, without her now, but what
> hard is sometimes!

That paper was published in that form as unedited work in progress
to be read by Isabel's class. In it, she developed objectivity as she
wrote. She put herself in the place of her sister and came to understand
why Elsa was upset by Isabel's attitude toward their mother. Such
understanding is more apt to come to us when we write at different
times about the same experience or relationship. Time—which is the
accumulation of experiences—changes us.

At this moment in American publishing, magazine and book editors
are increasingly printing thoughtful histories of individual experience.
Seldom do they publish essays of ideas or summaries of trends unless
they are accompanied by little stories or case histories to give the
ideas life and authority. Here, for example, is Joyce Maynard's con-
tribution of April 12, 1979, to the column *Hers* in *The New York
Times*. Like Isabel Marquez, Joyce Maynard gathers a number of
experiences and reflections to build her statement about her relationship with her grandmother.

> My mother called last week to tell me that my grandmother
> is dying. She has refused an operation that would postpone,
> but not prevent, her death from pancreatic cancer. She can't
> eat, she has been hemorrhaging, and she has severe jaun-
> dice. "I always prided myself on being different," she told
> my mother. "Now I *am* different. I'm yellow."
>
> My mother, telling me this news, began to cry. So I be-
> came the mother for a moment, reminding her, reasonably,
> that my grandmother is 87, she's had a full life, she has all
> her faculties, and no one who knows her could wish that she
> live long enough to lose them. Lately my mother has been
> finding notes in my grandmother's drawers at the nursing
> home, reminding her, "Joyce's husband's name is Steve.
> Their daughter is Audrey." In the last few years she hasn't
> had the strength to cook or garden, and she's begun to say
> she's had enough of living.
>
> My grandmother was born in Russia, in 1892—the oldest
> daughter in a large and prosperous Jewish family. But the
> prosperity didn't last. She tells stories of the pogroms and
> the Cossacks who raped her when she was 12. Soon after

that, her family emigrated to Canada, where she met my grandfather.

Their children were the center of their life. The story I loved best, as a child, was of my grandfather opening every box of Cracker Jack in the general store he ran, in search of the particular tin toy my mother coveted. Though they never had much money, my grandmother saw to it that her daughter had elocution lessons and piano lessons, and assured her that she would go to college.

But while she was at college, my mother met my father, who was blue-eyed and blond-haired and not Jewish. When my father sent love letters to my mother, my grandmother would open and hide them, and when my mother told her parents she was going to marry this man, my grandmother said if that happened, it would kill her.

Not likely, of course. My grandmother is a woman who used to crack Brazil nuts open with her teeth, a woman who once lifted a car off the ground, when there was an accident and it had to be moved. She has been representing her death as imminent ever since I've known her—25 years—and has discussed, at length, the distribution of her possessions and her lamb coat. Every time we said goodbye, after our annual visit to Winnipeg, she'd weep and say she'd never see us again. But in the meantime, while every other relative of her generation, and a good many of the younger ones, has died (nursed usually by her), she has kept making knishes, shopping for bargains, tending the healthiest plants I've ever seen.

After my grandfather died, my grandmother lived, more than ever, through her children. When she came to visit, I would hide my diary. She couldn't understand any desire for privacy. She couldn't bear it if my mother left the house without her.

This possessiveness is what made my mother furious (and then guilt-ridden that she felt that way, when of course she owed so much to her mother). So I harbored the resentment that my mother—the dutiful daughter—would not allow herself. I—who had always performed specially well for my grandmother, danced and sung for her, presented her with kisses and good report cards—stopped writing to her, ceased to visit.

But when I heard that she was dying, I realized I wanted to go to Winnipeg to see her one more time. Mostly to make my mother happy, I told myself (certain patterns being hard to break). But also, I was offering up one more particularly fine accomplishment: my own dark-eyed, dark-skinned, dark-haired daughter, whom my grandmother had never met.

I put on my daughter's best dress for our visit to Winnipeg, the way the best dresses were always put on me, and I filled my pockets with animal crackers, in case Audrey started to cry. I scrubbed her face mercilessly. On the elevator going up to her room, I realized how much I was sweating.

Grandma was lying flat with an IV tube in her arm and her eyes shut, but she opened them when I leaned over to kiss her. "It's Fredelle's daughter, Joyce," I yelled, because she doesn't hear well anymore, but I could see that no explanation was necessary. "You came," she said. "You brought the baby."

Audrey is just one, but she has seen enough of the world to know that people in beds are not meant to be so still and yellow, and she looked frightened. I had never wanted, more, for her to smile.

Then Grandma waved at her—the same kind of slow, finger-flexing wave a baby makes—and Audrey waved back. I spread her toys out on my grandmother's bed and sat her down. There she stayed, most of the afternoon, playing and humming and sipping on her bottle, taking a nap at one point, leaning against my grandmother's leg. When I cranked her Snoopy guitar, Audrey stood up on the bed and danced. Grandma couldn't talk much anymore, though every once in a while she would say how sorry she was that she wasn't having a better day. "I'm not always like this," she said.

Mostly she just watched Audrey. Sometimes Audrey would get off the bed, inspect the get-well cards, totter down the hall. "Where is she?" Grandma kept asking. "Who's looking after her?" I had the feeling, even then, that if I'd said, "Audrey's lighting matches," Grandma would have shot up to rescue her.

We were flying home that night, and I had dreaded telling her, remembering all those other tearful partings. But in the end, I was the one who cried. She had said she was ready to die. But as I leaned over to stroke her forehead, what she said was, "I wish I had your hair" and "I wish I was well."

On the plane flying home, with Audrey in my arms, I thought about mothers and daughters, and the four genera- tions of the family that I know most intimately. Every one of those mothers loves and needs her daughter more than her daughter will love or need her some day, and we are, each of us, the only person on earth who is quite so con- sumingly interested in our child.

Sometimes I kiss and hug Audrey so much she starts cry- ing—which is, in effect, what my grandmother was doing to my mother, all her life. And what makes my mother grieve right now, I think, is not simply that her mother will die in a day or two, but that, once her mother dies, there will never again be someone to love her in quite such an un- reserved, unquestioning way. No one else who believes that, 50 years ago, she could have put Shirley Temple out of a job, no one else who remembers the moment of her birth. She will only be a mother, then, not a daughter anymore.

Audrey and I have stopped over for a night in Toronto, where my mother lives. Tomorrow she will go to a safe- deposit box at the bank and take out the receipt for my grandmother's burial plot. Then she will fly back to Winni- peg, where, for the first time in anybody's memory, there was waist-high snow on April Fool's Day. But tonight she is feeding me, as she always does when I come, and I am eating more than I do anywhere else. I admire the wedding china (once my grandmother's) that my mother has set on the table. She says (the way Grandma used to say to her, of the lamb coat), "Some day it will be yours."

In the past, reading an impressive writer, you may have said, "How could she have thought so much about the subject, seen so many dif- ferent sides of it?" Now you know. This is the way professional writers go at writing a whole book of fiction or nonfiction bearing upon a central theme. They give themselves and the subject many opportu- nities to appear to each other. Try it. You don't have time for a full book but you can do as much as Isabel Marquez did.

WRITING TWENTY-ONE: At three or more separated times, write of something that has intrigued you. You can show it (or him, her, them) existing or acting at different places or times if you wish. Take advantage of those different places or times acting upon you. Maybe you've changed your mind from first to second time, or maybe your whole view keeps shifting. Remember you don't have to lecture your reader. Isabel Marquez didn't.

Usually we are more persuaded by the record of a life than by a sermon, and the best ministers fill their sermons with little stories, as Jesus Christ did. And Buddha. And Mohammed.

[George Bernard Shaw often sent his early drafts of his plays to his friend Ellen Terry, the actress, for criticism. Once she said she feared to suggest changes on his manuscript. He wrote back:]

"Oh, bother the MSS., mark them as much as you like: what else are they for? Mark everything that strikes you. I may consider a thing fortynine times; but if you consider it, it will be considered 50 times; and a line 50 times considered is 2 per cent better than a line 49 times considered. And it is the final 2 per cent that makes the difference between excellence and mediocrity."

chapter 18
sharpening

REHEATING a piece of writing after it has cooled, tempering it, and sharpening it is enjoyable—if you know how. Otherwise it may turn out worse, brittle or misshapen. In years of experience with editors and other readers who criticize his writing, a professional comes to identify some of the common weaknesses in all writing, and he looks for them when he sits down to improve his first or second draft of a piece of writing.

He looks for the excessive use of the verb *is* (and all forms of *to be*), of *it*, of adjectives, adverbs, and passive verbs.

The verb *is* links other words, or proclaims something exists; it does not say much on its own. Writing dominated by *is* also suffers from too many nouns and adjectives, which the verb connects. It lacks the force and liveliness of writing filled with verbs that communicate specific action, like *careen, screech, tickle, swallow,* etc.

Too many uses of the word *is* drive a writer to stuffing his sentences with the words *it* and *there*. A writer who speaks honestly and wants his reader to know something that has counted for him seldom lets

224

his sentences get sick in these ways; but he has gone to school, been asked to write Engfish. He can't help being susceptible to these diseases. Here's a paragraph of free writing by a healthy writer:

> He doesn't have legs. Not ones that feel or move. It's been that way almost four years now. Wheels. I was scared to talk at first, felt like a kid asking what it is that everyone's talking about. But we did. We used to goof around and tell dirty jokes. I always felt a little fake. Dan and I took him to the bathroom every day. Had to be done in a special way. Were there once. Dan asked a question. I don't remember. I answered, "What do you think I am, a cripple?" That's what I said. I didn't look at anyone, just the wall. For about half an hour, I felt very whole, but my stomach was tin foil. They were quiet, both of them. Quiet as being alone. I wished someone would cut off my arms.

In that passage, *is* and *it* don't dominate. The word *there* appears only once, and denoting a place, not wasting space as it often does when used merely as a handle in front of the word *is*: "There is a need for change." The adjectives and adverbs that appear pull their weight. In several sentences the writer avoids using adjectives to describe his feelings, and instead employs a telling fact or metaphor: "I didn't look at anyone, just the wall," "I wished someone would cut off my arms." In this way he avoided the weakness of commonplace adjectives. He didn't write: "I felt just awful," or "I was never so embarrassed in all my life."

In the above passage the only danger words that perhaps need replacing are *It's been* in the first line and *it is* in the third. Sentence number three might read better if it said: *"He's* been that way almost four years now." And the fifth if it didn't contain the bracketed words: ". . . felt like a kid asking what [it is that] everyone's talking about." But on the whole, this is a sharply written passage.

To show Is-ness and It-ache at their worst, here's another passage on the same subject.

> One of the worst feelings in the world is when you are being stared at. It makes you feel like your slip is showing or your pants are ripped. They mean no harm; it's just their way of being curious. It makes it hard for someone who is physically different. It is a shame that these people have to be unknowing.

Both writers apparently hated to see persons "physically different" made fun of. The second writer was an Engfisher who couldn't free himself to put down powerful facts. So he presented his sick sentences. If you're writing with a high degree of honesty, you will never find your words as ill as his when you sit down to write a second or third draft. But all writers at times put down sickly expressions. In the passage above, circle the uses of the verb *to be;* check them; and underline the adjectives. You will see how little meaning the words communicate. The passage isn't worth sharpening. With its wasted words cut, it still doesn't compel the reader:

> Being stared at makes you feel like your slip is showing or your pants are ripped. The starers are just curious, they mean no harm. They don't realize how much they hurt someone who is physically different.

In any sort of writing, the excessive use of *it* piles up other unnecessary words in a sentence.

Original. By a recent poll it was revealed ...

Revision. A recent poll revealed ...

It has a way of picking up bad company. *It seems* are two words that frequently do bad things together.

Original. It seems that of the both groups, the boys are more conscious than the girls about subtleties of dress.

Revision. The boys are more conscious than girls about subtleties of dress.

Often writers say *seems* when no seeming is involved whatever, but rather clear and certain feeling or fact.

Note how cutting the uses of the verbs *would be* and *wasn't* (forms of *is*) allows the following sentence to be reduced from 34 to 23 words:

Original. Today an act like this would be considered a tragedy in a boy's life if he wasn't allowed at least a couple of hours to himself for the care and parting of his hair.

Revision. Today a boy denied a couple of hours to himself for the care and parting of his hair would consider himself tragically mistreated.

A helpful strategy in replacing *is* in a sentence consists of finding another verb which carries more meaning and allows you to drop a number of other unnecessary words.

When you notice a lot of adjectives and nouns and pronouns popping up in your sentences, you'll probably find that they were created by the excessive use of *is* or other forms of *to be*.

Original. It was the style for the girls in that school to wear hair ribbons.

Revision: The girls in that school wore hair ribbons.

One way to transfuse blood into a sentence anemic with Is-ness—substitute a metaphorical verb for *is*.

Original. The poor subservient freshman is an inferior because he is not a leader in organizations, says the Student Association president.

Revision: The poor freshman wags his tail as an inferior. He is never a leader in organizations, says the Student Association president.

Shakespeare was a master of the metaphorical verb. In *Macbeth* he made Malcolm say:

> This tyrant whose sole name *blisters* our tongues,
> *Was* once thought honest.

Suppose Shakespeare had written with Is-ness:

> This tyrant whose sole name *is* a blister on our tongues,
> *Was* once thought honest.

Again, one use of the verb *to be* is enough in the statement.

REVISING SEVEN: In one of your past longer pieces of writing circle every use of the forms of the verb *to be*. Consider which need to be eliminated and revise the sentences in which they appear. Remember that Is-ness stands for a *weak* use of a form of *to be*. No writer can write many sentences in a row without usefully employing *is*.

REVISING EIGHT: Check another of the long writings you have already done. Look for the weaknesses mentioned in this chapter, eliminate them, and make your paper both more concise and concrete. In your writing you should be hunting for uses of *it* and *there* which don't carry solid meaning but act merely as convenient handles for introducing other expressions. For example:

Original. In some churches there are large choir stalls that partially surround the minister.

Revision. In some churches large choir stalls partially surround the minister.

But sometimes these words operate well as handles. They are hard to replace in these two sentences:

> It is cold out tonight.
> There are only four houses on the other side of the street on our block.

Too often, vague uses of *it* and *there* lead a writer to wasting other words as well:

Original. It is the task of the school to train all the students.

Such an It-ache as that may be cured by making a noun the subject of the sentence. At the same time, an editor would probably change the possessive construction "of the school" to "school's," a more informal but vigorous expression:

Revision. The school's task is to train all the students.

A sentence doesn't ache from a healthy use of *it* or *there*. For example:

> The ball rolled and rolled until it hit the fence.
> "He's sitting over there," said the witness, pointing.

In these sentences *it* represents the ball and *there* tells a place. These are different uses from those involved in *It is* and *There are*.

Dullness also results from the excessive use of passive verbs.

Passive. It was brought to our attention by the manager that we had not sent out the invoice.

Active. The manager told us we had not sent out the invoice.

Passive. The play was a performance that was observed by George with amazing indifference.

Active. George observed the play with amazing indifference.

Passive verbs suggest that nobody is doing anything. Just sitting around being acted upon.

Passive. The object that was stepped on by me was a ladybug with lavender spots.

Active. I stepped on a ladybug with lavender spots.

Passive. The scheme was conceived by John at four in the morning.

Active. John conceived the scheme at four in the morning.

Dullness may also be imparted to sentences by excessive use of the verbs

make   go   get
have   move   come

They aren't full of specific meaning. Circle each use of them in your writing and question it: can the verb be replaced with a more particular and meaningful one? For example, *making* might be supplanted by

constructing   gluing   joining   stringing
building   piling   digging   sticking

and many other verbs. Even these are fairly general; for example, a writer might say "I *cemented* two stones together" rather than "I stuck two stones together." Choosing more precise and vigorous verbs puts life into writing because life is particular, not general.

Like Is-ness, the shoddy use of *make, have, go, move, get,* and *come* leads to a frightening waste of words:

Original. This land *has* the appearance of being arid.

Revision. This land looks arid.

These verbs frequently seed sentences with unnecessary nouns.

Original. He finally *came to* his decision. He would run.

Revision. He finally decided he would run.

You should remember that these suggested revisions are made out of context. The last revision above saves three words from the original sentences, but if the author's purpose was to slow down the reader and delay the divulging of the decision, he might better use the original version, which carries a different rhythm.

Beginning writers often insist on establishing the ownership of an object with the verb *have* before they let the owner use the object. Good way to clog the story.

Original. He *had* a bicycle. He rode it to work every morning.

Revision. He rode his bicycle to work every morning.

The principle involved in sharpening is to fill words with precise meaning or get rid of them. Beginning writers splatter adjectives and adverbs like buckshot. Consider this passage:

> **I summoned up courage and *boldly* set forth through the pathway. Suddenly loomed in sight five male patients sit-**

ting outside only a few feet from me. Too late to turn back, I consoled myself with the idea that an attendant was probably *unobtrusively* hidden from view but there, nevertheless, for protection.

Then the thought dawned on me that I was in the wrong and didn't deserve protection because I was trespassing—there were blockades which I had ignored, set up in front of the pathway. The patients, perhaps sensing my *nervous* anticipation, *possibly* evident in my *faltering* steps and *nervous* eye movements, said "hello" to me.

My *natural* reaction to this situation bothers me. In Psych class we consider mental patients just "sick people." I don't want to be guilty of sharing the *common* feelings of the *general* public.

Here in line 1, *boldly* is unnecessary with "summoned up courage" and "set forth," both expressions which imply boldness. In line 5, *unobtrusively* is unnecessary. Seldom does anyone hide obtrusively. In lines 10 and 11, *perhaps* is an honest word but the other italicized words overdo the notion of sensing nervousness. A sharp cutting is needed.

Original. The patients, perhaps sensing my nervous anticipation, possibly evident in my faltering steps and nervous eye movements, said "hello" to me.

Revision. Perhaps sensing my anticipation in my faltering steps and nervous eye movements, the patients said "hello" to me.

In line 13, *natural* is not an accurate word for what the writer wants to say. *Instant* or *stereotyped* would make more sense. In line 15, *common* is unnecessary. *Sharing* and *general* say enough by themselves.

Remembering the *repeat-and-vary* principle, the good writer avoids ruts. He doesn't allow himself to supply for every verb an adverb and for every noun an adjective until the pattern becomes monotonous and the words flabby. He avoids or changes dead patterns like these:

He slowly walked up the stairs, nonchalantly pushed on the door, and casually entered the room.

At the picnic were sticky-fingered children, rosy-cheeked mommas, and large-stomached fathers.

When he finishes his first or second draft, a good writer tests the adjectives and adverbs: are they pulling their weight? Do the other words around them render them unnecessary? See how freshly and powerfully Shakespeare uses an adverb in giving Regan, King Lear's daughter, these words about her father:

> 'Tis the infirmity of his age: yet he hath ever but *slenderly* known himself.

A fundamental in using adverbs and adjectives is not to let one of them smother the effect of another strong word. Don't let your straight man steal the attention from the comic. If you write

> She was *unusually* hideous.

you have lessened the force of *hideous* by making the reader attend to the weak word *unusually*. If you write

> It was a tremendously tall skyscraper.

you have lessened the force of *tall*. In fact, both *tremendously* and *tall* are tired and should be replaced with words that fix the height of the skyscraper in actual or metaphorical scale.

> I stood a hundred feet away and yet my neck ached from looking up to the top of the building.

This chapter has talked about weak uses of certain words. All of them may be used adequately or strongly by a skillful writer. Note in this beautifully phrased passage from "Self-Reliance" that Emerson uses many strong verbs but also forms of *to be*. He plants four adjectives within the space of seven words. He finishes with a sentence that carries the normally vague and weak verb *go*.

> Travelling is a fool's paradise. Our first journeys discover to us the indifference of places. At home I dream that at Naples, at Rome, I can be intoxicated with beauty and lose my sadness. I pack my trunk, embrace my friends, embark on the sea and at last wake up in Naples, and there beside me is the stern fact, the sad self, unrelenting, identical, that I fled from. I seek the Vatican and the palaces. I affect to be intoxicated with sights and suggestions, but I am not intoxicated. My giant goes with me wherever I go.

The power of this passage comes from its ideas as well as from its expression. Emerson is true to his thoughts and feelings, and therefore his words carry surprise. The words that precede or follow ordinarily weak verbs like *to be* or *goes* are full of meaning—*intoxicated, giant, fool's paradise.*

Sharpening writing is not as simple and easy a matter as this chapter suggests. Many of the changes dictated here are debatable, and only a person considering the total context of a word or phrase can see whether or not it should be retained. Find ways of probing your sentences so that you see alternative ways of stating them. *Is, there,* and *it* frequently are wasted and breed other unnecessary words. But they're good words in their place. You'll find writers as brilliant as Bernard Shaw using *it is* when the words are not absolutely necessary, as in the quotation at the head of this chapter:

> And it is the final 2 per cent that makes the difference between excellence and mediocrity.

This *it* doesn't ache much. It could be eliminated and the sentence written

> And the final 2 per cent makes the difference between excellence and mediocrity.

but the words *it is* in this passage act as emphasizers. They slow down the reader and make sure he gives attention to *2 per cent.*

The moral of this chapter is not to do away with all uses of the cited words, but to learn where to look for possible weak spots in your sentences. I originally wrote the first sentence of the paragraph above in this way:

> Sharpening writing is not as simple and easy a matter as this chapter makes it appear.

Spotting the *it* in the sentence, and thinking about removing it, I saw that I could drop three words, *makes, it,* and *appear,* and substitute only the word *suggests.*

REVISING NINE: Look over two of your past free writings and attempt to eliminate from them weak passive verbs, empty verbs like *make* and *have,* the overuse of adjectives, and the unnecessary use of intensifying words like *tremendously* and *great big.*

When the college professor is asked to write an article for a learned journal, he too often shifts into Engfish and says:

> Unquestionably the textbook has played a very important role in the development of American schools—and I believe it will continue to play an important role.

You may have the urge here to say, "So have spitballs." The professor goes on:

> The need for textbooks has been established through many experiments. It is not necessary to consider these experiments but, in general, they have shown that when instruction without textbooks has been tried by schools, the virtually unanimous result has been to go back to the use of textbooks. I believe, too, that there is considerable evidence to indicate that the textbook has been, and is, a major factor in guiding teachers' instruction and in determining the curriculum. And I don't think that either role for the textbook is necessarily bad.

The professor begins his statement with the weasel word *unquestionably*. The very point he's going to try to make in the paragraph he calls unquestionable before he starts. From then on he throws (*lobs* would be a better word; nothing has force in this paragraph) a bunch of dull generalizations in his reader's face. Something has played a *role* in the *development* of something. How many times have you heard that vague line? What role? An *important* role. What does that mean? What kind and rate of development? How did the schools develop as a result of the textbook? What a mishmash of educational language: "need established . . . many experiments . . . virtually unanimous result . . . considerable evidence . . . major factor." These are Weasel Words. They don't say anything for sure yet they keep insisting they are certain and unquestionable. The professor talks about impressive experiments but never mentions one. He doesn't think it's "necessary to consider these experiments" yet he employs them as the only evidence for his argument. Note his last sentence:

> And I don't think that either role for the textbook is necessarily bad.

That's the only possibly exciting sentence in the paragraph. Someone has apparently said that using a textbook to guide teachers' instruction or determine the curriculum is bad. Who said that? Why? The writer needs to say, but he isn't fixing to say anything for sure. He won't give the reader anything he can examine and be sure about. He's just talking through his weasel nose.

Every writer talks weaselry at times. This language is hard to see because it's so common.

> It was *sort of* a flop.
> He was *kind of* a hero to me.

That, *incidentally*, is four fouls.

Going through the weeds there was *almost* like walking in a swamp.

His father, *by the way*, is a crook.

> *"I've got a sort of idea but I don't suppose it's a very good one."*
> Winnie the Pooh (A. A. MILNE)

In hurried conversation such weaselries should be forgiven, but not in writing, where the author has a chance to revise and tighten. The weakness of *sort of* and *kind of* is that they don't tell the reader whether the writer really thought "it" was a "flop" or "he" was a "hero." If the writer wanted to communicate that the play was not completely a flop but a failure only in the first act, he should have said so. If he wanted to say that "he" was a hero in one way but not in another, he should have told in what way. Otherwise, he should have simply said: "It was a flop" and "He was a hero to me." Usually *sort of* and *kind of* take the punch out of the words they precede. They lessen rather than increase meaning. If you scatter them throughout your writing, your reader will eventually suspect you don't mean anything you say. Note these weasel words:

The *final* conclusions of the workshop.

There is a *limited amount* of seating space.

Throwing mud in her face wasn't *too* nice.

Falling down the stairs isn't *exactly* fun.

But being in that wreck was an *especially* devastating experience.

Mary was a *remarkably* lovely queen.

Other words frequently used in weasel fashion are *relative, particular,* and *various.*

This is a *relatively* minor matter and need not concern us long here.

If the reader doesn't know relative to what, he can't extract much meaning from *relatively.*

This is a *particularly* fine example of social organization.

Fine already tells the reader the example is above ordinary. *Particularly* steals attention from *fine.*

> In his travels around the world, the captain has encoun-
> tered many diseases in *various* countries and *various* envi-
> ronments.

This is straight cornmeal mush. Most readers would like it better
fried crisp and served with hot syrup. If the writer wants to make his
point with power, he should say "about two thousand diseases in
fifty-six countries and in environments ranging from ice floes to
tropical rain forests."

Most academic writing is loaded with weasel words and phrases;
for scholars are taught to be cautious, to qualify. But there are
times to be cautious and times to be bold. Watch this pedantic phrase
weasel its ways into an otherwise straightforward sentence:

> Last week the world was contained in a blue plastic egg
> filled with jelly beans and a set of rabbit teeth—*at least it
> was* for five-year-old Jack.

The author doesn't really mean to hint that anyone else's world
beside Jack's was filled with that bunch of jelly beans and set of
rabbit teeth, but she heard a weasel squeal somewhere and echoes
it in her sentence.

As I write this chapter warning others of weaseling, I remember
that when I was writing another text, an editor pointed out that
almost always when I used the words *in fact*, I followed them with
an unsupported personal opinion. Frequently writers try to make
up for weak opinions by introducing them with one of the following
expressions:

indeed	surely	honestly
obviously	certainly	frankly
of course	needless to say	sincerely

The most dishonest man I ever knew constantly prefaced his remarks
with the expression, "I would be less than candid if I did not say—."

Writers are often dishonest with themselves: they speak apolo-
getically, defensively, pompously, or condescendingly when they do
not feel apologetic, defensive, pompous, or condescending. A teacher
who once submitted a poem to an editor of a magazine, hoping for
publication, referred to her manuscript in her covering letter as "This
bit of fluff, modeled after 'The Children's Hour.' " Her comment
sounds like the introductory remarks many persons make before they
speak in a group meeting: "Now I don't claim to be an expert in this
subject and what I have to say probably isn't worth much . . ." Then

they make a fifteen-minute speech. One is tempted to say to the teacher: "If you think your manuscript is fluff, don't send it to the magazine"; and to the apologetic speaker: "If you don't think you're qualified to speak, don't speak. Or if you are qualified, don't waste our time telling us you aren't."

"What do you know about this business?" the King said to Alice.

"Nothing," said Alice.

"Nothing whatever?" persisted the King.

"Nothing whatever," said Alice.

"That's very important," the King said, turning to the jury. They were just beginning to write this down on their slates, when the White Rabbit interrupted: "Unimportant, your Majesty means, of course," he said, in a very respectful tone, but frowning and making faces at him, as he spoke.

"Unimportant, of course, I meant," the King hastily said, and went on to himself in an undertone, "important—unimportant — unimportant — important —" as if he were trying which word sounded best.

Some of the jury wrote it down "important," and some "unimportant." Alice could see this, as she was near enough to look over their slates; "but it doesn't matter a bit," she thought to herself.

LEWIS CARROLL

. . . childhood word-play, adolescent slang and double-talk, often derivative, but natural and exciting. In general the schools have made it their business to kill this kind of playful interest, and they have had the backing of society in this effort . . . most professionals with highly developed skills are fond of playing with those skills.

W. NELSON FRANCIS

chapter 19 words speaking to words

WORD PLAY

EVERYTHING is peaches and cream. Like something the cat dragged in. Like hunting for a needle in a haystack. Things have gone all to pot. Great oaks from little acorns grow, and a stitch in time saves nine.

A college student looking at a list like that wrote: "Everything is clichés and Pream." That's word play. *Pream* rhymes with cream, *clichés* reminds one of the sound of *peaches*. Pream is a powdered substitute for cream. Another student said he felt like someone who had dragged in the cat. And a number played with the word *pot*.

A cliché is a much-used expression. At what point it becomes overused and offensive is difficult to say, for some listeners expect more freshness than others. A case can be made for clichés. Their familiarity reassures and soothes, say their defenders. Surely one cannot rid all his conversation of them. Proverbial sayings are also old and yet cherished all over the world. In the United States we say,

He who laughs last laughs best.

In Liberia people say,

You are leaning on a dry bamboo.

Mosquito says: If you want a man to understand you, speak in
his ears.

We generally take the drowning child out of the water before
slapping it.

You'll enjoy reading Liberian proverbs more than American ones
because they're new to you.

Naturally, conversational clichés are easier to take than written
clichés, for they are gone on the wind; but people who suffuse their talk
with them misuse their friends.

WRITING TWENTY-TWO: Think of other dull word combinations
like *grave responsibility, definite contrast, grim tragedy, bitter truth.*
Play with them until you come up with ten new combinations or twists
that you think work.

Doing that, one student wrote; "It's both a pressure and a privilege
to be here." Another wrote: "Home is where the garbage is," and
"Love Is a Many-Splintered Thing," and "I want a girl just like the
girl that turned down dear old Dad."

The secret of productive word play is simple: Let yourself go. All
great persons—artists, scientists, engineers, architects, cooks, designers
—fool around. If their play produces something usable, they use it.
Maybe a new kind of soup. If not, they feel no pain or guilt. You
can't feel guilty about play and become a creative person. In this game
you must be loose with language. Sinful. Show no respect for the tried
and blue. Expect a lot of misfires, like bad firecrackers. The girl who
wrote the story about the bus driver delivering schoolchildren (printed in Chapter 8) ended with a masterful play on the saying that man
has feet of clay, meaning he is subject to error and weakness.

I watched the bus drive away on wheels of clay.

Word players aren't so much playing chess as just playing around.
They may decide to put the play to practical use, although they don't
need to. The more you play with words, the more often you'll find
playful statements crossing over into serious expression. E. E. Cummings,

an American poet, constantly sawed up his words and tacked pieces on them. He looked at the word *mankind* and decided to write it *manunkind*. Then he used that new word in the first line of a bitter poem about the evils man has committed in the name of progress. It begins:

> pity this busy monster,manunkind

This was not simply a trick by Mr. Cummings. For years he had written against war and man's cruelty to man.

Play with titles of articles or books, with titles for your own writings. First study newspaper and magazine article titles. Note the puns, the newly created words. Here are some examples:

(a) *How to Cheat on Personality Tests*, by William H. Whyte, Jr.
(b) *A Problem of Design: How to Kill People*, by George Nelson
(c) *Arms and the Boy*, by Wilfred Owen

"Arms and the Boy," a title of a poem, plays on the first line of Virgil's *Aeneid*, which begins: "Arms and the man I sing . . ." The poet Wilfred Owen is suggesting that the reader should remember that boys rather than men are often killed in war.

(d) *The Beast in Me and Other Animals*, by James Thurber
(e) *Bed of Neuroses*, by Wolcott Gibbs
(f) *Golf Is a Four Letter Word*, by Richard Armour

The word play in all these titles is pointed. It makes a reader think twice and see significance. When Sidney Cox, a writing teacher at Dartmouth College, published a book of reflections and musings about writing—not a program of specifics for learning to write—he called it *Indirections: for Those Who Want to Write*. He was playing on the word *Directions*.

> . . . the light of magic suggestiveness
> may be brought to play for an evanescent
> instant over the commonplace surface of
> words: of the old, old words, worn thin,
> defaced by ages of careless usage.
>
> JOSEPH CONRAD

Try to write the truth in your language and at the same time let your words speak to each other. One day a student playing with words wrote:

> November, and the cornfields are brown and broken and
> they rattle in the freshening wind. Meanwhile across the
> cornflakes heavy voices grumble the usual. A word of mean-
> ing drowns in a sea of crunch.

When he handed this paragraph to a teacher, he appended this
comment:

> I was just playing with words and sounds and pictures.
> Somehow it reminds me of T. S. Eliot's coffee spoons [in
> "The Love Song of J. Alfred Prufrock"]. Know what? I'll
> bet if the thing were printed, someone would analyze it.

Here the writer is dishonest. The passage is more than meaningless
sounds and pictures. In his play he must have had in mind tension
between the fresh wind in the cornfields and the stale breakfast
table conversation. It's a delightful and valid statement which makes
its point in a sidelong manner. If incorporated into a larger context,
it might become the most powerful paragraph of a paper. What a
writer says unconsciously may carry more meaning than what he plans
meticulously.

WRITING TWENTY-THREE: Try playing with words as you do
a free writing. After Eric and his grandmother had discussed a
number of extinct prehistoric animals, Eric asked, "Can those dino-
saurs ever get unstinct?" A girl watching a class fall silent when a tape
recorder was brought into the room said, "Most people turn off when
the tape recorder turns on." Start writing about something and consider words that oppose it *in meaning.* And in *form,* as Eric did. When
you think of writing that someone's remark "left little room for doubt,"
you might say, "left only a small closet for doubt." Or to reverse the
idea—"left a large attic for doubt." Write for fifteen minutes. Try to
speak a truth that counts for you, however large or small. You don't
need to force the play. The best play occurs when the player gets outside himself and becomes hooked by the game. While he is trying to
beat out a bunt he doesn't say to himself, "I will enjoy the game." He
legs it to first as fast as he can.

Note how the words in the following paragraph speak to each other:

> On Sundays the machine usually behaves better in accept-
> ing coins. Several times it has fooled me with its ready-to-
> serve manner. I walk down the eight flights from third
> floor, put in my change, push the Coke button and am

answered by the delightful sound of a falling cup and a
nice long rebellious belch from the machine: I get 10¢
worth of Coke cup and air.

WRITING TWENTY-FOUR: There are kind, constructive, and
happy families who never engage in word play. I was brought up by a
mother who never played with language. Not until I was thirty did
I realize word play was easy. I thought it an esoteric game like *jai alai.*

Often the best writers allow their words to become playful. They
relax and watch the words go down on paper, waiting for opportunities,
but not pressing. The young woman who wrote the following paper
hammered at *beans,* repeating the word again and again. Note how
several of her words speak to each other: *green and fresh . . . shriveled
up and dead; white fluff . . . black fluff; fat . . . skinny.* She's restrained
in the use of this technique; it becomes not a silly forced game but a
graceful, natural method of expression

BEANS

I'm sitting in my room in the middle of the night looking at
green beans. Beans surround me. Beans from the ceiling,
beans from the book cases, beans dangling from dresser across
to the desk. We canned forty quarts of beans and ate fresh
beans for weeks, and the beans keep coming. I have a funny
feeling I don't even like canned beans. Maybe home canned
beans are better than store canned beans.

The beans in my room aren't canned. They're dried. I've
heard about "leather britches dried beans" the way the
settlers used to preserve them before Kerr and Ball and
freezers were around. I threaded the beans on kite string and
hung them around the room to dry.

As I was threading the beans I can remember thinking
how nice it would be all winter to be reminded of the boun-
tiful summer and the fresh taste of squeaky green beans. I
could picture it—there would be days of blizzards, we'd be
snowed in, stuck for weeks, and there'd be a huge kettle of
soup always warm and yummy with lots of beans in it.

But now I don't know. Those thoughts were nice when
the beans were green and fresh and I was just threading
them. Now I'm sitting in my room looking at them. They
are shriveled up and dead. They're brown and crunch. They

have white fluff growing on them in clusters. Some of them
have black fluff. I can't get excited about a blizzard in the
winter any more. I can't get excited about being snowed in
for weeks. A pot of beanless soup sounds pretty good right
now.

I used to think I was born at least two hundred years too
late and that I missed my spot in time. I've always had a lot
of pioneer spirit, never been afraid to improvise or do things
without help. I like the feeling of having food stored in the
basement and kitchen—enough so that it wouldn't matter if
we were stuck all winter, we'd still eat hearty on food we
preserved ourselves. It's a comfy secure feeling, like everything is in order, we've done a lot of work to get things
ready for winter, and now we can face the harsh season.
As winter approached the settlers must have felt that way
too. I wonder if their beans looked as awful as mine. No
wonder you never hear about a fat settler. You could get
pretty skinny looking at my beans.

All that work, threading them. I can't get over it. I think
I'll pick out some of the least moldy ones and try them.
Maybe they're not as bad as they look. Maybe water has a
magical healing effect on them. I just thought of a huge pot
of soup again.

Write freely for at least twenty minutes on a subject that has caught
you lately. Listen to the words making their sounds and thoughts. Then
let it happen. Some of your next words will begin speaking to those
you've already put down.

Wait a day and study what you wrote. Just because some of your
words speak to each other doesn't mean your paper can't be improved.
In the writing above, the noun *beans* can stand frequent repetition but
forms of the word *look* may be developing a little white fluff on them.

METAPHOR

Metaphor, the statement of one thing in terms of another, is related
to word play. A student writes in her journal:

After having three dates during the weekend, one of my
roommates spent several hours baking cookies for her Army
boy friend. A girl from down the hall came in and said,
"Those cookies are half Bisquick and half guilt."

This habit of seeing likeness between things apparently different is one we all command at times. A fifth-grade child says:

A tree in spring is a double-barreled shotgun exploding.

As a writer you need not waste time trying to decide whether or not what you're writing is a metaphor, simile, or fabulous reality. The point is whether or not you're getting your words to speak to each other. For example, the following sign,

HILLTOP MARATHON
ROAD AND WRECKER SERVICE
Located on E. Main Hill
DON DARLING AND JOHN LOVETT
OWNERS

contains words that speak to each other and create what might be called a fabulous reality, but a skillful writer might make them work for larger purposes, in an extended context. The professional writer stores material like that in his mind or records it in his journal, then pulls it out when the occasion is ripe. The sign above shows Darling and Lovett are engaged in helping persons in trouble. They ask money for the services. A writer who was talking about persons who appear kindly but act only to make money might say they remind him of a sign he once saw . . .

Strangely, a writer skillful with metaphors seldom commands them to appear. He collects visual and auditory impressions and waits for them to form into metaphors while he's writing. He draws them from his close knowledge, intimate experience. He doesn't calculate or manufacture them. Watch this metaphor rise out of the materials:

> Formica-topped desks never scratch. I can't bur or mar them. Number 248 cubicle that I have been assigned holds compact, practical drawers and desk firmly bolted to a wall, unmoveable, without handles. I never knew how much handles on a drawer meant to me until I was deprived of them. I actually thought at first that I like formica tops. But my fingers don't like the formica. It's not grooved and soft like a battered old oak desk.
>
> Nothing in my room cares about me.

This is the metaphorical habit—to see likenesses and differences in unexpected but valid comparisons. College students frequently speak
this way when they don't think they need to come up with Engfish.
During a campus controversy over the desirability of removing credit
for physical education courses or dropping them altogether, a freshman
wrote:

> Supporters of our PE program at Western should be
> hung in a locker.

A student wrote in her journal:

> What's my mind doing now? Nothing of importance. It
> feels like I've got a bathing cap on one size too small.

Another woman wrote:

> We went to the basketball game tonight. That's kind of a
> funny sport that goes back and forth fast across the court
> like one of those balls connected by a rubber band to a
> paddle.

WRITING TWENTY-FIVE: Try writing two papers, each of twenty
minutes or more in which you extend a metaphor so it affects the whole
writing. Here's an example:

> In small towns everything's just scattered around, like
> Augusta. There's a car without an engine or wheels rusting
> in a driveway. A dried-up antique gas pump stands on the
> sidewalk of the main street without a gas station around
> it. An abandoned building next to the restaurant is long
> and flat and the broken windows that ring the structure
> stare into one huge empty room. Impossible to figure out
> what it ever housed. I feel like I should pick things up in
> Augusta and straighten them out like I do in my living
> room, put the gas pump and car away in the junk drawer
> and sweep the old building under a rug.
>   Order is easier to ignore.

There are dangers also in metaphors. When you forget the dead
and hidden ones in the language, you may compose foolish sentences.
For example:

> Changing the course of a fast, deep river would normally
> be a lost cause, but this is one cause the North High family
> cannot afford to lose hold of.

This is a metaphor used by a student editor to ask others to help him reform the school newspaper. In it, he forgets what he's saying and asks the readers to keep hold of a river. He should remember that water is impossible to grasp.

Here's an excerpt from a paint company's directions for using artists' colors:

> Where very thin glazes are desired, Liquitex colors mixed with the Medium may be quickly and lightly rubbed over the surface with fingers and thumb in the manner of oil glazes. On the other hand, unwanted color or glaze may be wiped off.

The writer committed a blooper in using the phrase "On the other hand." He forgot its dead metaphor. Just before that he's talking about literal fingers and thumb. Like a thousand other phrases in everyday language, "on the other hand" was once a brilliant metaphor. Now people use it so unconsciously they need to be jogged with the vaudeville gag: "On the other hand—she had a wart."

WRITING TWENTY-SIX: Write two 10- to 20-minute free writings in which you talk of things you love. Let yourself describe them in metaphor and simile that come from your deepest knowledge about objects or processes or occupations. Don't be satisfied with simple, brief metaphors: "His face was like a sunny day." Develop a metaphor, let its parts speak to each other and create new and continuing comparisons, as this beginning writer did:

> **When I think of barnacles I laugh because if they were attached to my bottom I'd feel important—like the Queen Mary. Maybe I ought to think like this when I take a bath and slide across the porcelain ocean at the end of a narrow day.**

> *Alice didn't dare to argue the point, but went on: "And I thought I'd try and find my way to the top of that hill—"*
>
> *"When you say 'hill,'" the Queen interrupted, "I could show you hills in comparison with which you'd call that a valley."*
>
> *"No, I shouldn't," said Alice, surprised into contradicting her at last: "a hill can't be a valley, you know. That would be nonsense—"*

> *The Red Queen shook her head. "You*
> *may call it 'nonsense,' if you like," she*
> *said, "but I've heard nonsense compared*
> *with which that would be as sensible as*
> *a dictionary!"*
>
> LEWIS CARROLL

EXPOSING THE ROOTS OF WORDS

Once you've caught the habit of making words speak to each
other, you'll find yourself examining what each word says by itself,
who its parents were, and what it says when its original meanings are
reactivated. Then your language won't be soggy but fresh and crackling. In *Walden* Henry Thoreau began writing a sentence,

> We meet at meals three times a day, and give each other a
> new taste

and he remembered the metaphor in the word *taste*. Because he didn't
allow the word to become abstract in his mind, he was able to finish
the sentence in this way:

> of that old musty cheese that we are.

and on another page he said:

> If you have built castles in the air, your work need not be
> lost; that is where they should be. Now put the foundations
> under them.

William Hazlitt said:

> Miracles never cease, to be sure; but they are not to be had
> wholesale, or *to order*.

And so beginning writers can do when they allow themselves to think
about what their words are saying. In an education book a student
saw the question

> What is a good English teacher?

and she wrote underneath it:

> Who is a good English teacher?

With that little move she showed up the pedant who thinks he can
create good teachers by listing their qualities or making up a job
description. Steve Tod recorded what a mother said to her three-year-

old, "Mary Jane, get out of your Coke!" and showed he recognized that the verb was meant literally there.

To *belittle* is a word now almost always used figuratively. It takes on new power in this passage where the writer thought about its literal meaning and utilized it.

> I am an amateur mechanic I guess. I can fix the car or truck as a rule when something goes wrong. I put a whole new ignition system in the truck and two thermostats and a water pump—it was hot that day—and I change plugs, points, and oil, and I put a fuel pump on the old Studebaker and a carburetor, and I change tires and do body work and can start a car without pushing it or using jumpers by jacking it up in back, spinning the rear wheels, and popping the clutch in third gear. I guess I'm kind of a mechanic. I even completely rebuilt my cycle. It's still not all together yet, but I'll be out belittling hills with it by spring.

To put new meaning into old words or restore meaning now dead is to do a favor to your reader who would prefer going to sleep in a bed than in your writing. In this little unfinished journal entry a writer has started to consider seriously the word *woman*.

> Even my own mother doesn't know quite what woman is. Too often she tries to pass herself off as lady instead. Though—there are real ladies I admire. I want to be able to see the lady and the woman incorporated into one vital human being.

Such thinking about the meaning of words is not trivial. Customarily reformers and innovators and system builders breathe life into dead words. In 1947 the philosopher-psychologist Erich Fromm began to construct a new philosophy of the personality. He wrote:

> Responsibility and response have the same root, *respondere* = "to answer"; to be responsible means to be ready to respond.

and also:

> Respect is not fear and awe; it denotes, in accordance with the root of the word (*respicere* = to look at), the ability to see a person as he is, to be aware of his individuality and uniqueness. To respect a person is not possible without knowing him . . .

Sometimes a writer spins out a whole story without realizing that it is building up layer by layer a new or supercharged meaning for an old word. In the following story, a college senior uses five good-sized paragraphs to build her ironic meanings for the common terms *death* and *life*. Stories of the death of relatives are frequently sentimental, carrying more emotion than the action warrants, or insisting on a stereotyped response that doesn't fit the particular experience. Not so with this account.

> She greeted me when I bent over. I thought she said, "My girl," but I wasn't sure. Her speech was almost unintelligible. She was half sitting, half lying in a huge bed and the fluorescent lighting that flooded the ward and turned the sheets and curtains a glowing, blazing white made her face an ugly pinkish yellow and robbed it all of the contouring shadows that might have humanized it. Her eyes were shut, her jaws slack, her whole face vacant and over-relaxed. Her wrists were tied to the sides of the bed. And IV needles had been pushed into her arm and secured by a piece of now blood-spotted gauze. The green tubes of the suction machine were held in her nostrils by a metal clip, and a criss-cross of adhesive tape.
>
> Suddenly, an animal spasm went through her body. She half sat up. Her frame jerked and twisted. Her arms strained to reach and tear away the tubes. The identification band on her wrists—a blue plastic ring like a child's dime-store bracelet—shook up and down on her thin wrist. Her head went back, her mouth opened wide, and she gasped for air, her throat throbbing. I waited for her eyes to open —I waited for many minutes until I understood that she would never look at me again. Then I walked out . . .
>
> I stood outside waiting for one of my elders to say, "Take these tubes out, and leave her alone." I thought "They'll never get their hands on me. I may have to walk into the woods to die in peace, but they'll never make my death an endurance contest." We waited an hour and then two. There was no place to sit down and nothing to do. Finally Aunt Millie, who was a registered nurse, and had begun to take over the situation said, "Why don't you folks go down to the lounge? I'll stay here and take care of her."
>
> It was a reasonable suggestion only we had no place, no function outside her room. We drifted down to the lounge

and sat with our coats thrown over the backs of our chairs and our eyes turned inwards. I flipped through a pile of magazines, trying to distract myself with a picture essay on Japanese women, menu suggestions in a Campbell's soup ad, and the other slick, glossy things one finds in *Life*.

Aunt Millie came up to the lounge around twelve o'clock and said, "I'll stay, if you'd like to go home now. I'll call." Aunt Millie hadn't been to see Grandma in a couple of years. We picked up our coats and shuffled out.

The house was cold when we got home. I went right upstairs and got into bed. It didn't seem like I'd lain there long before I heard the telephone ring. I went downstairs late the next morning and sat on the davenport. Mom came in and said, "Grandma died about two o'clock last night, Sarah." I looked up and said, "Thanks, Mom," but didn't feel anything. I didn't care. That death was only a biological fact, as pointless and trivial as the eight horrible hours of vegetative life they'd forced on her.

In that hard story that tamps down so much feeling, the author played seriously with the words *death* and *life*. Because she had the habit of putting down names of things making up her experience, she found herself writing the name of a magazine that also played upon her subject, and she used that name with double meaning. Playing with words may be a funny or solemn act. Either way the words can speak to each other and set up a dialogue that the reader can enjoy and learn from —a second communication beyond the direct one between writer and reader.

irony. 2 a: *the use of words to express something other than and esp. the opposite of the literal meaning.*

Webster's Seventh New
Collegiate Dictionary

chapter 20
writing
indirectly

YOU DON'T HAVE to write in a straight line that runs right at your reader. You can shoot words off on a diagonal, a little off target, and expect the reader to see where the bull's-eye really is. Making a point indirectly gives it surprise.

You may turn upside down what you say. Exaggerate. You may say exactly the opposite of what you mean. Take up a serious subject lightly or a trivial subject heavily. A funeral is no place for jokes, but a writer can write humorously about funerals. Evelyn Waugh did and called his novel *The Loved One,* a story about an ostentatious burying park in California. Jonathan Swift wrote ironically about poverty and called his essay "A Modest Proposal for preventing the Children of Poor People from being a Burden to their Parents or the Country" (by roasting them as food for the rich).

Here are some of the ways a writer speaks indirectly:

(a) *A writer may play dumb,* pretend to be holding one opinion while tipping off the reader to his true, and often opposite, opinion.

In chapter seventeen of *Huckleberry Finn,* Mark Twain, talking through Huck, speaks so indirectly, yet with such a straight face, that many readers don't see what he's saying in this description of the Grangerford house and family:

> It was a mighty nice family, and a mighty nice house, too. I hadn't seen no house out in the country before that was so nice and had so much style. It didn't have an iron latch on

the front door, nor a wooden one with a buckskin string, but a brass knob to turn, the same as houses in a town. There warn't no bed in the parlor, not a sign of a bed; but heaps of parlors in towns has beds in them. There was a big fireplace that was bricked on the bottom, and the bricks was kept clean and red by pouring water on them and scrubbing them with another brick; sometimes they washed them over with red water-paint that they call Spanish-brown, same as they do in town. They had big brass dog-irons that could hold up a saw-log. There was a clock on the middle of the mantel-piece, with a picture of a town painted on the bottom half of the glass front, and a round place in the middle of it for the sun, and you could see the pendulum swing behind it. It was beautiful to hear that clock tick; and sometimes when one of these peddlers had been along and scoured her up and got her in good shape, she would start in and strike a hundred and fifty before she got tuckered out. They wouldn't took any money for her.

Well, there was a big outlandish parrot on each side of the clock, made out of something like chalk, and painted up gaudy. By one of the parrots was a cat made of crockery, and a crockery dog by the other; and when you pressed down on them they squeaked, but didn't open their mouths nor look different nor interested. They squeaked through underneath. There was a couple of big wild-turkey-wing fans spread out behind those things. On a table in the middle of the room was a kind of a lovely crockery basket that had apples and oranges and peaches and grapes piled up in it which was much redder and yellower and prettier than real ones is, but they warn't real because you could see where pieces had got chipped off and showed the white chalk or whatever it was, underneath.

This table had a cover made out of beautiful oil-cloth, with a red and blue spread-eagle painted on it, and a painted border all around. It come all the way from Philadelphia, they said. There was some books too, piled up perfectly exact, on each corner of the table. One was a big family Bible, full of pictures. One was "Pilgrim's Progress," about a man that left his family it didn't say why. I read considerable in it now and then. The statements was interesting, but tough. Another was "Friendship's Offering," full of beautiful stuff and poetry; but I didn't read the poetry.

Another was Henry Clay's Speeches, and another was Dr. Gunn's Family Medicine, which told you all about what to do if a body was sick or dead. There was a Hymn Book, and a lot of other books. And there was nice split-bottom chairs, and perfectly sound, too—not bagged down in the middle and busted, like an old basket.

They had pictures hung on the walls—mainly Washingtons and Lafayettes, and battles, and Highland Mary, and one called "Signing the Declaration." There was some that they called crayons, which one of the daughters which was dead made her own self when she was only fifteen years old. They was different from many pictures I ever see before; blacker, mostly, than is common. One was a woman in a slim black dress, belted small under the arm-pits, with bulges like a cabbage in the middle of the sleeves, and a large black scoop-shovel bonnet with a black veil, and white slim ankles crossed about with black tape, and very wee black slippers, like a chisel, and she was leaning pensive on a tombstone on her right elbow, under a weeping willow, and her other hand hanging down her side holding a white handkerchief and a reticule, and underneath the picture it said "Shall I Never See Thee More Alas." Another one was a young lady with her hair all combed up straight to the top of her head, and knotted there in front of a comb like a chair-back, and she was crying into a handkerchief and had a dead bird laying on its back in her other hand with its heels up, and underneath the picture it said "I Shall Never Hear Thy Sweet Chirrup More Alas." There was one where a young lady was at a window looking up at the moon, and tears running down her cheeks; and she had an open letter in one hand with black sealing-wax showing on one edge of it, and she was mashing a locket with a chain to it against her mouth, and underneath the picture it said "And Art Thou Gone Yes Thou Art Gone Alas." These was all nice pictures, I reckon, but I didn't somehow seem to take to them, because if ever I was down a little, they always give me the fan-tods. Everybody was sorry she died, because she had laid out a lot more of these pictures to do, and a body could see by what she had done what they had lost. But I reckoned, that with her disposition, she was having a better time in the graveyard. She was at work on what they said was her greatest picture when she took sick, and every day and every night it was her prayer to be allowed to live till she got it done, but she never got the chance. It was a picture of a young woman in a long white gown, standing on the rail of a bridge all ready to jump off, with her hair all down her back, and looking up to the moon, with the tears running down her face, and she had two arms folded across her breast, and two arms stretched out in front, and two more reaching up towards the moon—and the idea was, to see which pair would look best and then scratch out all the other arms; but, as I was saying, she died before she got her mind made up, and now they kept this picture over the head of the bed in her room, and every time her birthday come they hung flowers on it. Other times it was hid with a little curtain. The young woman in the picture had a kind of a nice sweet face, but there was so many arms it made her look too spidery, seemed to me.

This young girl kept a scrap-book when she was alive, and used to paste obituaries and accidents and cases of patient suffering in it out of the *Presbyterian Observer*, and write poetry after them out of her own head. It was very good poetry. This is what she wrote about a boy by the name of Stephen Dowling Bots that fell down a well and was drownded:

ODE TO STEPHEN DOWLING BOTS, DEC'D.

And did young Stephen sicken,
   And did young Stephen die?
And did the sad hearts thicken,
   And did the mourners cry?

No; such was not the fate of
   Young Stephen Dowling Bots;
Though sad hearts round him thickened,
   'Twas not from sickness' shots.

No whooping-cough did rack his frame,
   Nor measles drear, with spots;
Not these impaired the sacred name
   Of Stephen Dowling Bots.

Despised love struck not with woe
   That head of curly knots,
Nor stomach troubles laid him low,
   Young Stephen Dowling Bots.

O no. Then list with tearful eye,
  Whilst I his fate do tell.
His soul did from this cold world fly,
  By falling down a well.

They got him out and emptied him;
  Alas it was too late;
His spirit was gone for to sport aloft
  In the realms of the good and great.

If Emmeline Grangerford could make poetry like that before she was fourteen, there ain't no telling what she could
a done by-and-by. Buck said she could rattle off poetry like
nothing. She didn't ever have to stop to think. He said she
would slap down a line, and if she couldn't find anything to
rhyme with it she would just scratch it out and slap down
another one, and go ahead. She warn't particular, she could
write about anything you choose to give her to write about,
just so it was sadful. Every time a man died, or a woman
died, or a child died, she would be on hand with her
"tribute" before he was cold. She called them tributes.
The neighbors said it was the doctor first, then Emmeline,
then the undertaker—the undertaker never got in ahead of
Emmeline but once, and then she hung fire on a rhyme for
the dead person's name, which was Whistler. She warn't ever
the same, after that; she never complained, but she kind of
pined away and did not live long.

What you have read is a mild satire of the décor of a house and
a strong satire of a sentimental little girl who wrote bad poetry. Obviously Huck thinks the house beautiful, but Twain suggests with
small cues that he doesn't. He might admire artificial fruit, but when
he has Huck mention "where pieces had got chipped off and showed
the white chalk or whatever it was," you should begin to suspect his
intentions in this writing. Think of the whole picture: the mantel
a garish display of painted scene; crockery birds, dog, cat; and turkey
wings. On the table an oil-cloth spread displaying a spread eagle—
more wings. The books: standard family pieces, revealing no individuality of mind in their choice, all perfectly piled as if never used.
The pictures on the wall patriotic and sentimental. The room is as
gaudy as a souvenir shop at Niagara Falls, and Twain wants the
reader to know this at the same time he wants him to see that Huck
Finn is completely inexperienced in judging such matters. The room
goes perfectly with Emmeline Grangerford's poetry, which Twain
hits more directly in hard satire.

Twain's indirectness enables him to make three points at once. He scores the Grangerfords' lack of cultural independence, shows his hero limited in experience, and slyly criticizes the American middle-class for its use of pseudo art objects in its homes.

(b) *A writer may directly say she doesn't understand, when she does,* as this high school student did in a poem:

> I wonder if the mail has come
>   (Not that I really care.)
> Our quarrel was really very dumb.
> I wonder if the mail has come!
>   (I shouldn't have said that 'bout her hair.)
> Should I have written? Do I dare?
> I wonder if the mail has come.
>   (Not that I really care.)
>
>   KATHY CURRIER

(c) *A writer may take on another character's views,* perhaps her own when she was young, and pretend she doesn't know any more now than she did then, as did this girl in an account of her childhood:

TOMATOES

I was four when I had my first encounter with a tomato. We lived in Santa Barbara in a gray house separated from our neighbor by a garden of green and black stripes. The old man, Mr. Swift, fussed in his garden each dewy morning and worried his tomato plants into growing green and tall.

One early summer morning I was playing in the outskirts of the garden and happened to notice ladybugs crawling on Mr. Swift's prize plants. I didn't want them chewing up the fruits of my dear neighbor's labor so I decided to help him. I knew he would thank me when he found out I had gotten rid of the speckled pests for him. The only trouble was I was afraid to touch the bugs, so I had to break off each leaf that had an orange dot on it. I had gone through six rows when my mother called to me through the screened window that lunch was ready. Mr. Swift never knew that I tried to help him because I wasn't able to finish my job. A mysterious telephone call during lunch upset my mother and she spanked me right in the middle of a fried egg sandwich and wouldn't let me go outdoors the rest of the day.

It's a wonder that poor Mr. Swift's garden ever grew. One evening after supper my mother sent me out in the yard to break up a tea party that had been going all afternoon. Three of my dolls lay asleep on the ground around the orange crate tea table, and I feared they would be sick because it had turned very cold. I bundled them in my wagon and was pulling them to the back door when I noticed the garden.

Someone had played a mean trick on poor old Mr. Swift. Each of his tomato plants was hidden under a sawed-off milk carton. I knew they couldn't breathe inside there and would die if I didn't uncover them. It didn't take as long as getting rid of the bugs because I could just kick over each box with my foot. It was dark when I finished and got my dolls in the house. My mother scolded me for tracking in mud; I had been too late though, because next morning all the plants lay wilted on the ground. My neighbor didn't understand when I told him they died because they couldn't get their breath—he said, "The wind did it." I don't think he was a very smart farmer.

I don't know if Mr. Swift planted tomatoes again the next year because that winter we moved to Nebraska. We lived on the corner one block over and two blocks down from Grandma's house. In the spring Grandma gave me some seeds so I could plant a garden of my very own and learn responsibility. I decided I would have tomatoes because I already knew all about growing them. Besides, maybe I could send some to poor Mr. Swift. Daddy helped me. He spaded up the garden and planted the seeds, and then I watched them grow. My mother let me use my allowance to buy a sprinkling can from the dime store so I could water my garden. Daddy showed me which were the weeds and I tugged them out by the roots so they wouldn't choke my tomatoes. My garden grew and Daddy put a tall slender stake for each plant to climb. I watered my garden four times the first day and at least once a month after that. My garden grew as I played with the three boys next door, but I never got any tomatoes to send to my old neighbor. My mother told me that the odd blue flowers on my tomato plants were called four o'clocks, and I picked a bouquet for her.

CAROLINE SIEBLER

When you write indirectly, you must be consistent in style and viewpoint. You cannot use the Alternating Current without blowing the whole electric circuit. You must take a position or attitude or mood or role and stay in it throughout your writing. You're working on at least two levels. On the first, you must move authentically at all times. If your name is Alice and you're traveling through a Wonderland, you must believe in it all the time. You may have doubts and express amazement at what you see, but finally you must believe. And the Queens and Humpty Dumptys you encounter must be naïve and small-minded at all times on the first level, no matter how cleverly on the second level you manage to make them appear normal human beings.

In the story "Tomatoes," the author maintains the child's point of view beautifully except in a few spots, such as when she uses the word "outskirts" and the phrase "fruits of my dear neighbor's labor." Look for others. When you play another role than your own, you must stay in a voice that is right for that role.

> *Either stick to tradition or see that your inventions be consistent.*
>
> HORACE

(d) *A writer may make fun of pompous or pedantic persons or milksop and toadying persons by mimicking their language and pushing it to further excesses.* This exaggeration is often called burlesquing. For example:

IMPORTANT THINGS TO REMEMBER

Some things in this course will be more important than others. The most important thing to remember is that the War of the Tulips was fought before the Treaty of Pootrecht. Other important battles were the Alley Ambush of 1412 and the Small Slaughter of 1303. These are all important, but not as important as the date of the War of the Tulips.

(e) *A writer may blow up a trivial matter so large that it bursts.* For example:

The students who support the campaign to bring greasy and crumbly potato chips back to our cafeteria have completely rejected the traditions of Rich Central and are attempting to maliciously destroy the unity of our school

. . . They are undoubtedly using innocent potato chips as a guise for their plot to overthrow the Cafeteria Honor Committee and instill chaos, disunity, and trash throughout the school . . .

This was the method Jonathan Swift used in *Gulliver's Travels,* a cutting satire of the way adult human beings conduct themselves in every department of life. In one part of the book he puffed people up and in another he reduced them.

(f) *A writer may attack himself, or someone else he thinks needs defending.*

To the Editor:

Frank Forest ticks me off too. His office implies representation of all the students at Western, even though only six per cent voted for him. Doesn't he know he has to speak for **ALL** the students?

What right does he have to be involved in any other organization besides Student Association? What right does he have in using any means possible to point out problems on the campus and in society? Who does he think he is—asking me to read the Kerner Commission Report, when I want to go out and hustle girls? Who is he to ask the Faculty why we must study Physical Geography while our cities burn? And even though he looks around his classes and sees more and more boredom and apathy, who does he think he is trying to correct it? Why does he keep bothering everybody? (He says because of wars, hate, racism, exploitation, authoritarian system); I say it's because of communist B.S.

And if all this isn't enough, who gave him the idea that he could grow his hair long? Doesn't he know he's gotta look like the rest of us good students? Imagine, he thinks he can get away from our mold!

As a responsible, mature student at Western, I will not let Frank Forest get away with this. I demand that he get his hair cut, not join any organization besides S.A. and the Chess club, not affiliate with those "dirty commies" and get back into the game.

It is time the student body asks Forest to be like past presidents (let's see, what were their names?). After he gets back into the game, think of the increased benefits for him and us. He can use his office as another glory to add to his record. We can continue getting drunk, going to boring irrelevant classes, living in dormitories (even until we're twenty), and when we send our kids to Kalamazoo Central [High School], we can thumb through our Physical Geography notes to find out what to do, or else call in the police. I can hardly wait.

(signed) Frank Forest

(g) *A writer may treat an act lightly that is ordinarily feared,* in order to reduce its power.

For example, Julie Beach, writing in a student newspaper, begins a column with these paragraphs:

> For those students who have not yet reached the grand old age of eligibility for a driver's license, here are a few helpful hints to get them through the ordeal.
>
> First of all, get plenty of sleep the night before the test is going to be taken. It helps one get a passing grade if the road signs can be read clearly.
>
> When walking out to the parking lot with the policeman, try to remember where the car is parked. It doesn't pay to put him into a grouchy mood by walking around the lot for half an hour.
>
> After getting into the car, remember to unlock the door on the passenger's side. If a tapping noise is heard, don't be alarmed. It is only the officer knocking on the window, trying to get in.
>
> The key should now be placed in the ignition, then turned. If for some unknown reason it won't turn, take it out and flip it over; it was probably in upside down . . .

(Reminder for persons working on tightening: in paragraph 2 the words "is going to be taken" could be omitted, and also the word "noise" in paragraph 4.)

(h) *A writer may turn upside down or outrageously distort the treatment of an event* in order to ridicule the straight, sober, or trite treatment it's usually given.

For example, sports writers frequently present a dull roundup of the year, in which they try to make every team's record look impressive. Steve Henson, sports editor for *The Torch* (newspaper of Rich Township High School Central Campus, Park Forest, Illinois, May

13, 1966), decided he had had enough of such trite stuff and wrote a spoof, part of which follows:

> ... You all remember Central's football team, better known as Bill Barz. Smashing through the season nearly undefeated (well, you can't win 'em all) Barz and his teammates beat up everybody (if not on the field then out in the parking lot after the game). Cinderella Quanstrom put on his helmet and glass slippers and really turned in a great season. We can't forget guys like Denny Zumbahlen and Larry Morris, who averaged 38 tackles per game—31 of them after the whistle had blown.
>
> The Olympian Gridders were undefeated at home, using the advantage of the home field, the home refs, and Central's own Mr. Matheny running the scoreboard. It was simple—how else could you beat somebody 51–0? "Football Player of the Year" has to go to little 6'8", 295 lb. Bill Barz, to go along with his other awards of all-conference, all-area, all-suburban, all-state, and all-world . . .
>
> The varsity cagers were a great team, though, and exciting to watch. Hundreds of records were set during the season. Hot Dog Madderom averaged about 40 points per game and set a game high record when he tossed in 68 points against T. F. South. Randy hit on an amazing 22 field goals in that game in only 97 shots from the field. His best performance was in the Oklahoma game. Randy really scored and made several fine passes. Ed Younker tied the world record of falling asleep during a game (17 times) and Bob Moyer hit the most number of free-throws without a miss by a manager: 2 (also a world record). Bob Ewing grew the longest beard by a 6-foot forward in the entire South Suburban area . . .
>
> The Rich Central golf team has not been up to par this spring. Don Richmond, the "most consistent performer," really tore up the course at Olympia Fields last week, with a 67; in fact some fairways are still being repaired. He shot a Country Club record 58 last Saturday, with an eagle on the 5th hole, birdies on the 7th and 8th, and by forgetting to play the back nine . . .

One of Steve Henson's strategies in this column is to begin a statement in conventional manner and then end it with a kicker:

... who averaged 38 tackles per game—*31 of them after the whistle had blown.*

... He shot a Country Club record 58 last Saturday with an eagle on the 5th hole, birdies on the 7th and 8th, and *by forgetting to play the back nine.*

Another of his strategies is to present an actual fact and invent new facts which carry it to ridiculous heights:

... to go along with his other awards of all-conference, all-area, all-suburban, all-state, and *all-world.*

The truth is that Rich Central teams had a good season; for example, the baseball team won the District Championship and the football team lost only one game. But the indirect writer doesn't speak pure and whole fact. He risks being misunderstood. Mr. Henson's spoofing is consistent enough to make most readers aware of his intent, but even though he said, "we remind you to not believe everything you read" one student complained in a letter, saying,

You stated that *no* one ever went to *any* of the wrestling meets, and you did not even recognize the existence of a wrestling team.

This proves you have never gone to a wrestling meet; regular, or any of their district, sectional, or state meets ... So shape up, and apologize for the unjust insult you tossed to our boys, or don't call yourself a fair sports editor.

Answering that letter, Mr. Henson said:

If you believed that I was not exaggerating when I said "nobody went to any of their meets" and that no wrestling team even existed, then you must have taken everything else in the column seriously too. You must have believed that I was not exaggerating when I said that Barz was 6'8" and 295 lb., or that Madderom scored 68 points against T. F. South, or that Zumbahlen and Morris tackled 31 men after the whistle, or that Ewing tossed the shot through the gym wall into the little theatre.

He shows by his answer that he realizes that indirect writing cannot alternate between straight and indirect expression. It must be consistent in its attitude.

At times all of us speak indirectly naturally and with ease. To a girl falsely modest about her pretty new dress, we say, "You look horrible,

Anne, absolutely rotten." In sarcasm we say to a person who has assigned us an unpleasant job, "Oh, this is lovely work—I wouldn't want
to do anything else." A common line spoken by a soldier in World
War II to another soldier digging a ditch was: "Whatya gripin' about?
You're learnin' a trade." We mimic the way a teacher acts or talks. In
dozens of ways, we speak with double tongue, knowing closely our
audience and sensing how far we can go in indirection without losing
them. As writers, we can learn to sustain and unify a piece of indirect
communication which cuts and cuts down, astounds and delights,
cajoles and teases.

WRITING TWENTY-SEVEN: Write quickly a piece of indirect
writing about something or someone you know well and feel strongly
about. Whatever your degree of factualness or exaggeration, make
your statement ring true. Don't attack or ridicule someone for something he didn't do or say and can't have done or said. All must be true,
at least in the sense of being representative. Play with ideas, approaches,
words. Then reconstruct, make consistent, tighten, sharpen, polish.
sharpen, polish.

A short note about imaginative writing. Beginning writers often
believe that really good writing, really impressive writing, must be
made up rather than based on fact. Really. Look at that word. It's got
real in it, like most good writing. Jonathan Swift wrote four stories of
trips to fabulous lands where his Gulliver met giant and tiny men,
people who lived in the sky, talking horses; but all the time Swift was
writing about England, that real land, like America or China, where
stupid and self-centered little men and big men go clumping around
talking large and talking small and looking bad to anyone who can
see them clearly, really. Lewis Carroll took his reader with Alice
through the looking glass to places where egotistic and pompous
queens and Tweedle brothers were certain of all sorts of foolishness.
Lewis Carroll was also talking about England. And so really that
most people in the United States and other countries think he's describing them. The best imaginative writing is based on the real.

I am also convinced that the more you know about your craft, the freer you can be from it. My interpretation of freedom has nothing to do with sloppy or careless technique that is a caricature of freedom. To me real freedom arrives when the artist's creative instinct can function without limitation and without consciousness of technical means.

GABOR PETERDI

chapter 21
the
order
of
words

A CHILD OF SIX speaks as if he knew his meaning depends a great deal on word order. He wouldn't think of saying:

Of wouldn't he think saying.

And he wouldn't mess up the agreement signals in this sentence by using words that signal oneness when they need to signal twoness:

Johnny and Bill has his own bike.

And he wouldn't say:

It was nice of they.

because in the American grammatical system words like *he, she,* or *they* preceded by prepositions signal their relationship by changing to the object form (*him, her,* or *them*). Kids know this by the time they're six or eight. But sometimes they run into an adult—maybe a teacher—who is so worried about someone saying,

> You and me should go to the show.

that they say,

> She did not give it *to* you and *I*

when their unconscious and normal feeling for the signal would make them say,

> She did not give it *to* you and *me.*

J. D. Salinger made his hero Holden Caulfield, in *The Catcher in the Rye*, talk in this highly self-conscious ungrammatical way:

> I think I probably woke he and his wife up . . .

When Eudora Welty said that beginning and professional writers have the same troubles—not being serious or truthful—she might have added that they both have the same troubles with grammar. Most editors find little that is grammatically weak about the writing they edit, and when they do, the weaknesses are usually confined to a few troubles to be expected in the writing of anyone using the American grammatical system. Frequently they involve (1) confusing word order, (2) lack of clear signal by pronouns, and (3) verbs that don't signal which nouns they belong to.

In reading over the first draft of your writing, look first for these possible weak spots.

Word order signals meaning:

Original. When green I love the woods most of all.

Is that when I am green (sick at the stomach) (young, like a green plant), or when the woods are green? If the latter, the sentence should read:

Revision. I love the woods when green most of all.

or

Revision. I love the green woods most of all.

Thoreau opened Chapter Two of *Walden* with this sentence:

Original. At a certain season of our life we are accustomed to consider every spot as the possible site of a house.

His grammar would have been slightly confusing had he written:

Misrevision. We are accustomed to consider every spot at a certain season of our life as the possible site of a house.

Now *spot* and *season* are too close to each other. The phrase *at a certain season* should be close to *accustomed*.

In your writing, place next to each other those words which belong together in meaning. In the following sentence, the words in italics and in small capitals belong together in meaning but are separated from each other in position:

> This task, which George found highly agonizing, *grew*
> under the heat of the afternoon sun *soon* to be *unbearable*,
> and he QUIT working at it steadily EVENTUALLY.

When the words are rearranged (and a Whichery removed), the sentence is improved:

Revision. Under the heat of the afternoon sun, this agonizing task soon grew unbearable and George eventually quit working at it steadily.

The new order makes more sense, but it reveals the sloppy thought on the part of the writer. If the task "soon" grew unbearable, then why did George wait until "eventually" (whatever that means) to stop working at it? Either the "soon" or the "eventually" should be eliminated. Better yet, the writer might tell the reader what he means by "soon" or "eventually." How many hours or minutes?

Not every sentence changes its meaning with a change of word order. For example:

Original. Our minds thus grow in spots . . .
Revision. Thus our minds grow in spots . . .
Revision. Thus grow our minds in spots . . .
Revision. In spots thus grow our minds . . .

American-English grammar does not do all its signaling of meaning by word order.

REVISING TEN: Examine your last two long pieces of writing for blunders and weaknesses in word order. Write down on a separate sheet of paper your weak sentences and your revision of them. Reading aloud will help you in this task.

All writers and speakers occasionally let one of the segments of their sentence dangle out on a limb where it can fall off the tree. The most distinguished example is probably a sentence in Thomas Jefferson's First Inaugural Address:

> About to enter, fellow citizens, on the exercise of duties
> which comprehend everything dear and valuable to you,
> it is proper that you should understand what I deem the es-
> sential principles of our government, and consequently
> those which ought to shape its administration.

What is "about to enter" is Jefferson, not "you," who are fellow citizens,
or "it," which here is one of those vague words which can't enter anything. A dangling construction fails to make clear who is doing what.

> While walking back from my English class, a squirrel
> came up and stepped on my foot.

Squirrels returning from English classes will upset anyone.
　　More examples of dangling constructions:

> Not finishing dinner until 8:30, another problem was in
> the making.
> By subtly mentioning to one set of parents that it would
> be nice if we could all be together, they usually take the
> hint and invite others.

But enough of these sinful errors. Good writers master grammar in
order to control their words, and meaning is their target. In a given
paragraph, they may use an expression that is technically a dangling
construction but nevertheless communicates their meaning clearly. For
example, here's the masterful English writer William Hazlitt beginning
the third paragraph of his essay on Sir James Mackintosh:

> To consider him in the last point of view first. As a poli-
> tical partisan, he is rather the lecturer than the advocate.

The first sentence doesn't show clearly who's doing the considering,
and the whole group of words isn't really a sentence at all. But it works,
and an editor would be a fool to change it.
　　The commonest word-order change made in manuscripts by editors
is to bring together subjects and verbs which have been thoroughly
separated.

Original. *Professor Rending,* in approaching his subject, stumbled in
　　circles, like a drunk.

Revision. In approaching his subject, *Professor Rending* stumbled
　　in circles, like a drunk.

The method here is to pull out the segment of a sentence which is
properly introductory, such as

> When he was altogether prepared,

from the sentence in which it occurs:

> President Wilson, when he was altogether prepared, presented his plan to the League of Nations.

and put it at the beginning.

Revision. When he was altogether prepared, President Wilson presented his plan to the League of Nations.

Often, such rearrangement allows the writer to eliminate a wasted expression such as a Whooery:

Original. Queen Gertrude is a weak person, who is, in spite of her faults, held in high regard by the three men in her life.

Revised. In spite of her faults, Queen Gertrude is held in high regard by the three men in her life.

All writers slip occasionally in making clear the reference between pronouns and their antecedents and the agreement between subject and, verb. Therefore editors routinely check for these slips and find them frequently:

> Sol and his buddy Georgie, who is his uncle's favorite baseball player, often *tries* to eat more than he can hold.

Revised. Sol and his buddy Georgie—his uncle's favorite baseball player—often *try* to eat more than they can hold.

> The haggling and the bickering and the many hours of long drawn-out close reading I had to do when I was tired— it was all too much for me.

Revised. The haggling and the bickering and the many hours of long drawn-out close reading I had to do when I was so tired were all too much for me.

Note that most slips in pronoun reference and noun-verb agreement occur in long sentences which interrupt themselves with qualifications and side-trips. Editors examine such sentences closely, expecting meaning may have slid into a ditch.

Commonly professional writers use *which* and *that* to refer to the the word immediately preceding:

> I like HAMBURGERS *which* are well done but not dry.

But increasingly these days, they are using *which* or *that* to refer to a whole action described in a number of preceding words:

> Renny approves of making changes now, which is all right with me.

You will do well to stay with the conservative practice of including a clear referent word immediately preceding *which* or *that* as in HAMBURGERS *which*. If you ignore this practice and create a sentence that can't be misunderstood by your reader, let it stand; but the odds are against you. Note that if the example contained three more words,

> Renny approves of making changes now in the plan, which is all right with me.

the reader couldn't be sure whether what is "all right with me" is the whole plan or the changes. The reader's understandable interpretation of the sentence is probably that *which* refers to *plan*, the word immediately preceding it.

These little matters of reference and agreement are the higgledy-piggledy of grammar. More crucial matters exist. When you think of word order—the way words come together in phrases and clauses (pieces, hunks, segments, absolutes, whatever you call them at the moment)—think of how you may control it to bring your writing alive.

Try telescoping three or four sentences into one, so that the first reaches out and grabs part of those that follow. Here are three sentences too closely related to stand separately:

Original. Immediately Juliet sees the only solution to her problem. That solution is suicide. This is a highly illogical choice.

You can tack on to the first sentence the essential elements of the second and third sentences:

Revision. Immediately Juliet sees the only solution to her problem—suicide, a highly illogical choice.

Such tacking-on must be done with care. If the sentences preceding those above have suggested that the author is judging Juliet's behavior, this revision may be clear. But if not, the reader might take the sentence to say that Juliet sees suicide as a highly illogical choice, a meaning which would jar against the notion embodied in "only solution."

Study the Tack-On sentences of good writers. You'll see that they frequently write down a subject and verb (and sometimes an object of the verb) and then simply add nouns or prepositional phrases, or phrases beginning with verb forms ending in *-ing* or *-ed*:

(a) *It would become a sorcery,*
          a magic.

ARCHIBALD MAC LEISH

(b) *There is a pulpit at the head of the hall,*
          occupied by a handsome gray-haired judge
                with a faculty of appearing pleasant and impartial
                     to the disinterested spectator,
                               and
                                    prejudiced and frosty
                     to the last degree
                     to the prisoner at the bar.

MARK TWAIN

(c) *Each of us lives and works on a small part of the earth's surface,*
                moves in a small circle,
                          and
     of these acquaintances
                knows only a few intimately.

WALTER LIPPMANN

(d) *There were several ladies on board,*
          quite remarkably beautiful or good-looking,
          most of them, alas,
                          now dead.

IVAN TURGENEV

(e) *Let us arrange the contents of the heap into a line,* with
          the works that convey pure information at one end, and
          the works that create pure atmosphere at the other end, and
          the works that do both in their intermediate positions,
                the whole line being graded so that we pass from
                     one attitude to another.

E. M. FORSTER

Occasionally an author uses the Tack-On method at the beginning
of his sentence:

(f) Approaching Concord, doing forty, doing forty-five, doing fifty,
     the steering wheel held snug in my palms,
     the highway held grimly in my vision,
     the crown of the road now serving me (on the righthand curves),
                now defeating me (on the lefthand curves),
     *I began to rouse myself from the stupefaction which
          a day's motor journey induces.*

E. B. WHITE

Most beginning writers need to nudge themselves into Tacking-On more often but the habit comes naturally to many persons. These statements were written by high school students not coached to Tack-On:

It is the great American tradition to shed your
anxieties and slothfully recline at the rim of a pond,
    resting and
    letting your unattended pole slip in the motionless wet.

While playing tennis I feel a sense
of freedom,
of being able to release the pent-up emotions from
       hours, days.

Man, who could have been so useful, is now dead,
not physically,
but emotionally and mentally.

Another way of exploiting the force of word-order in American-English is to place a word in an unusual or dominant position in the sentence.

> *[Ask] How many words out of their*
> *usual place, and whether this alteration*
> *makes the statement in any way more*
> *interesting or more energetic.*
>
> EZRA POUND

In many sentences the position of most weight for a word is the end. Frequently you can punch a word by putting it last in a sentence.

> **I went up to get a friend to go to class with. While waiting for her to get ready, I glanced around the dorm room. There were clothes, hairdryers, curlers, pressers, strewn all around the six-girl room. On the desk sat a book entitled *Social Disorganization*.**

Note how the power of the statement would be lessened had the last sentence been written:

A book entitled *Social Disorganization* sat on the desk.

Of Sir Walter Scott, William Hazlitt wrote:

The old world is to him a crowded map; the new one a dull, hateful blank.

Had he placed his words in normal order, he would have written less forcefully:

> The old world is a crowded map to him; the new one a dull, hateful blank.

Hazlitt's version forces the essential words to the end of each word group, where they gather power and achieve parallelism. To move a word out of normal position is to surprise the reader.

Normal Order. He was a lost man.
Unusual Order. He was a man lost.

Writers need to develop an ear for normal word order and respect that order. If they continually scramble it, they will confuse their readers rather than surprise them. The principle involved here is the old one mentioned in Chapter 12: repeat and vary. Vary the normal pattern, but sparingly. And don't forget to create a pattern of expectation in the first place.

REVISING ELEVEN: Take two of your past writings, one free writing and one a planned longer work, and go over each word and sentence to see where you can change word order and improve the clarity or force of your statements. Write in the changes on the original so you and others can see what difference they make in the writing.

> "He has got no good red blood in his body," said Sir James.
> "No. Somebody put a drop under a magnifying-glass, and it was all semi-colons and parentheses," said Mrs. Cadwallader.
>
> GEORGE ELIOT

chapter 22

observing conventions

FROM THE AGE OF FIVE onward most Americans know and practice the social conventions of their region and economic class. They say "thank you" and "you're welcome" and they eat with or without napkins or finger bowls or whatever is proper to the persons they associate with. Their ego is involved. They want to be liked, to feel right in the social circle they choose for themselves.

But most Americans don't know the publishing conventions of the educated world. They have been taught commas and semicolons as they have been taught "please" and "May I introduce my brother—" but each year in school they learn them for a test and forget them the following day. Why? Because they never expect to have their writing published, or even dittoed and passed around the class. Their ego is not involved.

But the torture of being required each year to learn again what they never learned and aren't going to remember once again this year is slow and unbearable. *Semicolon* becomes a dirty word. Like Mrs. Malaprop, they confuse *apostrophe* with *parenthesis* and *hypothesis* and *apotheosis*.

What should they do if they're sixteen or sixty and haven't learned the American conventional system for aiding readers in understanding the meaning of printed rather than spoken sentences? About the only chance they have is to study sentences in print and deduce for themselves the system. If they look to a textbook for rules, they will forget them again quickly and painfully.

If you're in this unhappy group of persons laden with guilt about commas and italics, begin observing. Construct generalizations which explain why certain mechanical conventions of print are used in the right-hand column of sentences below. For your convenience the lefthand column presents sentences naked and innocent of most punctuation or other signaling devices. Look at them first. Make your guess at what they need in the way of signals. Then study the signals printed in the right-hand column, which follow the normal conventions of writing published in most magazines or books. Note that they don't follow newspaper conventions, which are different from those of books.

DIALOGUE

Well, if we went to Raleigh we could get Mr. Isaacs Christmas candy. Before she could answer Mamas footsteps passed in the hall overhead so she said Don't you reckon we ought to stay closer-by than Raleigh? He turned to her. Look—are you sticking with me or not? She looked and said Yes. Let's go then. She scraped their dishes and left them in the sink and said I'll get my coat. Where from. My room. All right but come straight back.

"Well, if we went to Raleigh, we could get Mr. Isaac's Christmas candy."

Before she could answer, Mama's footsteps passed in the hall overhead so she said, "Don't you reckon we ought to stay closer-by than Raleigh?"

He turned to her. "Look—are you sticking with me or not?"

She looked and said "Yes."

"Let's go then."

She scraped their dishes and left them in the sink and said, "I'll get my coat."

"Where from?"

"My room."

"All right, but come straight back."

REYNOLDS PRICE

SEMICOLONS, COMMAS, PERIODS, DASHES, COLONS

Learn these marks in this order if you want to master punctuation quickly. The semicolon has only four or five major uses, the comma dozens. If you know a semicolon isn't called for, you can bet wisely that what you need is a comma.

UNPUNCTUATED

1. Well I agree you could say the atom bomb doesn't go boom

CONVENTIONALLY PUNCTUATED

Well, I agree. You could say the atom bomb doesn't go boom;

it just obliterates a few hundred thousand people.

2. The world needs a little loosening of discipline and the schools need a little tightening of self-discipline.

3. He was no good for he had fallen apart at both the seams and the cuffs.

4. Renny a boy without guts was my enemy but Pedro a boy without guts was my friend.

5. I like Jackson Michigan Michigan City Indiana and Indianapolis Indiana.

6. It was a large city however I walked its streets without fear.

7. She was however a girl one could get along beautifully without.

8. Those days when Grandpa was a boy are long gone now the snows are deep and my Jaguar won't start.

9. In the last analysis Bertram doesn't measure up to the job.

10. Although a writer can lie about facts he should never lie about feelings.

11. When the moon comes over the woodshed behind the university library it feels out of place because Robert Frost is not there.

it just obliterates a few hundred thousand people.
(or):
Well, I agree you could say the atom bomb doesn't go boom. It just obliterates a few hundred thousand people.
The world needs a little loosening of discipline, and the schools need a little tightening of self-discipline.
He was no good, for he had fallen apart at both the seams and the cuffs.
Renny, a boy without guts, was my enemy; but Pedro, a boy without guts, was my friend.
I like Jackson, Michigan; Michigan City, Indiana; and Indianapolis, Indiana.
It was a large city; however I walked its streets without fear.
(or):
It was a large city; however, I walked its streets without fear.
She was, however, a girl one could get along beautifully without.
Those days when Grandpa was a boy are long gone; now the snows are deep and my Jaguar won't start.
In the last analysis, Bertram doesn't measure up to the job.
(or):
In the last analysis Bertram doesn't measure up to the job.
Although a writer can lie about facts, he should never lie about feelings.
When the moon comes over the woodshed behind the university library, it feels out of place because Robert Frost is not there.

What a sight it is, to see Writers committed together by the eares, for Cere-monies, Syllables, Points, Colons, Com-

ma's, Hyphens, *and the like? fighting,*
as for their fires, and their Altars; and
angry that none are frightened at their
noyses, and loud brayings under their
asses skins?

BEN JONSON

12. I liked working there in the city next to the subway with its rattle its earth jar its grimy dirt that settled in the whorls of the ear and transferred itself from my sweating neck to my white collar by nine each morning.

I liked working there in the city next to the subway with its rattle, its earth jar, its grimy dirt that settled in the whorls of the ear and transferred itself from my sweating neck to my white collar by nine each morning.
(or):
I like working there in the city next to the subway—with its rattle, its earth jar . . .

13. She is sweet notwithstanding her sour tongue and pretty as cottage cheese.

She is sweet, notwithstanding her sour tongue, and pretty as cottage cheese.

14. I always found Archie that sad bag of a man worth his weight in tin.

I always found Archie—that sad bag of a man—worth his weight in tin.

15. We walked across the square a place deserted by everyone but the familiar urchins who were dipping their feet in the fountain as if it were a cold day in February.

We walked across the square— a place deserted by everyone but the familiar urchins, who were dipping their feet in the fountain—as if it were a cold day in February.

16. She was a beautiful plump hen of a woman whose legs were properly pipe-stems ending with gigantic feet and I loved her clucking and pecking her squawking and fluttering.

She was a beautiful plump hen of a woman whose legs were properly pipe-stems ending with gigantic feet; and I loved her clucking and pecking, her squawking and fluttering.

17. The Alsatians were losing the Martian war quickly they had no missiles or orbiting vehicles.

The Alsatians were losing the Martian war quickly; they had no missiles or orbiting vehicles.
(or):
The Alsatians were losing the Martian war quickly: they had no missiles or orbiting vehicles.

18. The General Velocipedes car was a beauty stinking heater buckling back wheels and valves that needed regrinding after a turn around the block.

The General Velocipedes car was a beauty: stinking heater, buckling back wheels, and valves that needed regrinding after a turn around the block.

SIGNALS FOR EMPHASIS

Conventionally, book and magazine writers and editors emphasize words with italics and quotation marks. When they use a word as an example of a word rather than as a regular part of a sentence, they usually put it in italics, which are indicated in handwriting or typescript by a single underline. (A double underline indicates small capitals; triple underline, capitals.)

19. The use of and is more difficult than most beginning writers realize.

The use of *and* is more difficult than most beginning writers realize.

20. Phrases like in terms of and with respect to can kill off an otherwise good speech.

Phrases like "in terms of" and "with respect to" can kill off an otherwise good speech.

More often than not, the words *say, call, refer to as* are followed by quoted words.

21. Those are what Mr. Wick calls "critical elements."

Frightened by Mrs. Clutched, their old third-grade teacher, many beginning writers use quotation marks around any word that would seem unusual in the sterile air of Mrs. Clutched's classroom. They say:

We had a "bunch" of good pitchers on our team and they used to "bug" each other constantly.

Nothing looks more square to an experienced editor or reader than this overuse of quotation marks. It implies either that the writer is a phony and won't admit that the words she's quoting belong in her vocabulary, or that the words *bunch* and *bug* are absolutely new to her readers in the use she has put them to. If they are slang, she should decide whether or not she wants to employ slang. If it's inappropriate to the subject and situation, she shouldn't use it. If it's customarily set in italics—and there you can see the principle behind italics and quotation marks: to help the reader when he needs help, to inform him of what he's not apt to see on his own when he's reading in a healthy state of perception—then she should use italics or quotation marks.

NUMERALS

Unless numerals are being used in an article or book constantly, the professional writer conventionally writes in words those numbers that can be written in two words or one, and all others in numerals. She never begins a sentence with a numeral; for without an opening capital letter, a sentence looks as if it is part of the preceding sentence.

22. We counted twenty-four eggs within one hundred feet but there were 142 in the whole area.

If a sentence requires a number like 136 (written in numerals because it can't be written in two words) and several other numbers, they are all written in numerals, for the sake of consistency:

23. ALWAYS: Three thousand and eighty-four men were ready; they each had 136 ounces of food, 32 feet of rope, 2 cans of suppressed napalm, and 12 rounds of ammunition.

NEVER: In the cages were rabbits in groups of 4, 3, and 6. 7 of them were kept in the barn in a larger enclosure, and 413 in all the buildings combined.

TITLES

Quotation marks aren't used around words that appear above a piece of writing as its title. That would be like writing,

My name is "John."

Exception: When the title consists of, or in part of, words borrowed from another source, those borrowed words may be enclosed in quotation marks. Even then, if the borrowed word or phrase is well-known, it need not be quoted:

To Be or Not to Be a Ham

Writers citing names of other published works are careful to follow a consistent signaling system. Usually they *italicize* (or *underline*) names of whole works—a novel, history, encyclopedia, anthology, play, magazine, newspaper. They *put in quotation marks* smaller parts of those whole works: a chapter, article, poem, newspaper report (its title is its headline).

24. Jerry Kobrins Why Gleason Got the Headlines is another star-centered article in TV Guide but Up at Yale by Neil Hickey seriously looks at what college students are writing that could raise the level of television drama.

Jerry Kobrin's "Why Gleason Got the Headlines" is another star-centered article in *TV Guide,* but "Up at Yale" by Neil Hickey seriously looks at what college students are writing that could raise the level of television drama.

25. The Old which is the first chapter of Renfrew's latest book The Gnu and the Auld is a masterpiece of humor.

"The Old," which is the first chapter of Renfrew's latest book, *The Gnu and the Auld,* is a masterpiece of humor.

SIGNALING POSSESSION

The apostrophe to signal possession is the hardest conventional sign to remember because it's slowly fading away in use. In formal names printed in capital letters, it's no longer used:

VETERANS ADMINISTRATION

In the days before dictionaries began to establish conventions firmly (Dr. Samuel Johnson's *Dictionary* of 1755 solidified spelling and other writing conventions in England, and Noah Webster's *Dictionary* of 1828 did the same in America), writers often used the apostrophe to indicate plurals, as did Ben Jonson in 1640 in the line quoted in this chapter:

> . . . Points, Colons, Comma's

(Capital letters were conventionally used in England and America then for most major nouns in a sentence), and in Chaucer's day (1400), possession was signaled by an *-es* ending on words:

> As dide Demociones doghter deere . . .
> That lordes doghtres han in governaunce . . .

Chaucer used no apostrophes for possession, although here the daughters in both lines belong to the fathers mentioned. Writing about two hundred years later, Shakespeare commonly used an *-s* ending to signal possession, but still without an apostrophe:

> It was a Lordings daughter, the fairest one of three . . .
> A womans nay doth stand for nought . . .

Conventions in publishing change like conventions in ladies' dresses but not as fast. At the moment, most printed books and magazines in the United States are employing the apostrophe to signal possession, even though it's no more necessary in most instances than in Shakespeare's day.

26. I got my moneys worth when all the ladies cakes were left in my car.

I got my money's worth when all the ladies' cakes were left in my car.

27. A womans nay doth stand for nought.

A woman's nay doth stand for nought.

28. Jamess trouble was not the Worthingtons trouble.

James's trouble was not the Worthingtons' trouble.

SCHOLARLY WRITING

Two common miswritings in scholarly work are the abbreviation for *page* or *pages* and the signal for paragraph indention.

WRONG: pg (pgs)   RIGHT: p. (pp.)
WRONG: P   RIGHT: ¶

Pg. may be some lazy person's abbreviation for *pig,* but it isn't the conventional abbreviation for *page.* Understandably persons make the sign of a double-stemmed capital P to indicate *paragraph,* but the proper sign has nothing to do with the letter P. It's a sign used in illuminated manuscripts before 1440, then without such long stems, and still in use today.

Footnotes are a pain to writers, readers, editors, and printers; but some scholarly tasks require them so that scholar-readers may trace easily the steps through which a writer made his case. Like all conventions, footnotes are being constantly changed in form, usually in the direction of simplicity.

In footnotes, *Ibid.* means "the same as above." The following set of footnotes reveals a standard pattern. Why do some *Ibid.* entries include page numbers and some not?

1 Fred M. Oliver, *Love Problems of High School* (New York, 1939), pp. 33-34.
2 *Ibid.*
3 *Ibid.,* p. 101.
4 Karl Heimson, "The Courting Pattern," *New Ways in Education* (Englewood Cliffs, Texas, 1956), p. 555.
5 Oliver, p. 101.
6 Heimson, p. 420.
7 *Ibid.,* pp. 419-425.
8 William G. Looney and James Brass Smith, editors, *Thinking and Talking* (New York, 1965), p. 13.
9 George Walker, "Sex," *The Teacher's Magazine,* vol. 14 (June, 1967), pp. 13-14.

Text of paper employing above footnotes:

Fred M. Oliver, psychologist at Nendy High School, Oak Pond, New York, cites the informal conversation of students. Jane, a senior, says "I'm mad for you, John," meaning in the new dialect of her group that she has decided to take John's part in his quarrel with his girl friend Susan.[1] This new game, played at several high schools in the area,[2] represents a clever playing with words—taking old slang or in-group expressions and giving them their literal rather than traditional meaning. "Cool it" to these students means to open the windows or turn down the thermostat.[3]

Conventional students in a Kansas high school do just the opposite. They develop a new language for love and dating which consists of giving new double meanings to the commonest expressions, like "Wash the linoleum" or "Is it cold out?"[4]

Oliver[5] and Heimson,[6] however, both state explicitly that they admire high school students' ability to invent new language. Heimson presents six pages of new expressions created by students in a high school of only one-hundred students.[7] Thirteen out of the twenty-five articles in a recent anthology on language center on the speech of American teenagers.[8] Parallels with these American developments have been found in Hungary by George Walker.[9]

This passage is footnoted in conventional form, but it is ridiculously overfootnoted. The reader couldn't stand that many footnotes in that short a space. The writer of these paragraphs is so overwhelmed by his sources that he has lost command of his own expression and line of development. If you are required to use footnotes, reserve them for documenting ideas or facts either so unusual and controversial or so detailed that they need to be credited to a writer. Footnote what readers are likely to want to check further.

A list of books, which occurs at the end of a paper, an article, a chapter, or a book, usually contains fuller information about the books: the publisher, number of volumes in a set, etc. In footnotes, names of authors are arranged in normal order: first name first. In a bibliography, they are arranged last name first, so that the order of the books in the list will be useful, easy to consult because arranged by authors' last names alphabetically:

BIBLIOGRAPHY

1. Heimson, Karl. "The Courting Pattern," *New Ways in Education* (Englewood Cliffs, Texas, Pinetree Press, 1956), 158 pp.

The "158 pp." indicates that the volume contains 158 numbered pages, a way to show the reader how extensive the book is.

BIBLIOGRAPHY

2. Looney, William G., and James Brass Smith, editors. *Thinking and Talking* (New York, Mouth Press, 1965), 450 pp.
3. Oliver, Fred M. *Love Problems of High School* (New York, Kissinger Co., 1939), 413 pp.

In short papers documenting notes make more sense at the end of the paper than as footnotes at the foot of each page. Footnotes are hard to type at the bottom of the page—the writer can't gauge how much room he needs. And they are hard to set in type—the printer can't gauge the room either, and he must shift to smaller type as well. An intelligent alternative to footnotes used frequently in scientific publications employs parenthetical references: (2: 33-34), which means that the book referred to is number 2 in the bibliography and the references are to pages 33 and 34 in it. Part of the above text would then be written this way, referring to the piece of bibliography given above, which would be printed at the end of the paper or article. The paper would contain no footnotes:

> This new game, played at several high schools in the area (2: 33-34), represents a clever playing with words—taking old slang or in-group expressions and giving them their literal rather than traditional meaning. "Cool it" to these students means to open the window or turn down the thermostat (3: 101).

Wise writers and editors adopt a pattern of documentation of sources that fits the purposes of the writers and, as much as possible, of readers. If the place of publication and publisher are not apt to be significant to readers, they are omitted from footnotes and supplied only in a bibliography. Almost always page references and dates of publication are given because they are useful to readers in locating material and in assessing the up-to-dateness of assertions and facts. All conventions need the help of common sense: the person who speaks outside in February with her head bare in order to observe a convention may find others soon observing her funeral.

Here are a few more models of conventional footnotes: For a book:

1 George M. George. *The Georgeness of the World* (New York, George Book Company, 1918), pp. 33-34.

For a magazine:

2 Margaret Mead, "Trends in Personal Life," *The New Republic* (September 23, 1946), 115: 348.

For a newspaper article:

3 "College Dating Changes Pattern," *The New York Recorder*, June 2, 1952, p. 13.
4 George Kriver, "Bronx Hospital Planned," *The Bronx Bomber*, June 3, 1967, p. 1.

For a government document:

5 *Dating Problems in Urban High Schools*, United States Health Service Publication 1090 (Washington, 1953), p. 7.

For an encyclopedia:

6 "Harvard University," *The Encyclopedia Britannica*, 14th edition.

For an excerpt from a book not read in the original but seen reproduced in part in another book:

7 Francis E. Merrill, *Courtship and Marriage* (New York, 1949), in Edwin R. Clapp
and others, eds., *The College Quad* (New York, 1951), p. 74.

For a personal interview or conversation arranged by the author:

8 Interview with John Rogers, Dean of Men, Northside High School, Chicago,
Illinois, April 4, 1967.

BORROWING WORDS

Conventionally, professional writers command their words and those
of others, but never imply they own the words of others.

They insert borrowed words naturally into their own sentences.

Wasting Borrowed Words:	*Commanding Borrowed Words*:
His dearest relative described him as "He was a great guy, full of fun, but gentle."	His dearest relative described him as "a great guy, full of fun, but gentle."

Professional writers don't refer to a statement they are quoting as a
quote, for they are doing the quoting, not the author. They call the
statement a *statement,* an *assertion,* an *argument,* etc. They remember
that quotes don't speak, only persons.

For example, one quote states: "The Undersecretary rejected the budget proposals of the whole Council."	For example, an unidentified London *Times* reporter states that "The Undersecretary rejected the budget proposals of the whole Council."

Professional writers remember that in conversation they must say
"I quote" but in writing they indicate this act by quotation marks.

War Magazine says, and I quote, "Wretches strew the beaches in a lovely pattern."	*War Magazine* says, "Wretches strew the beaches in a lovely pattern."

If you respect your writing, learn the craft and learn the conventional systems of signaling meaning to the reader. But don't use these
signals as a substitute for the order and clarity you must achieve with
words. If you want the reader to become excited, you must write
excitingly. You can't force excitement by putting three exclamation
marks at the end of your sentence! ! ! Three or four exclamation marks
are conventional only in comic strips.

suggestions for teachers

Many teachers around the country have broken loose and found a way of enabling their students to write alive. By hit and miss they have constructed a whole enabling process. But what may work for them and their students may not be congenial to others. Here's the process I have patched together. I don't say it is *the* way, but it has been tested. Every element in it contributes to three essentials:

- raising the level of truthtelling in a class;
- inducing students in the first week to forget their English-teacher-inspired fears and find authentic voices in writing;
- creating a seminar in which students help each other learn the disciplines of the writing craft.

These are unusual accomplishments. I don't bring them about for every student, but usually for a majority of those in every writing class.

The following steps create a climate that encourages truthtelling and, in turn, live sentences:

1. I read aloud an example of *Engfish,* the stilted word-wasting language of the schools. Point out its weaknesses. Read aloud a truthtelling student paper that speaks with authentic voice.

2. Tell students: "No one speaks truth always. We all lie, consciously and unconsciously. I ask you to try for truths. I'm going to try. You'll be astonished by the difference that's made by a constant effort to raise the level of truth in this room."

NOTE: Every line in this litany is designed to help students feel like telling truths. To risk truths in front of the group. To write for every person in the town, not just for the teacher. In this program a steady effort to *protect feeling.*

3. I begin with free writing, the best passages of which I reproduce and bring into class. Read them aloud. Prohibit negative comments for the first few meetings. If a listener doesn't like a passage, he's to say nothing. That's not lying; simply refraining from comment.

4. On the first day I face the effects of grades upon truthtelling. One expedient is to ask students to store their returned writing in a folder or envelope, and at the end of the course present it for a grade.

Those having the greatest number of writings that have scored with students and teacher receive the highest grades. But no grades earlier unless students ask to know how they're doing. Then I look over the folder and grade it as of that moment. A request for such early grading has seldom been made, because a constant evaluation of everyone's writing has been occurring in the seminar. Most students quickly find out how they're doing.

5. Ditto or otherwise reproduce the best writings and pass them out to all members of the class before having them read aloud. Announce that those who want a class response on a paper the teacher has not chosen for reproduction will be given that right.

The reproduction of papers is a burden, whether I retype the papers myself or ask students to write or type their best work on ditto masters. However the job is done, it's costly in time and money. But like the other steps described here, it enables students to reach readers with their writing. One expedient: I type ditto masters single-spaced in two columns to make them more readable, and thus save 50 percent on paper.

Another expedient, which John Bennett has used: ask students to write for 10-15 minutes at the beginning of every class period and then on the last day of the week choose the paper they think best. They take it back to their room, cut or expand it, and write or type it on a ditto master, to be run off for comment by the Helping Circle in subsequent meetings.

Because comments are made on papers in class where they count, where they can be judged by the writers as they compete for attention and belief, I don't need to waste time writing in their margins while I'm reading them. Many studies have shown that written marginal comments have little effect. Late in the course I might write a note to a student I think is ripe for a certain suggestion.

6. Pass out a reproduced writing to the group and read it aloud, or ask a student to read it aloud, or suggest that the writer (unidentified) read the paper if she wishes.

After the paper has been read, ask the group, "Well, how does that strike you?" At that point my experience is to encounter silence. It seems to grow and spread through the room as I become more nervous, fearing the writer will take the silence as negative criticism. The members of the class sit, eyes down, tongueless. I have for nine years failed to realize why the eyes are down. The students are on the spot. They're quickly reviewing the writing, trying to sort out the reasons for their feelings. Sometimes unsure of their response, they're reading the work again to locate it.

And I'm sitting there thinking, "Come on, you dumb people. Are you incapable of responding to human experience recorded truthfully?" For nine years I forgot that I had read the papers on initially receiving them, often typed them on ditto masters, and then heard them read again in class. So my students were encountering the paper for the first time and I for the third. I've made my sortings, enjoyed the opportunity for second and third revisions of judgments, and grown familiar with details.

Now I tell students that their reluctance to speak is intelligent and remind them of what they're doing during that silence. After a few moments for heads down—"Did anyone like anything in the paper?" If I get a number of positive responses, later, "Now, any suggestions for improvement?" Sometimes lively discussion erupts, sometimes continued reluctance; sometimes praise and help; sometimes confusion and pain.

The heads-down period is necessary: time to review first reactions, to collect thoughts and examples, to ponder a response that will be focused rather than fatuous, helpful rather than damaging.

7. I always ask students to comment on a piece of writing before I do. Teacher's comments later, or last. Otherwise students step back into traditional school where the game is to find out what teacher thinks and go along with it. Hour after hour, year after year, students have played that game. Even in this program they will revert to it unless the basepaths are obliterated.

8. I try to build the students' confidence and move the class forward on it. At first reproduce good writing so that students can advance from success to success. As the course proceeds with assignments, some students do not score. I ask them to do free writing again.

After they've received praise from the group, writers are usually strong enough to listen to others tell them that a subsequent work is weak in large ways. Eventually every writer must learn to use negative comments to improve her work.

9. When I give regular assignments (for example, "Tell an incident in your childhood that struck you hard"), I add that persons who find the assignment wrong for them at the moment can come to me and say they're writing on another topic of their choosing. I want to help people become powerful writers, not to make them jump through identical hoops.

10. Once or twice a semester I bring in a piece of my own writing done for one of the assignments, or for some project I'm working on, and allow it to be judged along with the work of students—without divulging beforehand who wrote it.

11. By subtle and direct means I let the class know that I'm not asking for True Confessions. Truthtelling here doesn't imply, "I'm baring my soul, and I must tell you that once I—" This book demonstrates the power of telling facts, of objectifying experience so

a reader can live it vicariously and a writer can re-experience it. Thus —objectivity, which is seldom the mark of True Confessions writing. My class is not designed to be therapeutic, but to produce strong writing. If it has a therapeutic effect, all right; but no psychiatrist worked in that room.

If I sense that a paper will be embarrassing or injurious when read aloud, I withhold the identity of the writer. Sometimes I ask writers about the wisdom of publishing their work to the class or outsiders. I'm reminded of a woman I'll call Mary in one Shakespeare class who said she was afraid to write journal entries. Her sixth-grade teacher had once asked the class to write honestly whatever came to their minds. "I won't reveal writers' names." Mary wrote of her at-traction to a boy who sat two rows behind her. The next day the teacher read aloud her paper as an example of poor sentence struc-ture and organization, and chastised Mary before the class for "slop-piness." That was the end of Mary telling truths that counted for her in school.

School is the last place an objective observer should expect to encounter students speaking or writing truths that count for them. Unwittingly it's designed to nurture copycatting and phoniness. The Test-Grade System requires students to read a book or listen to teachers talk and give them back exactly what was said. The outcomes of doing exercises in the drillbook are expected to be exactly alike for every student. If instructors say, "Tell the truth," it's their truths that they usually expect to hear; and if they're given a disappointing or offending truth they're apt to say, "I'm sorry, but I'll have to give you a D for that."

What brings about truthtelling is a feeling that one is free to tell it, and that this act will occur in a room of nine or more persons (the response of a smaller number can be too easily dismissed as "friendly" or "prejudiced") who are trying to respond honestly. That one expert—the teacher—is not the sole responder and judge.

What brings about live voices in writing—the sound of in-dividual human beings drawing upon all their powers—is a release through free writing at the beginning of a course and then a growing self-discipline in trying for truths.

In dozens of ways this process forces students to care for their writing. They have a real audience; they will become audience them-selves. This double position is a responsible one.

12. If the class numbers more than twenty, I frequently break it into smaller groups for reading of papers. But I keep the whole group as the central testing ground, where I comment as well as the students, where I can speak to the whole class for ten or fifteen minutes when I feel, like a teacher, that I have something for all of

them. But I never sit in on the small groups. Students must perceive that the responses of their classmates carry weight.

13. Promise publication of the best writing: The dittoed two-column handout is itself a kind of publication. My students have frequently said, "When I saw my paper *printed* [it was actually only dittoed] in the handout, I could spot faults immediately." Thumbtack good writing on bulletin boards in the halls. Try to find resources for publishing a magazine or handout to be distributed beyond the classroom. As writers, the wider our readership, the more we feel pressure and desire to tell truths that count.

Those thirteen points make up the core of a writing program. Not all teachers will find them essential. I caution readers against taking this book blindly, chapter by chapter, assignment by assignment. More activities are provided than most students can satisfactorily carry out in a semester or a year if like professional writers they're revising and rewriting and abandoning some pieces. I wrote the book so that teachers could select those parts which make a program fulfilling and comfortable for them.

All kinds of writing are presented here, not to furnish a hodgepodge, but from an inner necessity. For all good writing—no matter what its type or form—has much in common with all other good writing. A precise statement of the parts of a vacuum cleaner and how to use it is more like Shakespeare's *Macbeth* than it is like a vague and lifeless description of a vacuum cleaner. A beginning writer would be mad to isolate a type of writing, like exposition, and concentrate on it as if the strategies of drama and story have nothing to do with her task. But that's what she's asked to do by most composition courses.

In this approach to writing, instead of seeing their errors paraded before them and the class, students are forced to look at their best work and go on from there—frequently from success to success. Like professionals, they're aiming to produce a number of strong writings, not thinking simply of periodically supplying a teacher with a paper to be graded. They write more than is presented to the group. They put aside writings which didn't go well after several tries. They take a short paragraph with good bones and put flesh on it. They add and cut drastically. They sharpen and polish.

They're advised to do these things by their classmates and teacher and textbook. They feel the pressure of possible publication. Some teachers using this book have begun exchanging a group of student papers with a similar class in another part of the city or nation, and then exchanging student responses to the writings. A way toward more objective evaluation.

Free writing liberates students to use their speech competencies without fear of being castigated for faulty form. The act of writing so fast often moves them into a kind of trance in which nearby distractions fade and they focus on the act so that their words seem to be writing themselves. In that condition (which scientists have isolated by study of brain waves as most often occurring when a person is drifting into or out of sleep) writers can remember their past experiences more fully and vividly. Part of that experience has been reading and listening to the cadences of the words of skillful writers and speakers. Much of what people have heard and read has been printed on their brains—the sounds of television-uttered sentences, the rhythms of film sequences, the economical humor of cartoon characters—and at a propitious time they can pull up from this reservoir patterns of language and form useful to their purposes.

For several years in directing writing seminars at the Bread Loaf School of English in Vermont, I noticed that some members did a bad job of reading aloud another person's paper to the group. They stumbled, skipped words, overenunciated, read pompously, and distorted and sometimes destroyed the meaning of what they were reading. I wondered why, for they were all teachers accustomed to reading aloud in front of groups. When I read a paper to the seminar, I usually read better than the others. Finally, I decided the reason was that I had seen the paper before, had a memory of its drift of meaning. To test my supposition, I introduced a new routine into the seminar.

Each day we all wrote freely for fifteen minutes on an open topic. Then I asked everyone to trade papers with another person. They separated themselves in the room and mumbled their way aloud through the other person's paper with one point in mind—to get the meaning of each sentence. We reconvened as a large group and two or three persons read aloud someone else's paper.

The readings were much better than they had been before. I didn't see the usual expressions of pain on the writer's face as the reading was carried out, and the involuntary responses of the listeners were much stronger—the laughs, the sudden intakes of breath, the tightening of hands, and other body language that showed involvement with the writing.

Then we went back to the original pairs and read our partner's paper aloud to him or her, so that every paper that had been written in that room was read aloud sensitively for meaning. All that reading took only about fifteen minutes.

Right away the feeling in the room became happier and more positive. No longer did writers feel others in the room were out to murder their writing. The way the readers had performed their work showed some appreciation for it. The readings were so good that ideas and feelings came through to all the listeners even though there was no written text in front of them.

I wondered whether high-school and college students given the same opportunity would read as well as these teachers. At first I thought, "Of course not." And then I remembered how different were the teachers' "before" and "after" performances. I knew that anyone past the age of six would read better having gone through rehearsal for meaning.

Why? Where would that dramatic reading talent come from? The answer was easy to find once I had asked the question—from their speaking habits. Anyone in any society learns early on how to speak with intonation that fits or enhances the meaning of one's sentences. In speaking the sentence "Take the pie out of the oven" no one would would emphasize the word *of*. We all know how to "read aloud" our own sentences in conversation because we're spinning out our meaning when we speak them. We control rhythm, sound effects, and emphasis skillfully, employing diminuendos and fortissimos like musicians, unless the speaking situation frightens or freezes us. Or unless an English teacher lets us know we will be corrected for "bad grammar."

There are parallels between reading aloud and writing. Attention to meaning springs forth all sorts of unconscious language powers in us. Concern for *what* we are saying rather than showing off our language usually produces the most eloquent composing in both speech and writing.

If this book has one thing to say it is that in school and out we should capitalize on the fact—it's not a theory or a hope—that we are all language-using animals by the time we enter school. Like adult birds, we don't have to be taught to fly, but merely to fly in new and better ways. I can hear the traditional English teacher talking to the adult bird in Basic Flying 100: "Now these are your wings. You'll be quizzed tomorrow on the names of their parts."

Another helpful point for writers has been emphasized at Bread Loaf by Peter Elbow, author of *Writing Without Teachers,* and Don Graves, the director of the Writing Process Laboratory at the University of New Hampshire. It is that all writers want and need aid from other persons responding to their work, but often they are hurt rather than helped. Elbow's suggestion is for those listening to a piece of writing read aloud to their peers to play the Believing, rather than Doubting, Game. Customarily we're taught by the university tradition to receive ideas and creative works skeptically, to ask what might be said against them, and in that way to test their validity and quality. But Elbow says we might better understand them—and therefore be in a position to say helpful things about them—if we try to go along with whatever a speaker or writer is saying. Look for evidence on the side of the writer or speaker. Try to find reasons for believing the line of argument or the development of a story. In responding to a piece of writing, for example, not to say immediately, "I don't think a person in your grandfather's position would ever have acted the way you say he did," but rather to look for cues in the writing that might explain his unusual behavior. And if they aren't there, attempt to supply them.

Whenever writers are describing a line of action or presenting an idea, they're building upon their experience, knowledge, or thinking. Their statements are not convincing perhaps because they haven't put down key elements of that experience, knowledge, or thinking. Saying to them, "This third paragraph just doesn't do the job. I don't believe in what you're saying at all," may be a true report of your reaction, but it's not likely to help a writer gather forces to make the paragraph convincing. Elbow and Graves advise a critic in that situation to say something like, "What are you trying to say in that third paragraph? Is it. . . . . ?" to show you are in the ready-to-believe mode rather than the rejecting, condemning mode. Or if you're reacting to a report or a story, to say, "Why does Uncle Alonzo hit the child?" instead of saying, "I simply can't believe that Uncle Alonzo would hit that kid at that time."

Questions like these of a writer almost always elicit more convincing reasons or facts than appeared in the original writing. When you ask such a question, it's smart to have pencil in hand and write down the writer's spoken response, which often is an eloquent or graphic statement of what didn't appear in the writing, but should.

Playing the Believing Game doesn't mean going along with things you don't believe in. It means building a case for believing so that you encourage writers to do the best possible job of saying what they wish to say. If, when they're finished, you still don't believe what they're saying or feel its impact, you then have the right to reject the writing. The Believing Game is a means of tamping down our instinct to sound off like authorities about everything we hear, to make grandly disparaging remarks in order to impress the members of a group, to put others down in an often unconscious effort to put ourselves up. Again, so much of our behavior in regard to writing is unconscious. We need to observe that behavior consciously at times and do our best to improve it. In fact, when we help writers improve writing, we usually feel prouder of ourselves than when we cut them down and send them home feeling incompetent and defeated. Teachers, of all people, should realize this and try to make themselves and their students helpful players of the Believing Game.

list of sources

Page

11 Henry David Thoreau, *Journals,* July 14, 1852.

12 Ralph Waldo Emerson, "Nature," *The Complete Essay and Other Writings,* edited by Brooks Atkinscn (New York, The Modern Library, 1950), p. 17.

13 Quoted in Clara M. Siggins, "Then It Got Buggles," *College Composition and Communication* (February, 1962), 6. 56.

13 Friedrich Nietzsche, *Beyond Good and Evil* (Chicago, Regnery, Gateway Edition, 1955), p. 77.

15 Gene Baro, "News and the Newsman," *The Reporter* (September 21, 1967), p. 50.

15 Eudora Welty, *Delta Wedding* (New York, New American Library, Signet Edition, 1963) p. 220.

15 Eudora Welty, quoted by Reynolds Price, "A Kind of Valedictory," *The Archive,* Duke University (April 1955), p. 2.

16 Samuel Johnson, source unknown.

18 Samuel Butler, *Works* (London, Jonathan Cape, 1923–26), XVIII, 210.

22 Wallace Stevens, "Adagia," *Opus Posthumous* (New York, Alfred A. Knopf, 1957), p. 158.

24 Donald Hall, "A Clear and Simple Style," *The New York Times Book Review* (May 7, 1967), p. 30.

26 E. M. Forster, *Aspects of the Novel* (New York, Harcourt, Brace, 1927) p. 197.

26 Henry Moore, "The Painter's Object," *The Creative Process,* edited by Brewster Ghiselin (New York, New American Library, Mentor Edition, 1955), p. 77.

27 Alfred Kazin, "The Language of Pundits," *Atlantic Monthly* (July 1961), pp. 73–74.

28 Wallace Stevens, "Adagia," *Opus Posthumous* (New York, Alfred A. Knopf, 1957), p. 162.

30 Jean Shepherd, "A Midtown Stroll After Midnight," *The New York Guidebook,* edited by John A. Kouvenhoven (New York, Dell Publishing Co., Inc., 1964).

31 John Ciardi, "Work Habits of Writers," *On Writing, by Writers,* edited by William W. West (Boston, Ginn, 1966), p. 153.

33 Sidney Cox, *Indirections* (New York, Viking, Compass Books, 1962), p. 130.

35 William Hazlitt, "On the Familiar Style," *The Hazlitt Sampler* (New York, Fawcett World Library, 1961), p. 228.

35 Benjamin Franklin, quoted in Carl Becker, *The Declaration of Independence* (New York, Alfred A. Knopf, Vintage Books, 1958), pp. 208–209.

37 Wallace Stevens, "Adagia," *Opus Posthumous* (New York, Alfred A. Knopf, 1957), p. 169.

41 Samuel Butler, *The Note-Books* (London, Jonathan Cape, 1926), p. 97.

42 Henry David Thoreau, *Walden and Other Writings* (New York, The Modern Library, 1937), p. 88.

43 Lewis Carroll, *Through the Looking Glass* (New York, Random House, 1946), p. 36.

Page

43   Norman Podhoretz, *Making It* (New York, Random House, 1967), p. 106.

47   Henry David Thoreau, *Walden and Other Writings* (New York, The Modern Library, 1937), p. 86.

48   Bernard Shaw, *John Bull's Other Island* (New York, Harper & Brothers, 1942), p. 209.

50   Jack London, *People of the Abyss* (New York, Harcourt, Brace, 1946), p. 213.

51   Ralph Waldo Emerson, "Thoreau," *Lectures and Biographies* (Boston, Houghton Mifflin, 1893), p. 362.

53   Thomas Henry Huxley, To Charles Kingsley, September 23, 1860, in Leonard Huxley, *Life and Letters of Huxley* (New York, D. Appleton, 1901), I, 235.

57   Michihiko Hachiya, *Hiroshima Diary* (Chapel Hill, University of North Carolina Press, 1955), pp. 11, 91–92.

58   Mario Roveda, "Through the Gates," *Unduressed* (Western Michigan University, April 7, 1968), p. 2.

61   Darcy Cudlip, "First Car," *Ibid.*

64   Sidney Cox, *Indirections* (New York, Viking, 1962), p. 131.

70   Frank O'Connor interviewed by Anthony Whittier, *Writers at Work: The Paris Review Interviews*, First Series (New York, Viking, 1959), p. 169.

70   Kathleen Bolinger, "Linus's Blanket," *Unduressed* (Western Michigan University, December 16, 1968), p. 5.

73,74   Samuel Butler, *The Note-Books* (London, Jonathan Cape, 1926), p. 106.

79   Marianne Moore interviewed by Donald Hall, *Writers at Work: The Paris Review Interviews,* Second Series (New York, Viking, 1965), p. 82.

81   T. S. Eliot interviewed by Donald Hall, *Ibid.*, p. 96.

83   Anton Chekhov, *Letters of Anton Chekhov*, edited by Avrahm Yarmolinsky (New York, Viking, 1973), p. 123.

89   William Hazlitt, "On Paradox and Common-place," *Table Talk* (London, J. M. Dent, 1952), p. 146.

90   William Hazlitt, "On the Ignorance of the Learned," *Ibid.*, pp. 70–71.

92   John Stuart Mill, *On Liberty* [1859] (New York, Appleton-Century-Crofts, 1947), p. 36.

96   William Shakespeare, *The Merchant of Venice*, III, i.

97   Richard Thurman, "Not Another Word," *The New Yorker* (May 25, 1957), pp. 37–44.

114   Stuart Chase, "Writing Nonfiction," *On Writing, by Writers*, edited by William W. West (Boston, Ginn, 1966), p. 327.

115   William Wordsworth, "The Prelude," *Complete Poetical Works* (Boston Houghton Mifflin, 1904), p. 1956.

115   Mark Twain, *Huckleberry Finn* (New York, Houghton Mifflin, 1958), pp. 3–4.

116   J. D. Salinger, *The Catcher in the Rye* (New York, New American Library, 1953), p. 144.

117   Sidney Cox, *Indirections* (New York, Viking, 1962), p. 6.

121   Grace Wendell, "We Were Getting Along," *Unduressed* (Western Michigan University, April 14, 1969), p. 12.

Page

124 Truman Capote interviewed by Pati Hill, *Writers at Work: The Paris Review Interviews,* First Series (New York, Viking, 1959), pp. 294–295, 296–297.

132 Dr. Seuss, *Horton Hatches the Egg* (New York, Random House, 1940), n. p.

138 Ralph Waldo Emerson, "The American Scholar," *The Complete Essays and Other Writings,* edited by Brooks Atkinson (New York, The Modern Library, 1950), p. 47.

139 James Baldwin, *The Fire Next Time* (New York, Dell, 1964), pp. 14–15.

139 N. H. and S. K. Mager, editors, *The Pocket Household Encyclopedia* (New York, Pocket Books, 1953), p. 168.

139 Irma S. Rombauer and Marion Rombauer Becker, *The Joy of Cooking* (Indianapolis, Bobbs-Merrill, 1953), p. 313.

140 Henry David Thoreau, source unknown.

142 Dave Connor, "Barbaric?" *Unduressed* (Western Michigan University, April 14, 1969), p. 2.

146 *The Heart of Emerson's Journals,* edited by Bliss Perry (Boston, Houghton Mifflin, 1926), p. 333.

147 Henry David Thoreau, *Journals,* April 22, 1851.

148 Henry David Thoreau, *Journals,* October 4, 1851.

152 Sidney Cox, *Indirections* (New York, Viking, 1962), p. 132.

153 Oscar Wilde, *A Woman of No Importance,* quoted in *The Wit and Humor of Oscar Wilde,* edited by Alvin Redman (New York, Dover, 1952), p. 33.

156 William Carlos Williams, "The Dance," *The Collected Later Poems* (New York, New Directions, 1950), p. 11; and "Poem," *The Collected Earlier Poems* (1951), p. 340.

158 Wallace Stevens, "Adagia," *Opus Posthumous* (New York, Alfred A. Knopf, 1957), p. 176.

158 Norman Podhoretz, *Making It* (New York, Random House, 1967), pp. 139–142.

161 Mary McCarthy interviewed by Elisabeth Niebuhr, *Writers at Work: The Paris Review Interviews,* Second Series (New York, Viking, 1965), p. 302.

165 American Humane Association, Denver, Colorado, undated pamphlet.

166 Frederick Douglass, *Life and Times of Frederick Douglass* (New York, Collier Books, 1962), pp. 484–485.

167 Donald Hall, "A Clear and Simple Style," *The New York Times Book Review* (May 7, 1967), p. 30.

168 Erich Fromm, *Man for Himself* (New York, Rinehart, 1947), p. 105.

169 Patricia Moyes, "What Is Your Cat Trying to Tell You?" *Woman's Day,* (February 20, 1979).

171 Harriet Beecher Stowe, *Uncle Tom's Cabin* (New York, Washington Square Press, Pocket Books, 1963).

176 Barnett Newman, "For Impassioned Criticism," *Art News* (Summer, 1963), p. 58.

180 George Felton, review of Roger McGuinn's *Thunderbyrd* in *Focus* magazine (April 15–30, 1977), Columbus, Ohio, p. 8.

Page

182 John S. Wilson, "Nina Simone at the Village Gate," *The New York Times* (February 24, 1979).

187 Kenneth Clark, "The Value of Art in an Expanding World," *Hudson Review* (Spring, 1966), p. 23.

187 Samuel Butler, quoted in Henry Festing Jones, *Samuel Butler* (London, Macmillan, 1920), II, 294–295.

189 Ezra Pound, *ABC of Reading* (New York, New Directions, 1960), p. 62.

191 James Thurber interviewed by George Plimpton and Max Steele, *Writers at Work: The Paris Review Interviews*, First Series (New York, Viking, 1959), p. 87.

192 Eudora Welty, "Must the Novelist Crusade?" *Atlantic Monthly* (October, 1965), p. 106.

195 Robert Lipsyte, *The New York Times* (August 5, 1966).

200 Samuel Butler, *The Note-Books* (London, Jonathan Cape, 1926), p. 102.

212 Henry David Thoreau, *Journals*, August 4, 1841.

219 Joyce Maynard, "Hers," *The New York Times* (April 12, 1979).

224 Bernard Shaw, in *Ellen Terry and Bernard Shaw: A Correspondence*, edited by Christopher St. John (New York, The Fountain Press, 1931), pp. 113–114.

231 Ralph Waldo Emerson, "Self-Reliance," *The Complete Essays and Other Writings,* edited by Brooks Atkinson (New York, The Modern Library, 1950), p. 165.

234 A. A. Milne, *The House at Pooh Corner* (New York, E. P. Dutton, 1928), p. 96.

236 Lewis Carroll, *Alice in Wonderland* (New York, Random House, 1946), pp. 140–141.

237 W. Nelson Francis, "Pressure from Below," *College Composition and Communication* (October, 1964), pp. 147–148.

239 E. E. Cummings, "XIV," *Poems, 1923-1954* (New York, Harcourt, Brace and World, 1954), p. 397.

239 Joseph Conrad, preface to *The Nigger of the "Narcissus"* in *Three Great Tales* (New York, Alfred A. Knopf, Vintage Books, n.d.), p. ix.

244 Nancy Hunter, "In Small Towns," *Unduressed* (Western Michigan University, April 14, 1969), p. 1.

245 Lewis Carroll, *Through the Looking Glass* (New York, Random House, 1946), p. 29.

246 Henry David Thoreau, *Walden and Other Writings* (New York, The Modern Library, 1937), pp. 123, 288.

246 William Hazlitt, *The Spirit of the Age* (London, Oxford University Press, 1935), p. 13.

247 Erich Fromm, *Man for Himself* (New York, Rinehart, 1947), pp. 99, 101.

250 Mark Twain, *Huckleberry Finn* (New York, Houghton Mifflin, 1958), pp. 85–88.

255 Kathy Currier, "Triolet," *Aurora 66*, Portage Northern High School, Portage, Michigan, p. 23.

257 Horace, *The Art of Poetry* in *The Complete Works,* edited by Casper J. Kraemer, Jr. (New York, The Modern Library, 1936), p. 401.

258 Frank Forest, *Western Herald* (Western Michigan University, October 21, 1968), p. 2.

Page

259 Julie Beach, "Driving's a Dilemma," *The Lakeview Crystal* (Lakeview High School, Battle Creek, Michigan, February 4, 1966), p. 4.

263 Gabor Peterdi, *Printmaking* (New York, Macmillan, 1959), p. xxii.

264 J. D. Salinger, *Catcher in the Rye* (New York, New American Library, 1953), p. 157.

266 William Hazlitt, *The Spirit of the Age* (London, Oxford University Press, 1904), pp. 130–131.

269 Archibald MacLeish, "Poetry and the Press," in *Thought and Statement*, edited by William G. Leary and James Steel Smith (New York, Harcourt, Brace, 1960), p. 481.

269 Mark Twain, "The Evidence in the Case," *Ibid.*, p. 373.

269 Walter Lippmann, "Stereotypes," *Ibid.*, p. 221.

269 Ivan Turgenev, "A Fire at Sea," *Ibid.*, p. 25.

269 E. M. Forster, "Anonymity, An Inquiry," *Ibid.*, pp. 440–441.

269 **E. B. White, "Walden,"** *Ibid.*, p. 39.

270 Ezra Pound, *The ABC of Reading* (New York, New Directions, 1960), p. 64.

270 William Hazlitt, *The Spirit of the Age* (London, Oxford University Press, 1904), p. 76.

272 George Eliot, *Middlemarch* (New York, Houghton Mifflin, 1956), p. 52.

273 Reynolds Price, *A Long and Happy Life* (New York, Avon Books, 1960), p. 121.

274 **Ben Jonson,** *Timber, or Discoveries,* in **English Prose,** 1600–1660, edited by Victor Harris and Itrat Husain (New York, Holt, Rinehart, and Winston, 1965), p. 330.

index